The European Labour Movement and European Integration

A publication of the Graduate Institute of International Studies, Geneva

The European Labour Movement and European Integration

Barbara Barnouin

Frances Pinter (Publishers)
London and Wolfeboro, N.H.

© Frances Pinter (Publishers), 1986

First published in Great Britain in 1986 by
Frances Pinter (Publishers) Limited
25 Floral Street, London WC2E 9DS

Published in the United States of America in 1986 by
Frances Pinter (Publishers) Limited
27 South Main Street
Wolfeboro, NH 03894-2069

British Library Cataloguing in Publication Data

Barnouin, Barbara
   The European labour movement and European integration.
   1. European Trade Union Confederation
   I. Title
   331.88′094   HD8372
   ISBN 0-86187-650-4

Library of Congress Cataloging in Publication Data

Barnouin, Barbara.
   The European labour movement and European
integration.

   Bibliography: p.
   Includes index.
   1. European Trade Union Confederation—History.
2. Trade-unions—European Economic Community countries—
Political activity.   3. International labor activities.
4. European integration. I. Title.
HD8372.E86B37 1986   331.88′091   86-5901
ISBN 0-86187-650-4

Typeset by Joshua Associates Limited, Oxford
Printed by Biddles of Guildford

Contents

List of Tables and Figures

List of Abbreviations

ACLI	Associazione Cristiane Lavoratori Italiani
ASI	Althydusamband Islands (Iceland)
BSRB	Bandalag Starfsmanna Rikis og Baeja (Iceland)
CCOO	Comisiones Obreras (Spain)
CES	Confédération Européenne des Syndicats Comité Economique et Social
CESL	Confédération Européenne des Syndicats Libres
CFTC	Confédération Française des Travailleurs Chrétiens (France)
CFDT	Confédération Française Démocratique du Travail (France)
CGB	Christlicher Gewerkschaftsbund (Germany)
CGC	Confédération Générale des Cadres (France)
CGIL	Confederzione Generale Italiana del Lavoro (Italy)
CGT	Confédération Générale des Travailleurs (France)
CGT-FO	Confédération Générale des Travailleurs–Force Ouvrière (France)
CGT-Lux.	Confédération Générale des Travailleurs–Luxembourg
CIC	Confédération Internationale des Cadres
CIDA	Confederazione Italiana delli Administratori (Italy)
CISL	Confederazione Italiana Sindicati Lavoratori (Italy)
CISL	Confédération Internationale des Syndicats Libres
CLE	Comité de Liaison d'Employeurs
CNG	Christlichnationaler Gewerkschaftsbund (Switzerland)
CMT	Confédération Mondiale du Travail
CMTU	Confederation of Maltesian Trade Unions (Malta)
CNV	Christelijk Nationaal Vakverbond (Netherlands)
COREPER	Committee of Permanent Representatives
CSC	Confédération des Syndicats Chrétiens (Belgium)
DAG	Deutsche Angestelltengewerkschaft (Germany)
DGB	Deutscher Gewerkschaftsbund (Germany)
EBFG	Europäischer Bund Freier Gewerkschaften
ECF-IUF	European Committee of Food, Catering and Allied Workers within the IUF
ECFTU	European Confederation of Free Trade Unions
EC of ISETU	European Committee of the International Secretariat of Entertainment Trade Unions
ECSC	European Coal and Steel Community
ECU	European Currency Unit
EEC	European Economic Community
EFA	European Federation of Agricultural Workers' Unions in the Community
EFTA	European Free Trade Association
EFTA-TUC	European Free Trade Association–Trade Union Confederation
EMF	European Metalworkers' Federation

EO–WCL	European Organization of the World Confederation of Labour
ERO	European Regional Organization (of the ICFTU)
ESC	Economic and Social Committee (of the EEC)
ESF	European Social Fund
ETUC	European Trade Union Confederation
ETUI	European Trade Union Institute
EURO–FIET	European Organization of the International Federation of Commercial, Clerical and Technical Employees
FCP	French Communist Party (France)
FGTB	Fédération Générale du Travail de Belgique (Belgium)
FLA	Föderation Luxembourgischer Arbeiter (Luxembourg)
FNV	Federatie Nederlandse Vakbeweging (Netherlands)
FTF	Fällesradet for Dansk Tjenestemands–og Funktionärorganisationer (Denmark)
ICCTU	International Confederation of Christian Trade Unions
ECFTU	International Confederation of Free Trade Unions
ICP	Italian Communist Party
ICTU	Irish Congress of Trade Unions (Ireland)
ILO	International Labour Office
ITUC	Interregional Trade Union Council
LCBG	Letzbuerger Chrëstleche Gewerkschaftsbond (Luxembourg)
LO Denmark	Landsorganisationen i Danmark (Denmark)
LO Norway	Landsorganisasjonen i Norge (Norway)
LO Sweden	Landsorganisationen i Sverige (Sweden)
MNC	Multinational Corporation
NATO	North Atlantic Treaty Organization
OECD	Organization of Economic Cooperation and Development
OEEC	Organization of European Economic Cooperation
PSUC	Partido Socialista Unificado de Cataluña (Spain)
PTTI	Postal, Telegraph and Telephone International
SAK	Suomen Ammattiliittojen Keskusjärjestöj (Finland)
SCE	Standing Committee on Employment
SCP	Spanish Communist Party (Spain)
SEK	Cyrpus Workers' Confederation (Cyprus)
SGB	Schweizerischer Gewerkschaftsbund (Switzerland)
SPD	Sozial Democratische Parteid Deutschlands (Germany)
STV–ELA	Solidaridat de Trabajadores Vascos (Spain)
SVEA	Schweizerischer Verband Evangelischer Arbeitnehmer (Switzerland)
TCO	Tjänstmännens Centralorganisation (Sweden)
TUAC	Trade Union Advisory Committee
TUC	Trade Union Congress (Great Britain)
TURK–SEN	Cyprus Turkish Trade Unions Federation (Cyprus)
TVK	Toimihenkilö-ja Virkamiesjärjestöjen Keskusliitto (Finland)
UGT	Union de Trabajadores de España (Spain)
UIL	Unione Italiana del Laboro (Italy)
UNICE	Union des Industries des Communautés Européennes

Acknowledgements

In the preparation of this study I have received help, encouragement and criticism from a number of friends and scholars to whom I wish to express my gratitude. First of all I am very grateful to Professor Harish Kapur for his friendly advice, constant encouragement and pertinent criticism without which this study would not have been completed. It would take too long to mention the names of all the personalities of the European labour movement who have given me the benefit of their considerable professional experience, but I must particularly thank Heinz O. Vetter, Mathias Hinterscheid, François Staedelin and Dr Ernst Piehl for having shared with me many a thought pertaining to the problems examined in this study. I must also thank the ETUC Secretariat for having permitted me to have access to its archival material without which it would have been impossible indeed to do full justice to some of the important points I have treated here.

Foreword

Western European integration is not the task of governments and European institutions alone. It would indeed be condemned to superficiality were it not supported by representative socio-political forces including, of course, the labour movement.

By focusing attention on the role of the labour movement in this developing process of integration, Barbara Barnouin has filled an important gap that existed in the literature.

The attempt to capture the complex and dynamic interaction between the ETUC and the EC institutions is particularly commendable. It provides a rare insight into some of the realities of European life which are seldom appreciated by the outside world. It also shows that the increasingly important social and employment problems facing the Community can no longer be dissociated from economic considerations and cannot be solved without the co-operation of the European labour movement.

The book has the additional merit of highlighting some of the existential problems the European labour movement is facing due to the present unemployment situation.

Alois Pfeiffer
Member of the
Commission of the European Communities

Introduction

Studies in the field of international relations have traditionally focused their attention on states as actors. Though this 'state-centric view of world affairs'[1] has been challenged by some scholars, it continues, nevertheless, to occupy an important place in international relations despite the emergence of myriad political forces and institutions that play a crucial role in intersocietal relations and international politics. In fact, over the last few decades these important non-governmental groups have continued to increase in number.

The national labour centres are clearly one of the prime examples (and perhaps the most palpable one) of this pluralistic development. The strategic role they have played, and continue to play in the determination of policies within the national frontiers of their respective countries, is indeed multi-dimensional, leading many observers to consider them as having acquired a position of preponderance in industrialized societies. Their influence and role, however, are not limited to the national borders of nations. Their basic ideology of international solidarity has led them, ever since their foundation, to be active also at the international level.

This is particularly true of West European labour organizations with respect to European integration. As early as the late 1940s, they had expressed an interest and willingness to cooperate in the establishment of a large European market which would promote the reconstruction of European economies and facilitate the solution of numerous social problems arising in the aftermath of the Second World War. In their view, the general level of prosperity in Western Europe could be increased only through close cooperation among Western European states; at the same time, it would eventually lead to the creation of a federated Europe that would be a guarantee for the establishment of a lasting peace in the area.[2]

The economic and political evolution of Western Europe, however, did not lead to the achievement of these far-reaching goals. Instead, the labour unions were faced with two important though less ambitious developments. The first was the introduction of an increasingly complex transnational technological phenomenon that resulted in the fragmentation of production of a wide variety of industrial goods. Many goods were manufactured in one country, assembled somewhere else and were finally given the finishing touches in yet another country. As this trend progressed, all avenues of resolving socio-economic issues purely within a national framework became exceedingly difficult. The second development was the establishment of the European Economic Community. Though this slow-moving and pragmatic institution did not correspond to the European labour's ideal of a Federated Europe, it was nevertheless invested with concrete, albeit limited, supranational authority. It could hardly be ignored. A pragmatic response was needed to what was clearly a pragmatic development.

The European labour unions attempted to adapt themselves to the new situation by becoming more and more pragmatic and by finally constituting themselves—not without difficulties—into a European Confederation whose principal objective would be to safeguard and defend the interests of its members at the European level.

In the ongoing process of West European integration, it could be argued that a study of this major pressure group, operating at national and European levels, therefore became highly relevant; for the European labour movement—adapting as it is to the changing situation—could only contribute to the further integration of Europe. Though this element in itself is a sufficient justification for this study, there are a number of other non-negligible considerations:

(1) The institutional framework the European labour movement has established to carry out its European policies transgresses national frontiers. In fact, it goes even beyond the EC borders. Its European organization, the European Trade Union Confederation (ETUC) comprises 23 million workers from the whole of Western Europe and constitutes the largest pressure group within the European Community. Its activities at both national and European levels with respect to European policy can be regarded as a significant factor in the advancement or in the deceleration of the integration process.

(2) Decisions on socio-economic developments in modern industrial societies have to be based on cooperation between relevant social groups. The harmonization and coordination of industrial, economic, regional and social policies at the Community level—which have an impact on the living and working conditions of the majority of the European population—cannot be undertaken without the effective participation of the groups concerned, including of course the trade unions.

(3) The progress of European integration beyond the technical limits imposed by the Rome Treaties might depend on the level of regionalism attained by the labour movement and on its ability to participate effectively in the overall integration process.

(4) The ETUC's interaction with the European Community still remains a relatively unexplored area of research. Hardly any work has been done on the subject, and whatever is available either deals with the period before the formation of the ETUC or, alternatively, is a straightforward account that does not take into consideration the complexities of the subject that become increasingly apparent on consultation of the archival documentation.

The documentation used in this study is wide-ranging. Almost all the published literature that is available on the subject was used for the elaboration of the different basic themes on which attention has been focused. But three additional sources were really crucial for this research: first of all, the author was able to consult the ETUC's unpublished archival documentation. The importance of this documentation can be gauged from the fact that the core of this study is based principally on this source material. Most of the material regarding the foundation of the ETUC, the different problems it had to face and the framework it had established regarding its objective, composition, etc., emanated from this precious source material which has hitherto not been consulted by any researcher. Secondly, the author was able to interview some of the major actors who were directly involved in the integration of the European labour movement and who were the real architects in designing a policy towards the EEC. Thirdly, the author—as a member of the DGB President's staff—participated personally in the various meetings in which many of the issues presented in the study were discussed.

Notes

1. 'Transnational Relations and World Politics', Ernst Nye and Robert Koehane, eds, *Transnational Relations and World Politics*, Cambridge, Harvard University Press, 1971; Karl Kaiser, 'Transnationale Politik: Zu einer Theorie der multinationalen Politik', *Politische Vierteljahreszeitschrift*, **1**, 1969, pp. 80–180.
2. ICFTU, *Report, 1949*, London, November–December 1949, pp. 40, 83, 79, 243.

Chapter 1

European trade unions and European integration: a historical overview

In Europe after the devastation of the Second World War, the primary concern of the labour unions was the maintenance of world peace, the recovery of their national economies, the reconstruction of their ruined industries and the elevation of their impoverished labour force to a new level of economic and social welfare.

In this connection, the European economic recovery plan clearly was a major milestone in the post-war history of the European labour movement. For one thing, it generated a split within the World Federation of Trade Unions (WFTU). The socialist unions parted company with the communist unions, thereby confirming the political and ideological partition of Europe between Eastern and Western zones of influence; for another, it acted as a major catalyst for the non-communist labour movement to unite and collaborate within the newly established International Confederation of Free Trade Unions (ICFTU), which grouped the socialist-oriented labour unions on a world-wide level.[1] But the element that played a primordial role in the forging of ties and the insertion of a European spirit among the non-communist trade unions was the American insistence on the establishment of an overall European recovery plan jointly formulated by all the democratic forces in Europe, including the trade unions. In fact, the trade unions themselves were already convinced that economic cooperation among European nations was a necessary condition for achieving a higher level of prosperity. Such cooperation, in their view, should follow a well-conceived plan stimulating the establishment of large economic entities—larger than the nation–states—within which free exchange of goods could take place. Narrow nationalism was rejected since it would only lead to the artificial protection of national markets by high tariff walls and other trade restrictions. The most urgent initial action, therefore, would be to take 'immediate constructive steps towards economic integration and peace, unification of Europe, including the incorporation of Germany in the European Communities'.[2]

As a first concrete step in this direction, the Schuman Plan to establish a European Coal and Steel Community (ECSC) aroused considerable interest among trade unions in the countries concerned. The Coal and Steel Community was expected to encompass two million workers from these two industries, which would inevitably have to undergo structural changes as a result of the establishment of such a large-scale market. The Committee for the Schuman Plan, established by the ICFTU, therefore saw as its major task the coordination of activities between governments and trade union delegations with the aim of clarifying the role of the High Authority in the proposed Community, in particular with respect to its employment and social policies, and to assure viable ICFTU participation in the operational phases of the project.[3]

That the ICFTU was largely successful in its endeavours was at least partly due to the fact that social and political considerations at the time made it necessary for the governments to seek labour support in order to assure the successful operation of the ECSC. This was particularly true in the case of Germany—a major coal and steel producer among the six countries involved— where trade unions had acquired unprecedented status and strength and were regarded as a guarantee in the process of denazification and democratization. In France and in Italy, but also to some extent in the Benelux countries, the governments favoured the possibility of strengthening the socialist trade unions as against the communist unions, which had denounced the Schuman Plan as a capitalist plot against workers' interests.

The Treaty establishing the ECSC thus contains social provisions concerning compensation payments and re-employment schemes for workers who might have to be displaced by the unavoidable restructuring of the industries concerned. In addition, three labour representatives were appointed as members of the High Authority, one of whom, Paul Finet, held the presidency for a time. Moreover, direct representation of labour from non-communist trade unions was assured in the Consultative Committee of the ECSC, which was concerned with all the major decisions made by the High Authority.

There were four major fields in which the ECSC established policies of direct interest to labour: readaptation for workers displaced by structural changes in the industries concerned; the resolution of the housing problem, an issue of major importance in post-war devastated Europe; the assurance of mobility of labour among the participating countries; and the adoption of industrial safety, health and hygiene programmes that were for the first time under study in Western European countries.[4]

The preparation of the Rome Treaties

In the early 1950s the European Regional Organization (ERO) of the ICFTU, established to deal with the Organization for European Economic Cooperation (OEEC), the ECSC and NATO already supported the idea of European integration. A trade union programme, bearing the imprint of its General Secretary, Walter Schevenels, was formulated equating economic integration with the survival of Europe. It called for social integration, the progressive adaptation of fiscal systems and free movements of goods, capital and workers under the aegis of a European supranational authority vested with vast political power.[5]

When the European idea was evoked at Messina in June 1955 by ECSC foreign ministers, the ERO rapidly responded by convening a conference through which it lent its full support to European economic integration and publicly expressed the hope that it would be accomplished 'within the framework of a policy of full employment and social progress in general, including an upward adjustment of social conditions'.[6] More specifically, the

Conference emphasized the need for the harmonization of economic and social policies, for greater mobility of labour, for the establishment of a European investment fund, for an integrated transportation system and for an organization for peaceful development of atomic energy.[7]

The ERO's support for the proposed European Economic Community (EEC) was again reiterated the following year. While expressing the hope that labour would have an important voice in the preparatory stages of its formation as well as in its institutions, it made a number of suggestions for the strengthening of the positions of the European Assembly and the European Commission as against the European Council of Ministers. The Assembly, in its view, should enjoy the attributes and the powers of national parliaments. But the major concern of the trade unions was to obtain their own participation in all EEC institutions, where they hoped to seek firm guarantees for the protection of workers against any disruptions that might occur during the transitional period of the integration process.[8]

Parallel to these efforts, pursued within the framework of their own European trade union structures, the labour unions also participated in the Action Committee for the United States of Europe established by Jean Monnet. In fact, they were regarded by Monnet as being among its most active members ever since the Committee was founded. In his view, their pro-European attitude had been amply proved in the past. Constituting themselves into a movement that was sensitive to social and political transformations, and representing a considerable force, they were perceived as a highly supportive element for any movement they chose to espouse. Reflecting, in particular, on the German situation at that time, Monnet considered that the Social Democratic Party's (SPD) transformation from original scepticism regarding European integration to that of cautious support was largely due to the DGB's influence.[9]

The attitude of the trade unions to Jean Monnet's action was equally favourable. They considered his committee as a highly valuable instrument for the revival of the European idea. Emphasizing their positive attitude towards the Committee, one of their representatives pointed out that

> Not only did the free trade unions follow the appeal launched by Robert Schuman, but, everytime the objective began to be threatened, they did everything to find solutions that would permit them to continue towards European unification. For example, all free and democratic trade unions actively participated in the Action Committee for the United States for Europe, and were behind its President, Jean Monnet, whenever he launched new initiatives. [Translation][10]

It should also be noted that Monnet's Committee, in turn, was an important meeting point for the Socialist and Christian trade unions; for it was here in this Committee that the two trade unions met regularly for discussions on European issues without any apparent contradictions on the great majority of the problems considered therein. This rapprochement within that institution, it could be argued, contributed to their subsequent reunification within the ETUC.

Trade unions in the European Community

While the basic attitude of the labour movement continued to favour European integration, its commitment to the Common Market was, however, somewhat dampened by the fact that trade unions were unable to exercise any major influence during the preparatory stages of the Rome Treaties, and were subsequently powerless in the determination of the course of the European integration process. Their objective of establishing a European political union with transnational democratic structures, permitting control over political and economic decisions at all levels was hardly realized in the Rome Treaties; if anything, they were faced with a system that tended to widen the powers of the Council of Ministers, considered to represent national rather than European interests.[11]

At the operational and decisional levels too, they witnessed a decline of trade union influence. The earlier Schuman Plan pattern of viable labour participation, for example, was not applied to the European Community. They did not have any representation in its executive organs. At first, an Economic and Social Committee was not even included by the governments.[12] When it was finally established, after considerable pressure by the trade unions, it was a consultative body with a diminished role, where labour unions were joined by other groups and where recommendations for membership were assigned to member states, which presented to the Council a list of acceptable names from which a choice could be made. This was in marked contrast to the ECSC Economic and Social Committee where the power to nominate members lay with the representative organization. Social policy also played a minor role within the Community. It had been relegated to a secondary level and was conceived as an adjunct to economic policies. No provisions were made for the establishment of a European social policy. Apart from a few paragraphs pertaining to the free movement of labour, to a European Social Fund for readjustment purposes, to specific measures concerning equality of wages for men and women doing the same work and to vocational training, national autonomy on social policy matters was maintained. The Commission was given the responsibility of studying social policy in the Community and of promoting cooperation between the member states in social matters rather than fixing goals to be reached by legislative decisions of the Community organs.[13]

The disappointment of the labour movement was further compounded by the fact that these half-hearted measures for an integrated Europe coincided with the resolution of most of the pressing social and economic problems that had surged forward in the immediate aftermath of the Second World War. The net result was that the European trade union structures established to deal with the European Community were relatively weak. The socialist and the Christian trade unions established separate structures in the form of loose coordinating bodies with little interaction between them and with no decision-making powers. The communist trade unions showed no signs of contradicting the anti-European stand of the Soviet Union. If anything, they became openly anti-integrationist and established an action committee against the 'Europe of Monopolies' in 1957.[14]

It was only in the latter part of the 1960s that a number of developments caused a renewal of trade union interests in the European Community. First of all, there was a change of governmental attitude on the trade union role within the Community, particularly in France and Germany, where a new leadership with different views on socio-economic issues and on European integration was projected onto the political scene. The importance of this new development can be gauged from the fact that it was precisely these two countries which had previously obstructed any viable progress in these sectors. France, under De Gaulle, had refused to accept any integrative process of the Community that would result in the weakening of its constituent units. In his perception of European nations none of the supra-national European institutions had any place.[15] Germany, under Erhard, had persistently blocked all efforts to increase the role of socio-economic forces within the Community. First as Minister of Economy and then as Chancellor (from 1948 to 1966), he had considered all attempts to increase the dialogue with trade unions and employers with a view to enhance their participation in the Community as contrary to the rules of the free market economy.[16]

All this changed in the late 1960s. With Pompidou at the helm of French affairs, the process of European Integration was given a new life with his acceptance of 'European Political Cooperation on Foreign Policy' and with the removal of the French veto on the enlargement of the Community.[17] With the nomination of Willy Brandt as the head of the German government, a certain amount of planning in economic and social policies was introduced that required increased consultations with social partners on these matters.[18]

The second element that pushed the trade unions to concern themselves more with Community affairs pertained to the developments in the business world. The customs union plus the Community's industrial policy had facilitated the acceleration of mergers or takeovers between business corporations. The internationalization of the production and marketing processes had become the most impressive trend in large companies' economic activities. Confronted with this new transnational phenomena, it was hardly possible for the trade unions to continue to function at the limited national level.[19]

Thirdly, the increasing strength of the employers' organizations, especially the 'superior interest-organization of the European federations of industries'[20] represented an additional challenge to the trade unions. This new power element, in their view, could only be counteracted by a strong trade union front, that crossed national borders at the industry level and by a viable consensus among the labour unions.[21]

The new political, economic and technological tendencies within the Community thus constituted a major catalyst in pushing the trade unions to operate collectively on the European front. It also made them increasingly conscious of the fact that trade union structures on the EEC level had become highly inadequate, and that they had to establish a new European organizational framework that was better suited to meet the new situation. This was done in 1969. Whereas the socialist unions established a European organization of labour forces from the EEC member states, the European Confederation of Free Trade Unions (ECFTU),[22] the Christian unions created the European Organization of the World Confederation of Labour (EO–WCL) during the same year.[23] Although these organizations included member unions from their respective Internationals, they operated independently of them. Focusing their principal attention on European issues, they had, for the first time in international trade union history, opted for a considerable degree of regional autonomy from their Internationals.[24]

The Communist trade unions—which during the preceding decade had gradually changed their approach to the Common Market—had obtained, for the first time, recognition by the Commission and had established a liaison office in Brussels.[25] At the Community level, this new movement in the direction of greater integration and pronounced social policies found its first and formal expression during The Hague Summit Conference in 1969. The Community gave notice of its intention to progress beyond the customs union towards a more effective economic and monetary union in which social policy would be a necessary and important component. This trend was continued and even reinforced during the early seventies when the Council, in 1971, formally expressed its intention to associate the different socio-economic categories with the management of the 'Economic and Monetary Union' to be established within the EEC. 'It is inconceivable', it declared, 'that the Community should be built up and strengthened in its economic and monetary aspects without taking account of social requirements at a time when they are becoming increasingly important in the planning of economic life in all member states'.[26]

This was re-emphasized at the Paris summit meeting in 1972. On this occasion, the German Chancellor, Brandt in particular argued that social justice and progress should no longer be considered by the Community as an appendage of economic growth, and that an effective social policy would revive the interests of people in European policies and institutions.[27] The meeting instructed the Commission to elaborate a common social policy programme that should also provide for an increased participation of the social partners in the EEC decision-making process.[28]

The introduction of a stronger social component in EEC policies—in the promotion of which trade union pressure at the national levels should by no means be underestimated—undoubtedly accentuated the trade union interest in European issues and finally contributed to the development of a new two-pronged trend in the European labour movement. One, as the European Community became increasingly complex, the trade unions were gradually drawn into the dynamics which they had themselves desired and which they had at least partially provoked. This was compounded by the general awareness that domestic socio-economic conditions had become largely inter-dependent rendering national solutions ineffective. Two, if the growing involvement with the EEC led to a gradual regionalization of the European trade union structures, it also contributed to its qualitative detachment from the Internationals. In sum, the European labour movement was rapidly evolving into a major pressure group at the European level, involved with the 'nitty-gritty' of day-to-day interaction with the Community. Also, it became rapidly apparent that the 1969 trade-union regional structures would not be sufficient to cope with the developments within the EEC, particularly with its enlargement, the negotiations for which were already in progress. The expected entrance into the Community of the ten-million-strong British TUC and the domestically influenced Danish and Norwegian trade unions required another re-examination of labour structures at the European level.

Furthermore, it had also become increasingly evident in the early 1970s that even the ideological structures—that hitherto maintained a division amongst European trade unions—had become, to a large extent, outdated.

Notes

1. George Lefranc, *Les Expériences syndicales internationales des origines à nos jours*, Paris, Aubier, 1952, pp. 98–136; Hans Gottfurcht, *Die internationale Gewerkschaftsbewegung von den Anfängen bis zur Gegenwart*, Cologne, Bundverlag, 1966, pp. 47–55.
2. ICFTU *Report*, 1949, op. cit., p. 243.
3. ICFTU, *European Regional Conference*, Brussels, 1–4 November 1950, p. 4.
4. Meyer Bernstein, 'Labour and the European Communities', reprint from a symposium on European Regional Communities, *Law and Contemporary Problems*, Duke University School of Law, Durham, N.C., 1961, pp. 572–85.
5. Walter Schevenels, 'The ICFTU's European Regional Organisation', *Free Labour World*, Brussels, January 1954, p. 4.
6. European Regional Organization of the ICFTU, 'Report on the European Trade Union Conference for the Revival of the European Idea', Brussels, August 1955, *ICFTU Archives*.
7. Ibid. See also: ICFTU, *Report*, July 1957, pp. 116, 117.
8. ICFTU-ERO, 'Observations Relative to the Draft European Market Treaty Submitted to the President of the Ministerial Committee by the Free Trade Unions Organisations of the Community', Brussels, 30 January 1957, *ICFTU Archives*.
9. Jean Monnet, *Mémoires*, Paris, Fayard, 1976, pp. 605–7.
10. Quoted in Pascal Fontaine, *Le Comité d'Action pour les Etats-Unis de l'Europe*, Lausanne, Centre de Recherches Européennes, 1974, p. 51.
11. Marguerite Bouvard, *Labor Movements in the Common Market Countries: The Growth of a European Pressure Group*, New York, Praeger, 1972, p. 50.
12. Gerda Zellentin, *Formen der Willensbildung in den Europäischen Organisationen* (Kölner Schriften zur Politischen Wissenschaft), Cologne, Athenaeum Verlag, 1965, p. 16 ff.
13. Treaty of Rome, Art. 48–51, 117–19, 123–8. On the EEC's social policy, see also: Colin R. Beever, *Trade Unions and the Common Market*, London, PEP, 1962, pp. 73–109; Jean-Jacques Ribas, *La Politique Sociale des Communautés Européennes*, Paris, Dalloz 1969; Bernt Heise, *Sozialpolitik in der europäischen Wirtschaftsgemeinschaft*, Göttingen, 1966; Bouvard, op. cit.; Doreen Collins, *The European Communities: The Social Policy of the First Phase*, London, Martin Robertson, 1975.
14. Bouvard, op. cit., pp. 43–55, 79–85; Ulrich Wacker, 'Zur Europapolitik der französichen Gewerkschaft CGT', in *Arbeiterbewegung und Westeuropäische Integration*, Frank Deppe, ed., Cologne, Pahl-Rugenstein, 19776, pp. 278–82; Werner Feld, 'The French and Italian Communists and the Common Market', *Journal of Common Market Studies*, **6**, No. 3, March 1968, pp. 249–65; Gerda Zellentin, *Die Kommunisten und die Einigung Europas*, Frankfurt-on-Main, Athenaeum Verlag, 1964, pp. 73–4.
15. Jean Lecerf, *La Communauté en péril: histoire de ;'unité Européennee 2*, Paris, Gallimard

(Collection idées), 1975, pp. 142–58; Walter Hallstein, *Die europäische Integration*, Düsseldorf, Econ Verlag, 1979, pp. 115–18.

16. Zellentin, 'Formen der Willensbildung . . .', op. cit., p. 25; see also Herbert Muller-Roschach, *Die deutsche Europapolitik 1949–1977*, Bonn, Europa Union Verlag, 1980, pp. 71–170.

17. Lecerf, op. cit. pp. 172–80, 336–39; *Die Europäische Politische Zusammenarbeit*, R. Rummel and W. Wessel, eds., Bonn, Europa Union Verlag, 1978, pp. 57–70.

18. Hermann Adam, 'Die Konzertierte Aktion in der Bundesrepublik', *WSI–Studien*, No. 21, Cologne, Bund Verlag, 1972, pp. 5–10.

19. Ernst Piehl, *Multinationale Konzerne und die internationale Gewerkschaftsbewegung*, Frankfurt-an-Main, Europäische Verlagsanstalt, 1974 (Schriftenreihe der Otto Brenner Stiftung, No. 2) Chapter 4, pp. 132–207.

20. Volker Jung, Norbert Koubek, Ernst Piehl and Ingrid Scheibelange, 'Aspects of Union Policy in Western Europe: Economic Concentration and Political Integration as a Challenge for the Trade Unions', translated from *WWI–Mitteilungen*, No. 10, 1971, p. 5.

21. Ibid., pp. 10–11; see also Emil Joseph Kirchner, *Trade Unions as a Pressure Group in the European Community*, Westmead, Saxon House, 1978, p. 28.

22. Bouvard, op. cit., p. 61.

23. EO–WCL, 'Die Stellung der Arbeitnehmer in einem sich veränderden Europa', *Tätigkeitsbericht des Ersten Kongresses*, Brussels, 7–10 May 1969.

24. Alberto Perez-Calvo, *L'Organisation européenne de la Confédération mondiale du travail*, l'Universitié de Nancy II, Centre européen universitaire, Nancy, 1976; EBFG, *Der EBFG gegenüber den Umwandlungen der Gemeinschaft*, Jahresversammlung 1971, Toulouse, 8–9 October 1971.

25. Europäische Gemeinschaften, Presse und Information, 'Ständiger Ausschuss CGT–CGIL', *Europäische Dokumentation*, Brussels, 1971.

26. EC Commission, 'Preliminary Guidelines for a Common Social Policy Programme', 17 March 1971, Brussels, *EC Bulletin*, 1971, No. 4, Supplement 2/71.

27. Full text of the Declaration of Chancellor Willy Brandt at the summit meeting, *Bulletin des Presse- und Informationsamtes*, Bonn, 20 October 1972, No. 147, pp. 1753–6.

28. *Déclaration finale de la conférence des chefs d'État ou de gouvernements des états membres ou adhérents des communautés européennes du 19 au 21 octobre 1972*. EBFG, op. cit.; see also Heinz Kuby, 'Machtverschiebung in Europea', *Gewerkschaftliche Monatshefte*, No. 22, 1977, p. 412.

Chapter 2

The enlargement of the European labour organization

The geographical dimension

For a number of years, trade union confederations from the EFTA states had shown an increasing interest in Common Market policies and had established in 1968 in Brussels a secretariat, the EFTA–TUC, comprising all ICFTU affiliates in the EFTA states. In view of the fact that the EEC was to be enlarged from six to nine or ten states, these trade union centres also became desirous to review the trade union structures in Western Europe. At a meeting convened for this purpose in Oslo in November 1971 between the ICFTU affiliates from EEC and EFTA countries, a few basic principles for increased cooperation between Western European trade unions were agreed upon.

It was recognized that 'the increased economic and technological inter-action between Western European states affecting national economic growth and employment situations precludes an effective representation of workers' interests on the national level alone'.[1] Furthermore, it was emphasized that the development and increase in strength of multinational corporations in Western Europe required a new and coordinated approach by the trade unions to enable them to effectively represent workers' interests towards these companies. Finally, the development of a more active social policy within the enlarged Community was again underlined as a major objective of trade union action.

The meeting decided to institute a working group, which, on the basis of these principles, would discuss the form and manner of increasing cooperation among West European trade unions. The group's target would be to make concrete proposals on the structure and objectives of an organizational framework. As the working group began to undertake this assignment, a series of differences arose among its members which—after several meetings—became so accentuated that it appeared increasingly difficult to reach a consensus on a number of basic issues. While there seemed to be general agreement that a new European labour organization should be established, divergence of opinion emerged on major questions such as the geographical extension of the organization, its aims and objectives and its links to the ICFTU.

One of the major difficulties arising at the very start of the negotiations was related to the negative or at least ambivalent attitude of the British Trades Union Congress (TUC) towards the Common Market.[2] Parallel to the government negotiations on Great Britain's entry into the Common Market in 1970–1, the ECFTU had proposed the establishment of a working group, with the participation of the TUC, to formulate trade union objectives in connection with the enlargement of the Common Market. Although the principle of forming such a committee had been accepted by the TUC, it never became operational, since TUC resolutions in 1970 and 1971 forbade its organization to participate with the other European trade union confederations in the formulation of a common position on the government negotiations.[3] As these negotiations progressed, it became increasingly clear that the TUC's attitude towards its country's entry into the Common Market coincided with that of the British Labour Party.

In a report adopted by the Annual Congress in 1970, the TUC clarified its views regarding the objectives the British government should try to achieve in its negotiations with the EEC. These objectives centered mainly around the problem of the costliness of the British contribution to the EEC budgetary requirements and its consequences for the British balance of payments. A second report, adopted by the Congress in September 1971, judged that government negotiations had failed to meet the objectives set by the TUC, and concluded that the annual cost to the British balance of payments would be at least 500 million pounds a year by the end of the transitional period.[4]

Since Great Britain had been suffering from chronic balance of payments' difficulties, the financial obligations which would ensue from her entry into the EEC, could—in the view of the TUC—be fulfilled only if deflationary policy measures were introduced. But the dangers of such a policy were that they could result in decelerating economic growth and therefore in increased unemployment. The TUC expressed, furthermore, the apprehension that British capital investment might move away from England into the industrial centres of the EEC, a process which could again diminish the growth of the British economy.

The TUC, therefore, manifested an overwhelming opposition to Britain's entry into the EEC unless a number of conditions were met. To its refusal to accept the financial obligations, the TUC added its refusal to accept the agricultural market in its present form, to accede to a possible monetary union or to any other form of 'supranationality'. In the TUC's view

the abolition of national currencies [within the EEC], while major economic difficulties exist between member states, could make it even harder to prevent industrial development taking place at the centre of the Community to the detriment of more outlying regions. The whole notion of economic and monetary union along the lines foreseen by the Community should not be uncritically accepted. It is not self evident that a group of the size of the EEC in fact needs a highly centralized economic system.[5]

Although some members of the TUC leadership might not have been as categorically opposed to Britain's entry into the Common Market or might have been more flexible concerning the conditions for joining the EEC, bound as they were by their Congresses' decisions, they could hardly do more than play an ambivalent role on the Brussels scene and take a restraining attitude towards the new European labour organization to be created.

Victor Feather, the General Secretary of the TUC, stated in an interview in January 1972 that, while he was not at all enthusiastic about Britain's entry into the Common Market, once England became a member, she would bring ten million organized workers which would match the eleven million then organized in the EEC. In his view, the sheer arithmetic of the new situation would enable labour to challenge the Community's economic policy-making bodies, and in particular the Economic and Social Committee which he characterized as a 'bladder of lard'. With regard to the continental labour movement, he criticized the 'constant in-fighting between Christians, Communist and Socialist Unions' while, on the other hand, emphasizing their social achievements.

As the major preoccupation for the British and European unions, he singled out particularly the role of the multinational corporations (MNCs) and the 'disproportionate and undesirable effect' they could have on policy decisions.[6] By giving top priority to MNCs in trade union action, Feather was highlighting the limitations of functioning within the narrow EEC framework. He envisaged a much broader forum for trade union action, a concept that was subsequently to dominate the TUC's attitude in the discussions that ensued regarding the geographical dimension of the European organization.

After the TUC Congress in September 1972 had again passed resolutions condemning by a strong majority the principle of Britain's entry into the Common Market and requesting unanimously the renegotiation of entry conditions, its leaders strongly encouraged the concept of an organization eventually including all trade union confederations in Western Europe. For the time being, however, they were prepared to accept the inclusion of all ICFTU affiliates of the region.[7]

In this concept, the TUC was supported by other members of the EFTA–TUC, especially the Nordic confederations. But the latter's argument was not based—as in the case of the TUC--on an ambivalent or negative attitude towards the Common Market, since the trade unions of Denmark and Norway were actively campaigning for the entry of their respective countries into the EEC. It was founded on more general economic considerations which, in their view, required intensified international cooperation between trade unions, in the whole of Western Europe, on a wide spectrum of economic and social issues. They believed that the 'preservation and creation of work and income is no more a national task, but an international matter as well, to be dealt with at least on the Western European level', since conditions for growth and employment are shaped in several countries at the same time. Thus, they considered it a primary task of the trade union movement in Europe to secure coordinated growth policies among the Western European governments.

With respect to the European institutions, the Nordic trade unions attributed great importance to the 'appearance of the Council as a decisional centre in Europe which has to be influenced by an integrated union movement, directing it towards socio-economic and political objectives corresponding to the conceptions of the labour movement'. They also stressed the importance of common actions towards MNCs in Europe. In general, however, they argued that

the question of trade union cooperation goes beyond jobs and growth. The broader aim of the labour movement, both on the political side and for the trade unions, would be to take part in and influence the formulation and evolution of society as we move into the post-industrial period, and as our national societies become increasingly integrated and interdependent. It is a question of gaining control over developments, to create the type of societies we desire. The aim must be to improve in a wide sense the life of those who live in these societies, and to give the man and woman an increasing possibility and ability to influence his and her own situation.[8]

In addition to these general conceptions, there existed a number of practical motivations which led trade unions of the EFTA–TUC to come out in support of a Western European labour confederation. The Scandinavians had established a long tradition of cooperation among themselves and had consolidated their trade union structure by setting up, in June 1972, the Nordic Labour Council—parallel to the political Nordic Council. The date is significant, since it shows their determination—while the negotiations about the new European labour organization were under way—not to allow any split within the Nordic cooperation scheme between members of the EEC and others. Including all the Scandinavian members of the ICFTU would however mean that the other ICFTU affiliates in Western Europe—the Austrian and Swiss confederations— could not be excluded from such an organization.[9]

A different framework for a European labour organization was advanced by some of the confederations of the ECFTU. The German DGB and the French FO, supported by the ECFTU Secretariat, for example, were in favour of an organization that was restricted to confederations within the enlarged Community. The DGB, in particular, was apprehensive about the degree of inefficiency such a large organization might engender with respect to the Community's institutions. It desired to establish a 'functional' organization with the specific task of dealing with Community affairs.[10] Furthermore, both the DGB and FO feared that a geographically extended organization might open the way for an ideological expansion beyond ICFTU members, thereby introducing an even greater degree of complexity and incoherence within the proposed organization. This apprehension was generally shared by the ECFTU Secretariat at that time. In its view, ICFTU organizations from the non-Community area should be admitted as associate members.[11]

The controversy about geographical extension was reflected in the debates regarding the aims and objectives that the new labour organization should adopt. While it was generally accepted that the organization should be an instrument of firm cooperation among Western European labour confederations, differences appeared as to the targets of such cooperation. Should it deal principally with the Common Market and its institutions, or should it—as proposed by the members of EFTA–TUC—deal with a number of more general trade union questions, leaving the Common Market issue as one among many?[12]

Although a meeting of European Trade Union leaders in Geneva on 6 June 1972 could not reach a consensus on the objectives of the organization, a majority favoured a large Western European labour organization.[13] Some of the former opponents to this solution had finally altered their views on this issue on the calculation that the weight of the EEC organizations in the new body would clearly outmatch the non-EEC organizations both in terms of their numbers as well as in terms of their membership figures. Thus, even in a large structure the preponderance of EEC organizations would be assured and—in spite of its more cumbersome structure—the possibilities orientating the European labour organization in a given direction could be largely maintained.[14]

Relations with the ICFTU

While the discussions about the establishment of a European labour organization were well under way, increasing concern was voiced within the ICFTU regarding the creation of an organization which—unlike the former European Regional Organization (ERO) of the ICFTU, to which its Western European affiliates had belonged—would not have any organic link with the ICFTU. Furthermore, the plans to create an independent labour organization in the European region were perceived, by most of the non-European ICFTU affiliates, as a serious threat to the very existence of the International.

Two consequences of such an action were particularly feared: one, the establishment of a European organization might lead to a high degree of regional involvement among the European ICFTU affiliates, possibly paralleled by decreased interest in the global labour organization in general and in the problems of developing countries and their unions in particular; two, the proposed European organization might gradually reduce the role of the ICFTU in Europe, thereby contributing to the weakening of the International itself.

These arguments were counteracted by the European organizations. L. Nielsen (LO Denmark) reminded the ICFTU that the ERO had been terminated in 1969 because of its inability to deal with internal European problems. Some speakers, furthermore, emphasized that the new organization would not be established as a competitor to ICFTU. It would be created for a series of practical considerations with precise targets and functions geared towards the Common Market.[15]

In the subsequent negotiations among Western European trade unions, the question of the new organization's relationship with the ICFTU did not pose a major problem. The vast majority of the confederations agreed not to recreate a regional organization of the ICFTU, but, at the same time, to continue to participate in ICFTU activities. It was also agreed that some type of working relations would be established between the executive organs of both organizations.

The deadlock

A number of events had, however, justified new doubts in the minds of those union leaders who were convinced that the best solution was a European Labour Organization that respected the Common Market's boundaries, but who had nevertheless shown some willingness to compromise on this matter. The TUC Congress in September 1972 had again passed a number of anti-EEC resolutions. Controversies about the financing of the European labour organization had arisen during the CESL–EFTA–TUC working group meetings, where the TUC refused to meet its obligations defined on the same lines as the other organizations. Also, there had been indications that the TUC—after Britain's entry into the EEC—would not participate in the different EEC institutions where trade unions were represented. Lastly, the vote on the referendum on Norway's entry into the Common Market on 24–25 September 1972 had yielded a negative result. Consequently, trade union representation in the EEC from Scandinavian countries had received a severe set-back. Thus, the Luxembourg meeting of European trade union leaders of October 1972, originally convened to confirm the date for constituting the new organization, became a scene of heated controversies.

It was particularly feared by some of the participants that an organization might be established which would by-pass the problems of the EEC. This apprehension was basically inspired by the British TUC attitude, which tried to side-track the establishment of a viable organization that possessed sufficient functional strength in terms of finances, secretariat, etc. Furthermore, concern also stemmed from the attempts by most of the EFTA–TUC representatives to dilute the European objectives of the organization through the introduction of many general trade union issues.[16]

The major difficulty arose, however, from the fact that the German DGB changed its attitude. Notwithstanding its preference in favour of an organization geared towards the EEC, it had up to then maintained a certain flexibility and willingness to compromise on this question. Reconsidering the issue at its meeting on 20 October 1972, the DGB Executive Board had, however, clearly come out against the establishment of an organization which was geographically not limited to the EEC. In its decision, the Board specified that only ICFTU members should be admitted and that its affiliates from EFTA states could become associate members. In the DGB's view, a homogeneous representation of workers' interests with respect to European institutions would be jeopardized by the participation of trade unions not directly concerned by EEC policies.

The Board furthermore expressed concern that the recent resolutions of the TUC Congress on Common Market matters might be an indication that the TUC considered an enlarged ECFTU as an instrument against the EEC.[17] It also expressed the fear that an enlarged ECFTU, including all ICFTU affiliates in Europe, would weaken the political weight of the ICFTU not only in Europe but also in the Third World, a situation which in turn would aggravate the conflict between trade unions in industrialized and developing countries.

The Scandinavian position on the other hand was reconfirmed by LO Denmark which considered the EEC decisions concern directly or indirectly those countries which were not members of the EEC. Since those countries do not have any influence on the EEC decision-making process, the forum of discussion created by an enlarged European labour organization would become even more significant for organizations from non-EEC countries. Trade unions in most of those countries, and particularly the Norwegian Labour Organization, which had strongly campaigned for the entry of its country into the EEC, had been favouring the strengthening of the EEC's relations with EFTA. The question of weakening the ICFTU by an enlarged European labour organization did, in their view, not occur, since the two organizations had distinctly different tasks to perform.

When the DGB Executive Committee, at its meeting on 7 November 1972, confirmed its former decision in favour of a functional EEC-orientated organization, LO Denmark and the British TUC thereupon declared that they would not become members of the new organization.[18] This dissident decision was evidently based on two different considerations: LO Denmark wanted to avoid a schism in the Scandinavian labour movement, whereas the TUC wanted to prevent internal conflict which might arise due to the anti-European decisions of its Congresses.

Under those circumstances, the solution to the problem appeared to rest on the shoulders of the DGB. An organization without the participation of two important confederations from the newly admitted EEC member states could hardly be considered representative of workers' interests within the Community. The persistence of the DGB in its attitude—however well founded— could lead to a major crisis in the European labour movement. Trade unions in Europe would not only be split into three ideological factions, but also divided into two regional blocs. Moreover, the continued existence of the present ECFTU would also be endangered, since cooperation with the partisans of an enlarged grouping (CISL and UIL, Italy and FGTB, Belgium) might not be assured in the future. Finally, its doors would in all probability also be closed to the Christian unions who, for a number of years, had been encouraging the elimination of idological barriers in favour of a united European labour movement.

Old issues revisited: the debate about a name

Two decisions taken by the European Council at its Paris summit meeting on 9 November 1972 were of major significance for the European labour movement: the Council decided to enhance the social policy in the EEC and to associate its social partners more closely to the decision-making process; and, secondly, it accepted an ECFTU proposal to prepare a social conference for April 1973.

These decisions underlined the urgency for the European trade unions to reach a consensus about a labour organization capable of functioning as a partner of the EEC institutions.

In an effort to find a compromise, without too much delay, a series of bilateral consultations took place between the different confederations involved. In particular, a delegation composed of three Scandinavian trade-union leaders headed by Thomas Nielsen, the Secretary-General of LO Denmark, visited the DGB headquarters for an exchange of views with the DGB Executive Board to reiterate their support for an enlarged labour organization and to confirm their willingness to function within an organization which might have a series of broad objectives, but whose principal task would be to represent workers' interests within the European institutions.[19]

After further deliberations the DGB Executive Board, in an extraordinary session, decided to reverse its former commitment to a restricted organization and to accept the 'large solution'.[20] This permitted the conference of European trade union leaders, convened in Luxembourg from 30 November to 1 December 1972, to reach an agreement on the geographical extension of the organization.[21]

A controversy, however, arose with respect to the name that should be given to the new European labour organization. This discussion—though apparently formalistic—in fact symbolized a series of diverging political and ideological concepts about the role of this organization. The debate centred around the question of whether or not to insert the word 'free' into the name of the new organization.

In order to demonstrate continuity in European labour policies—which hitherto had been carried out to a large extent within the framework of the ICFTU—the German, French, Austrian and Swiss unions defended the inclusion of the word 'free' into the name of the organization, 'free' being the traditional expression marking them off from communist unions since the split of the WFTU in 1948. In a lesser sense, it also represented the traditional separation from the Christian unions. 'Free' reflected the role and position of socialist-orientated trade unions in Western democratic societies, particularly their political and financial independence from parties and governments. Moreover, the insertion of the word 'free' underlined an implicit intention to avoid the opening of the organization to the Christian and Communist labour confederations.

Over the years, the Christian unions had developed a similarity of views with the socialist unions regarding European issues. Discussions about their possible affiliations to the new labour organization had already begun paralleling the discussion on its geographical dimension. Nevertheless, while the Christian unions appeared more acceptable than the communist unions, some reservations persisted regarding their admission. Accepting the Christian unions, ran the argument, might also facilitate the entrance of the communists, since one ideological opening might conceivably lead to another. Furthermore, it was argued that such an opening at an early stage might impede the process of internal consolidation which was deemed indispensable for the effective functioning of the organization.[22]

The ideological dimension

In spite of the reservations voiced by some of the European trade unions about the ideological expansion of the European organization, the question soon became unavoidable. Both the Christian and the communist unions showed increasing interest in joining the European organization. During the early stages of the debate on this issue, it became clear that the cases of the Christian and the communist unions should be approached differently. While the Christian unions had been consistently favourable to the European idea, the past hostility of the communist unions towards European integration could not be forgotten so easily and required a 'clear profession in favour of European integration'.[23]

The Christian trade unions

A Christian International, the International Confederation of Christian Trade Unions (ICCTU), established in the aftermath of the First World War, which was renamed World Confederation of Labour (WCL) in 1968, developed independently from the socialist and communist Internationals and with relatively little interaction with the two. Based on the doctrine of social Christianity, this labour movement sought to avoid both a socialist and an unrestrained liberal society in favour of a social system where individual liberty would be limited only by the requirements of general welfare.[24] The overwhelming majority of its member organizations are Roman Catholic and were—until recently—mainly located in Western Europe.[25]

Partly because of their closeness to Christian Democratic parties, the European affiliates of the WCL did, at an early stage, come out in favour of European integration, which they viewed as a supranational federation. One of the major objectives of such a federation would be to provide an equitable social order through the institutionalization of an active social policy, aiming at the realization of full employment, a European policy of social security and an efficient regional policy for the economically poor areas.[26]

Like the socialist trade unions, the Christian labour movement in Western Europe had supported the Marshall and Schuman Plans and had established, in 1955, a loose federation of trade unions for the European Coal and Steel Community which was to gather and to diffuse information to its affiliates. After the establishment of the European Economic Community, the WCL set up a regional organization for Europe, which, however, was not geared towards Common Market institutions only: it was to coordinate trade union action and to represent workers' interests within all European institutions, such as the OECD, the Council of Europe and EFTA.

As was the case with the socialist trade unions, the Christian organizations were also disappointed with the orientation of the Rome Treaties, which were, on the one hand, far away from the supranational political union conceived by them and, on the other, were considered socially inadequate. Notwithstanding their critical attitude towards the Common Market, the Christian trade unions participated actively in the work of those EEC institutions to which they had access.

Although the Christian trade unions were, in their principal demands (democratization of the Community institutions, enlargement of the Community, acceleration of the integration process)[27] fairly close to those voiced by the European ICFTU organizations, they had—for a long time—operated in a sphere of isolation. The limited number of affiliated organizations and their comparatively low level of membership had made their impact on the European community relatively marginal. By the mid-1960s, the problem of trade union efficiency arose time and again as Christian unions felt unable to influence governments, employers and the European institutions.

This problem was analysed in a report by the president of the European organization of the WCL (EO–WCL), who proposed that structural and organizational changes should be introduced to increase labour's efficiency in representing their members' interests within the Community. In particular, the report recommended that cooperation with the European ICFTU organizations on Common Market issues should be reinforced and institutionalized.[28]

In the past, some forms of cooperation between the Christian and socialist trade unions on the European level had already existed. With respect to the High Authority of the European Coal and Steel Community, a liaison committee between Christian and socialist organizations had been established in 1952 and, in a broader context, cooperation within the Trade Union Advisory Committee to the OECD had been gradually intensified over the years. Within the EEC framework, however, the record of cooperation between these two groups of organizations had been rather poor.

It was only in the second half of the 1960s that some cooperation had been established between the European organizations of the ICFTU and the WCL at the EEC level, particularly within the framework of the Economic and Social Committee. This cooperation appeared to develop in a fruitful way in spite of the fact that some friction persisted between the socialist and Christian Internationals, and in spite of the fact that serious difficulties existed at the national level in France and Belgium between socialist and Christian trade union confederations. A series of common positions on European issues had been published since 1967, and some elements of functional cooperation within the framework of the Trade Union Advisory Committee–OECD had already been established.[29] The socialist and Christian trade-union·congresses, for example, had both passed resolutions to the effect that consultations should take place between the two organizations to define practical strategies for increased collaboration.[30] In fact, a meeting between delegations of the two organizations had produced a proposal for the establishment of a joint committee with the mandate to work out a means for the merger of the two secretariats.[31]

In the meantime, however, negotiations between the ECFTU and the EFTA–TUC had brought into the open a series of problems which were considered of greater urgency than negotiations with the Christian trade unions. The proposals for merger therefore met with serious difficulties within the ECFTU and, in fact, were never implemented. It was felt by many ECFTU affiliates that ideological questions, which would inevitably arise in discussion with Christian unions, would unnecessarily complicate the already intricate negotiations with the EFTA–TUC.

The OE–CMT, on the other hand—a relatively small group at the European level in comparison to the ECFTU—wished to reinforce its position by working under the same umbrella with the socialist trade unions and was particularly keen to maintain the dialogue with them on this issue. Its second Congress in May 1972 confirmed its desire to establish a unified trade union structure at the European level.[32]

After some initial difficulties, a meeting finally took place between the two organizations in The Hague in 1972. It was generally recognized, on that occasion, that the forthcoming enlargement of the Community, the strengthening of the employers and the lack of influence of the European labour movement with respect to the European institutions had made it imperative to review the question of close and even institutionalized cooperation between the two organizations.[33]

The EO–WCL desired to participate in an enlarged working group established between themselves, the ECFTU and the EFTA–TUC that would enable them to participate in the creation of the new European labour organization.

This problem again met with a series of difficulties within the ECFTU. Due to divergences with the Christian trade unions at the national level, the Belgian FTGB and the French FO—basically reluctant about the admission of these unions into the proposed labour organization—were even more opposed to their participation in the negotiations about the establishment of such an organization. They therefore argued that relations with the EO–WCL should be the task of the new European labour organization once it had been established. The Secretary-General of the Belgian FGTB, George Debunne, contended moreover that should there be an ideological extension of the new organization, it should not in that case be restricted to the Christian unions, but should also embrace the communist trade unions, a proposal strongly criticized by the otherwise allied French FO. In the view of its General-Secretary, André Bergeron, admitting organizations belonging to the three Internationals would completely dislocate the free international trade-union movement and was, therefore, totally unacceptable to his organization.[34]

Another factor which further complicated the whole issue was the friction between the socialist and Christian Internationals. The ICFTU had become increasingly apprehensive about meetings that had taken place between the WFTU, and WCL and their regional organizations in February 1972 in Dubrovnik and in April 1972 in Brussels, where the forthcoming elections to the governing body of the ILO were the main topic. In particular, these meetings attempted to devise tactics to diminish the predominant role of ICFTU organizations within the workers' group of that body. These meetings caused consternation within the ICFTU about the 'double game' the EO–WCL was playing. On the one hand, it actively sought the cooperation of the European ICFTU affiliates at the EEC level; on the other it tried to undermine the ICFTU position within the ILO with the assistance of the communist International.[35]

After the establishment of the ETUC, the EO–WCL again expressed interest in participating in a united European trade-union organization. Its Executive Board decided to request another meeting with the ETUC on this matter, this time not to negotiate their entry into the ETUC but to establish a list of problems to be solved before negotiations proper would begin.

Within the ETUC, however, a general reluctance to admit the Christian trade unions appeared to prevail. With the exception of the Dutch, who were in the process of realizing a merger between the Christian and socialist trade unions on the national level, most organizations expressed reservations on this issue. While some insisted that the newly created ETUC should at first be allowed a phase of consolidation before it opened itself up to other organizations,[36] others favoured the entry of the Christian trade unions only under condition that the communists should also be admitted. This point had already been brought forward by the Belgian FGTB on earlier occasions and was now strongly supported by the British TUC, which was in favour of a largely open organization. It was also supported by the Italian CISL, which wished to pave the way for the eventual entrance of the Italian CGIL into the ETUC.[37] Others again expressed concern about the lack of any serious intention on behalf of the Christian trade unions to unify at the national and international levels. Notwithstanding these diverging reservations, all affiliates, with the exception of the FO, were in favour of continuing talks with the EO–WCL.[38]

During the ensuing negotiations, a series of problems became apparent on which the EO–WCL showed a high degree of willingness to compromise. Among the EO–WCL affiliates were two organizations which were not acceptable to the ETUC. One was the German CGB, a marginal organization the DGB had consistently attempted to eliminate from the German labour scene, and the Italian ACLI, a Catholic workers' movement strongly linked to the Vatican, which the Italian confederation refused to consider as a trade union.[39] These two organizations—it was assumed by the EO–WCL—would not request affiliation with the ETUC.[40]

In fact, it was not the EO–WCL as such which would affiliate to the ETUC, but candidates for membership would be its seven individual confederations: the Dutch NKV and CNV, the Swiss CNG and SVEA, the Luxembourg LCGB, the Belgian CSC and the French CFDT. The affiliation of these organizations would automatically lead to the suppression of the EO–WCL.[41]

The most difficult problem, however, pertained to the relations between the ETUC and the WCL. Whereas the EO–WCL wanted the ETUC to establish a relationship with the WCL similar to the one it had with the ICFTU, this proposal met with considerable resistance from ETUC organizations. In their view, relations with the WCL should remain within the jurisdiction of the ICFTU, which, for the last twenty years, had been trying to absorb the Christian International. No agreement could be reached on this issue, which deadlocked the negotiations. Although a few practical problems regarding this matter had been solved, major disagreements on basic issues continued to persist.

A breakthrough was finally accomplished in the beginning of 1974, after an agreement between the ICFTU and the WCL was reached to establish a common working group to study the possibilities of cooperation and unification of the two Internationals.[42] This agreement—which later appeared to be little more than a tactical move on behalf of the WCL—paved the way for the approval of the applications of the Christian confederations by the ETUC Executive Board that was ratified by a large majority of the ETUC Congress in March 1974.[43] Subsequently, the OE–CMT was dissolved at its extraordinary Congress in May 1974.[44]

The communist trade unions

While the admission of the Christian unions into the ETUC created relatively few problems, the debate around the entrance of the communist unions proved to be far more difficult. Contrary to the socialist and Christian unions, the Communist labour movement had consistently opposed every step towards European integration, in particular the establishment of the ECSC in 1952 and of the EEC in 1958. They viewed their establishment as a reflection of the Cold War, and as an instrument of the United States the purpose of which was to further extend its influence over Western Europe.[45]

The history of cooperation and dissent between West European communist and socialist trade unions had instilled strong misgivings among some of the socialist unions regarding any collaboration or even dialogue with communist unions. They were viewed as a danger for European trade-union unity and feared as a Trojan horse, likely to inject Communist policies (and thereby Soviet influence) into the European labour movement. Such apprehensions, however, were not echoed by all the Socialist trade unions. Some of them considered the inclusion of the two large trade union confederations of France and Italy as necessary for trade union efficacity in the region. Another important element in the debate was the evolution of the communist trade unions within their own countries on the one hand, and towards the Common Market on the other.[46]

The Italian Communist Confederation (CGIL)

The CGIL, in particular, had undergone a sea-change since the split of the Italian labour movement in the aftermath of the Second World War. After 1948, it was repeatedly used by its communist leaders as a political weapon. Different forms of agitation were developed against Italy's involvement in European economic integration and in other foreign policy issues.[47]

By 1954 the other confederation, the Christian Democratic CISL, founded after the 1948 split in the Italian labour movement, had gained strength at both factory and national levels at the expense of the CGIL. The combination of this factor with such external events as the 20th Congress of the Soviet Communist party, and the upheavals in Eastern Europe accelerated the downhill trend of the CGIL along with that of the Italian Communist party.[48]

The most important consequence of this development was the commencement of a process of re-examination of CGIL policies by its leadership. A number of modifications were introduced to adapt the trade union to the changing domestic and external realities. For the purpose of this study, the most important modification occurred regarding European integration. A few months after the establishment of the Common Market, the CGIL published its first official statement on the subject.[49] While stressing the fact that economic integration was basically valuable and could no longer be viewed as an instrument of the Atlantic Pact but as a viable economic institution, the declaration further pointed out that though the integration policies were

dominated by capitalist interests there had been nevertheless some amelioration of workers' living standards.

The conclusion drawn from this fact was that, in a European labour market,
unions, if divided, would be helpless before a powerful coalition of monopolies
and governments. This challenge could not be met by confrontation and verbal
attack, but required joint action by unions of all political affiliations.

At the fourth Congress of the WFTU in Leipzig in 1957, Guiseppe de
Vittorio, General Secretary of the CGIL, pointed out that the Common Market
was in the 'process of becoming a reality'[50] which should no longer be ignored
by the WFTU. In fact, he argued that it should be used to promote one of the
WFTU's major goals, the re-establishment of unity among trade unions in
Europe. A unified labour movement at the European level could transform the
Common Market from a capitalist-dominated institution to one which would
act in the interest of the workers.[51] Such evaluation of the situation did not
receive any support from the WFTU and its affiliates, who persisted in
opposing the Common Market. The CGIL argument was characterized as a
revisionist withdrawal before a *fait accompli*, when the basic aim should be the
liquidation of the EEC.

In the face of such lack of sympathy for the Italian point of view, the CGIL
gradually showed an increasing interest in greater national and regional
autonomy from the WFTU. It proposed a meeting of the WFTU's affiliates in
Common Market countries[52] with a view to examining ways and means of
establishing an information office in Brussels. When its French and Luxembourg counterparts refused to attend such a meeting, Sergio Lama, the General
Secretary of the CGIL, decided to set up such an office on his own in order 'to
escape from the absurd isolationism in which they have so far been voluntarily
confined'.[53] This fear of isolation also found its expression in the new CGIL
interest in cooperation with other left-wing forces at the international level. In
its view, 'the struggle waged by the working people at national levels in the
different sectors of the economy cannot produce the desired effect unless it is
elevated onto the international level'.[54]

Parallel to this new vision of the international cooperation, the CGIL
increasingly worked together with the two other Italian confederations, the
Christian CISL and the socialist UIL at the domestic level. By the mid-1960s
this cooperation had taken shape at the factory and enterprise levels and had
considerably increased trade union effectiveness.[55]

However, there did exist two major points of divergence between the CGIL
and the other confederations at that time. First was the issue of labour's
'autonomy' from political institutions that had become the centre of debate
between the CGIL and the CISL. Some of the CGIL leadership were strongly
criticized for its participation in the executive of the Italian Communist Party
(ICP). For a number of years, both the CISL and the UIL, as well as some of the
socialist leaders within the CGIL had demanded that the confederation break
all formal ties with the WFTU and the ICP. The CGIL, however, at its Congress
and at the Arica Conference in 1967, argued that as long as the CISL was not
willing to break its formal ties with the Christian Democratic Party and leave its
parliamentary group, the CGIL would also maintain its institutionalized

cooperation with communist organizations. By the end of the sixties, however, both confederations had accepted the principle of incompatibility between trade union and political office, a principle the CGIL considered a 'tactical imperative' for unity within the labour movement.[56]

The second issue pertained to goals and tactics to be followed by the labour movement in Italy. Here, too, an agreement was finally reached. The 'hot autumn' in 1969 with its series of important labour conflicts resulted in the emergence of a unified national 'reform strategy' that called for a wide array of social legislation to be negotiated directly with the government.[57] Although this reform strategy did not achieve some of its goals, it did redefine the place of the labour movement in national politics and led to a more unified approach to basic economic and social problems.

The process of *rapprochement* between the CGIL, the CISL and the UIL during the sixties and early seventies also led the CGIL to an increasingly more sophisticated approach to the Common Market, and a growing divergence with the WFTU on the issue of European integration. At its 1965 Congress, the CGIL strongly criticized the WFTU for its ideological and political rigidities that neither took into account national and regional particularities nor the different economic and social structures within societies. At this Congress, the CGIL demanded a modification of WFTU structures and statutes in order to allow for increased regional autonomy within the organization; but in the face of firm opposition, it gradually abandoned its fruitless attempts to bring about an internal change within the WFTU, and showed instead an increasing interest in the already prevailing trade-union structures at the European level.[58]

After the founding of the ETUC, Sergio Lama, General Secretary of the CGIL, in a basic policy statement, recognized the ETUC as a positive factor leading the European labour movement to a high degree of autonomy. He also expressed the desire to affiliate the CGIL to the European Confederation as soon as possible. The basic goal would be to participate in the 'battle for structural transformation and measures for the harmonization of social and economic policy . . . so as to respond to the needs for progress of the working people of the Community.'[59] Strongly supported by the two other Italian confederations, a meeting with representatives of the ETUC was proposed in order to discuss the possibilities of joining the organization.[60] In the ensuing meetings, the focal point of debate centred around the CGIL's affiliation to the WFTU. Its membership in the Communist International appeared to be a major obstacle for an understanding with the West European trade unions.[61]

At the Eighth WFTU Congress in Varna (15–22 October 1973), the CGIL had requested the organization to consider a change in membership status to permit some form of association. The Congress agreed with this suggestion and decided that in order to maximize the possibilities of new united action, it would mandate the next meeting of the General Council to determine rights and duties of associated members.[62]

However, without waiting for the decisions of the WFTU's General Council, the CGIL, in January 1974, unilaterally redefined its relations with the WFTU: it declared that it would participate in WFTU meetings with a consultative voice only, would move CGIL members from leadership positions within the WFTU and would no longer consider itself bound by any WFTU decision.[63]

After the third meeting between the CGIL and the ETUC, the latter delegation, which was mandated to clarify positions but not to take any decisions, reported to the ETUC Executive Committee. The relationship between the CGIL and the WFTU, in its view, had indeed changed and should the WFTU General Council refuse to accept the CGIL's interpretation of an associated membership the only alternative would be to exclude the CGIL from its ranks. The report also underlined the CGIL's positive attitude towards the European Community which not only recognized the reality of its existence but viewed it as an institution whose efficiency and orientations had to be reinforced in favour of the workers. Finally, the report also highlighted the fact that the CGIL's attitude towards the Italian political system had considerably changed over the last few years, in the sense that it had fully accepted the Italian constitution and the idea of political pluralism.[64]

However, before submitting any formal application for membership, the CGIL wished to be assured that such a request would be positively received. In that event it would dissolve its liaison office in Brussels which it had established together with the French CGT.

The ETUC Executive Committee, however, was divided on the question. The Italian Confederations CISL and UIL favoured the rapid admission of the CGIL into the ETUC. They emphasized that the communist dominated trade union operated in the same way as other trade unions in Western Europe, using freedom of organization, the right to strike and collective bargaining procedures to represent the workers' interests.[65] Also, after a series of common actions in the late sixties and early seventies, a trade-union federation of the three confederations (CISL, UIL, CGIL) was established during 1973. Furthermore, it was stressed that, in March 1974, twelve of the CGIL's leaders resigned from the PCI Executive Committee in accordance with the change introduced in the CGIL statutes, and that its statute within the WFTU had also been modified.[66] Finally, the CGIL, they argued, had undergone a constant evolution towards democracy. In 1968 it had declared its opposition to the Soviet occupation of Czechoslovakia, and had come out clearly in favour of a pluralistic democracy with free trade union rights in such a society.[67]

The entrance of the CGIL into the ETUC was also supported by a number of other trade unions, including the British TUC, followed by the Irish trade-union confederation, who reiterated the view that the principal aim of the founders of the ETUC was to create an organization capable of representing all European workers. The increasing tendencies towards unification and the strengthening of trade-union power on the national level should not, therefore, be undermined at the European level by excluding one or the other trade-union organizations for ideological reasons.[68]

The admission of the CGIL was also favoured by the Belgian FGTC, the French CFDT and the Austrian OGB, though, for slightly different reasons. The OGB and the FGTB both included communist minorities. Also, the FGTB had a history of conflict with the Belgian Christian trade union confederations (CSC) and considered that the admission of Christian trade unions into the

ETUC should be linked with that of the entrance of the communist trade unions. The Austrians—having criticized the division of trade unions in Western Europe between EFTA and EEC groups as a weakness that led them merely to react to political decisions instead of developing their own initiatives—did not wish to undermine the newly established trade-union organization containing both communist and socialist elements.[69] The French CFDT, having initiated 'common action' with the CGT on the national level, saw in the admission of the CGIL the necessary prerequisite for an eventual entrance of the CGT into the ETUC. Strong opposition, however, was raised by some of the major unions. The Scandinavian trade unions were at first opposed to the enlargement of the ETUC on the ground that the newly established European organization should, above all, attempt to reach a high level of internal consolidation. But they became less outspoken after the admission of the Christian trade unions.

The German DGB and the French FO were firmly opposed to any communist entry during the debate on this issue. The French FO, refusing any kind of dialogue or cooperation with the communist party or trade union in France since the split of the CGT in 1948, was against the entrance of a communist trade union. In fact, it had opposed the affiliation of the Christian trade unions mainly because it feared that it would provide an opening for communist confederations too.[70] The entrance of the CGIL, moreover, would, in its view, undoubtedly pave the way for the French CGT to enter the ETUC, a prospect to which it was thoroughly opposed.

The German DGB, since the existence of the German Democratic Republic, had been deeply opposed to all cooperation with communist parties and trade unions and actively combated any emergence of communist tendencies within its own ranks. A visit of a socialist member of the CGIL Executive Committee to the DGB headquarters, arranged to convince the DGB leadership of the good intentions of the CGIL, failed to obtain the desired result mainly because of the—in view of the DGB—ambivalent relationship between the CGIL and the WFTU.[71] Both the DGB and FO finally succeeded in obtaining a postponement of the decision on the issue by insisting that the ICFTU be consulted before any vote was taken.[72] They based their demand on a decision of the ICFTU Executive Committee stipulating that while bilateral contacts of its member organizations with WFTU affiliates were left to their discretion, multilateral contacts with any WFTU affiliates should be strictly confined to the ILO framework.

Within the ICFTU itself the issue of a CGIL affiliation to the ETUC was generally considered as a fundamental issue that touched the very foundations of the 'free' international labour movement. The original establishment of the ICFTU itself was largely attributable to the strong opposition that had developed towards communist trade unions in the late forties. And its very existence symbolized defiance of communism in many parts of the world.

The Asian affiliates of the ICFTU showed particular concern regarding developments in the European region. On an earlier occasion some had already expressed their fears about the weakening of the ICFTU through the establishment of an enlarged European trade-union organization. Now their apprehension had increased to the pitch of actually foreseeing 'the liquidation of the ICFTU'.

Among the most outspoken critics was P. P. Narayanan, Head of the Malaysian Trade Union Confederation, who cast serious doubts about the alleged political moderation of the CGIL. Quoting Liu Shao gi, he warned that 'a good Communist can always deny for years that he is a Communist'. He further pointed out that some people in the ICFTU 'have spent fifty years of their lives defending the frontiers of free trade unionism' and cited experiences of fighting communism in Asia. He also questioned the reality of trade union unity in Italy which he considered to be the prerequisite for the entrance of the CGIL into the European organization.

Another speaker questioned the possibility of establishing coordination on national policies with communist organizations. He cited experiences of such attempts in his own country, India, where, in his view, they had amply shown that the communist trade unions 'are not interested in positive progress, but in creating chaotic situations and restlessness in one country and all over the world'.[73]

It was argued by yet another speaker that the admission of CGIL would increase the respectability of communist trade unions in the Third World and thus blur the lines between free trade unions and those controlled by the Eastern bloc.

Devan Nair, leader of the Singapore trade union, went even further and castigated the Western European trade unions for not assuming the moral leadership that had fallen upon their shoulders after the withdrawal of the AFL–CIO from the ICFTU. To explain the high sensitivity of Asian trade unions with reference to this issue, he emphasized that 'communism in Europe means Shelepin in Asia, it means Shelepin plus Chou En Lai', reminding his audience of the high degree of competition between Soviet Russia and China in southern Asia. In his view, since both would attempt to use the International Labour Office (ILO) to establish influence in that area, the only defence was a strong ICFTU with clearly stated international principles. 'A European trade union organization which permits its values to be diluted by allowing communist organizations to affiliate' could do serious harm to the international trade-union movement. He warned that 'there are inevitable political and other consequences which will flow from whatever you decide in this part of the world . . .' and that 'the day must come when the non-communist, democratic trade-union centres in Asia will seriously have to think about other ways of protecting ourselves, and of pursuing our democratic goals and values in the Asian region'.[74]

Other speakers expressed concern that forging organic unity with communist organizations would lead to their actual domination over the European labour movement, a possibility which had many historical precedents.

These arguments were, however, refuted by some of the European trade union leaders. They pointed out that the socialist majority in the ETUC is fairly large, and could not be jeopardized by one communist organization. In fact, accepting the CGIL would not only weaken the position of the WFTU in

Western Euopre, if anything, it would increase the influence of socialist and Christian trade-union values on that organization.

The controversy between the European and non-European ICFTU affiliates was, however, so heated and the discord so insurmountable, that some feared a split of the ICFTU over this issue. In order to avoid any further dramatic developments, it was therefore proposed and accepted, that the ICFTU members should all re-affirm their attachment to the goals of that organization even if some expressed serious reservations about the admission of the CGIL.[75] In fact, it had become quite clear during this discussion that the ETUC had become an autonomous organization without a real organic link to the ICFTU, and that the ICFTU, on a matter of deep concern to a majority of its member organizations, could not exercise any viable influence on the decisions taken within the ETUC. When the issue finally came to a vote in July 1974, the CGIL was accepted by twenty-one votes to seven.[76]

Once the CGIL started participating in the ETUC, its behaviour did not differ from that of any other organization. The *rapprochement* in the mid-1970s between the German DGB and the CGIL on a bilateral level also fostered the integration of the CGIL into the ETUC, in particular after its complete defection from the WFTU.[77]

The CGIL, in a series of declarations, has confirmed its interest in the EEC although it is convinced—as is the rest of the ETUC—that a number of serious reforms have to be undertaken in order to reinforce the social component within the commercial policies. It stressed, in particular, the need to introduce a higher degree of democracy into the working methods and procedures of the EEC institutions, and to enable them to overcome pressing economic and employment problems. It sees in the ETUC the only instrument capable of developing a unified policy, representing workers' social and economic interests within the Community.[78]

The French Communist Confederation (CGT)

Closely following the Soviet line, the World Federation of Trade Unions (WFTU) had consistently opposed all attempts to establish a European political or economic union. All six WFTU affiliates in Western Europe, led by the French and Italian communist trade unions, had strongly criticized the formation of the European Coal and Steel Community, and had refused to participate in the Consultative Committee of the High Authority which was open to trade union representation.

The French CGT—echoing the general policy line of the WFTU—became particularly outspoken in its criticism of European integration. In its view, the Marshall Plan and the European Recovery Programme (ERP), characterized as 'Marshallization of Europe', was a form of American neocolonialism threatening national sovereignty and independence. It was perceived as a calculated scheme to foster American capitalist interests, channeled through West German industrial revival and expansion, which in turn was expected to lead to the 'prussification' of Europe.[79]

The ECSC was condemned as an 'arms pool', inaugurating the division of

Europe and constituting the economic component of NATO. In concert with the FCP, the CGT campaigned against the establishment of a European Defence Community on the ground that such an institution would undermine national sovereignty and the independence of the French army.[80]

This attitude persisted after the establishment of the Common Market. The Twenty-Third Congress of the FCP declared, for example, that the Common Market would 'increase the dependency of European countries on the US and the dependency of France on a reactionary and revanchist West Germany'.[81] Furthermore, the effects of the Common Market on workers' welfare were considered negative. It was feared that the exigencies of the Common Market to increase the competitiveness of the French economy would put undue pressure on the French working class, resulting in dwindling wages or declining social security benefits.[82] The basic principles of the EEC concerning free circulation of goods, free movement of labour and of capital, in the CGT view would result in:

(1) a ferocious competition based on very low wages and the least developed social security systems;
(2) the importation of unemployed workers from Italy and West Germany into France, and
(3) the depreciation of the French currency, and the eventual replacement of national currency by a European one that in turn would be determined by international cartels.

In line with this thinking, the CGT increasingly began to diverge from the CGIL, and played an important role—in cooperation with the WFTU secretariat—in systematically blocking all Italian attempts to introduce a certain degree of cooperation and coordination among communist trade unions in Common market countries. The meeting that was convened—of French, Italian and Luxembourg trade unions—under WFTU auspices, was totally deadlocked.[83] The measure of the FCP and the CGT opposition to European integration can be discerned from the fact that the French communist party leader, Maurice Thorez, publically dismissed the ICP's favourable position on integration as revisionist and illusory since, in his view, it proposed 'an allegedly positive policy calling for the "insertion" of the working class and its organizations in the Common Market'.[84]

Finally, domestic events introduced a degree of flexibility into the sectarian attitude of the CGT. The death of Maurice Thorez in 1964 and the commencement of some cooperation with the socialist forces in France, forged to defeat the Gaullist government in the 1965 elections, led to some changes in communist policy lines in general. These internal developments, compounded with the patient pressure exercised by the Italian communists on the French, finally led the latter to adopt a more pliable attitude towards the Common Market. Although their generally critical analysis of European integration basically remained unchanged, the CGT did recognize the need for the communist trade unions to change their tactical approach towards European integration. It came around to the idea of overcoming communist isolation and of developing common action as representatives of the communist workers within the European Community.[85]

The two trade unions therefore decided to establish a Standing Committee CGT–CGIL in Brussels in 1965. This committee was, however, recognized by the EEC institutions only in 1969, after the harsh labour battles in Italy and the social events in France in 1968 led their respective governments to include the CGIL and CGT representatives in the labour delegations to the EEC Economic and Social Committee.[86]

Soon after the establishment of the ETUC, the CGT took a series of initiatives to explore the possibility of its affiliation to the new European trade-union organization and its full integration into the workers' group of the EEC Economic and Social Committee. In its view, the EEC as well as the ETUC were biased against the CGT, which considered such an attitude to be 'in contradiction to the unitary relations between CGT and CFDT' on the national level and harmful to trade-union unity on the European level.[87] Nevertheless, it did not stop the communist trade union from pursuing a dual policy of periodically renewing its demand for affiliation and criticizing ETUC policy towards the Common Market.[88] This ambivalent but more positive attitude towards the ETUC can be attributed to a series of factors:

(1) since the establishment of a common liaison office with the CGIL in Brussels, the CGT reassessed its attitude about the EEC, especially in the sense that it acknowledged its existence as a reality—though still reiterating that its policies did not correspond to the interests of the working people in the Common Market. The EEC, in its view, remained an organization dominated by monopoly capitalism under the control of United States and West German political interests.

(2) the admission of the Italian CGIL into the European labour organization, and its leaving the liaison office, left the CGT isolated on the Western European labour scene. This was further accentuated by the CGT's feeling that it was discriminated against by the European institutions. In an attempt to overcome such prejudice and to strengthen its role within the European institution, it requested a meeting with Commissioner Ortoli in April 1976.[89] But it was not only with respect to the West European trade unions and the Common Market institutions that the CGT felt isolated. Within the WFTU, too, it was alone in its reassessment of the Community. The WFTU continued to demonstrate a spirit of rejection with respect to the EEC. In the mid-1970s, in a document on the 'crisis of the capitalist world', the WFTU made only one reference to the EEC, mentioning the inability of capitalist integration to secure a smooth development of capitalism, as the contradictions and confrontations within the Common Market have amply exemplified. Instead it focused strongly on the issue of multinational corporations and the necessity to contain their power by international labour solidarity.[90]

Criticism by the CGT towards this attitude within the WFTU and proposals to review their appraisal of the Common Market did not fall upon fertile ground, so that the CGT was compelled to admit—albeit cautiously—that its International did not have a strategy permitting the necessary action within the Common Market.[91]

(3) the adherence along with the CFDT to the 'common action programme' of the 'common front' established between the socialist and communist parties in France, also played a role in the CGT's reappraisal of Common Market institutions and the ETUC.[92]

Its attitude continued, however, to be ambivalent to both. While the CGT, between 1974 and 1980, took a series of initiatives to approach the ETUC and to renew a dialogue with the European labour confederation in view of becoming part of it, it maintained, at the same time, orientations that could be perceived as being in contradiction to its European aspirations.

Aside from the general perception of the Common Market as a forum of class struggle, the CGT periodically reiterated its criticism of some of the trade-union organizations with which it allegedly wanted to cooperate within the ETUC. Its attacks were directed against what it labelled 'reformist' organizations and in particular against the German DGB and its policy of codetermination, which the CGT could only interpret as a form of 'class colla-boration'.[93] This type of revolutionary jargon used by the CGT in its analysis of the European Community persisted and became a source of irritation to most of the European trade unions which were trying to cope with a series of EEC problems in a pragmatic and practical manner.

The problems that blocked the negotiations between the CGT and the ETUC were twofold. One was the continued affiliation of the CGT to the WFTU. From the very beginning it had become quite clear that the CGT did not intend to leave the WFTU, nor did it wish to alter its affiliation within the organization—unlike the CGIL. Furthermore, since the Christian and socialist-orientated trade unions were free to remain in their respective labour Internationals, the CGT considered all discussions on its affiliation with the WFTU as an interference in its internal affairs.[94] The other difficulty was the firm opposition of the French FO. This opposition could not be ignored since a general rule existed that no organization could be admitted without the approval of the organization of the same country that was already a member of ETUC.

All this was in marked contrast to the situation of the CGIL: it had been supported by the Italian trade union organizations already affiliated to the ETUC; and it had changed its terms of affiliation with the WFTU.

Since the CGT had on several occasions requested a meeting with ETUC representatives,[95] it was unanimously decided by the ETUC Executive Committee that talks on this issue should take place.[96] Although a series of meetings took place between ETUC and CGT delegations and although the CGT contacted individual ETUC affiliates in order to secure support for their application,[97] the talks proved cumbersome and did not make any progress. Irrespective of their attitude towards the CGT application, none of the trade-union representatives present in the Executive Committee seemed to wish to precipitate any action. If anything, some of them used all possible means to stall the negotiations and to postpone decisions on this highly controversial issue.

Reflecting this general mood, the ETUC president proposed the submission of a questionnaire to the CGT. Its reply, in his view, would provide a basis for a clear evaluation of the CGT's attitude towards the EEC, the ETUC and the French trade-union scene.[98]

Based on replies to the questionnaire, it was agreed to concentrate the discussions with the CGT around the following points:

(1) The CGT's relations with the WFTU and the attitude of both these organizations towards the European institutions;
(2) the CGT's attitude regarding the ETUC's majority decisions;
(3) the CGT's attitude towards the other trade union organizations in France.[99]

Shortly thereafter, these issues were discussed in a meeting between CGT and ETUC representatives. The report of this meeting raised considerable controversies within the ETUC's Executive Committee. Not only was it impossible to reach any decision on the matter, but some of the member organizations showed signs of increasing impatience with discussions on affiliations. They considered these debates time-consuming and detrimental to other business, particularly that of strategic conceptualization so necessary to face problems of European integration on a level beyond daily preoccupations.[100] It was therefore decided to postpone any discussions about the CGT issue for a sufficient length of time to allow ETUC affiliates a prolonged period of reflection on this controversial matter.

The question was rediscussed only in 1978 when G. Seguy, General Secretary of the CGT, took the initiative to approach the ETUC. The latter responded by reintroducing the same sort of questions that were discussed at the previous meetings. In addition, the French FO was requested to submit a detailed note explaining the reasons for its continuous opposition to the CGT's affiliation.[101]

In its answers to the ETUC's questions, the CGT strongly advocated its support to trade-union unity in France and pointed out that there already existed a broad basis for agreement between the CGT on the one hand, and the CFDT and the FEN (the teachers' union) on the other. Also, in its view, a certain degree of *détente* with the FO had recently developed. Regarding its relationship with the WFTU, it declared that no change from its previous position had occurred.[102] The fact that it had criticized the WFTU during its Ninth Congress for failing to provide a forum open enough to engender diversified debates was not to be interpreted as a disengagement by the CGT from the WFTU, but rather as an attempt to renovate the organization.[103]

With reference to its attitude to the European Common Market, the CGT reiterated its recognition of the reality of its existence. The most important phenomenon within the Common market, in its view, was the upsurge of multinational corporations, which endangered the basic interests of workers in Europe. This had not so far generated a sufficiently concerted and coherent opposition from the European trade-union movement. The trade-union movement—ran the argument—must therefore overcome the capitalist-government coalition, the major prerequisite for which was the termination of discrimination against the communist trade unions in France, Spain and Portugal, and their admission to the ETUC.[104]

The FO, however, maintained its strong opposition to the admission of the CGT. In the view of its Secretary-General, André Bergeron, the CGT's political concepts were basically opposed to those of the free trade-union movement. He perceived the CGT as an extension of the French Communist Party, as exemplified by its behaviour during the legislative elections in March 1978. Furthermore, argued Bergeron, 95 per cent of the leaders of the CGT on the national and regional levels, were members of the FCP. The most decisive factor for its non-acceptance within the ETUC, in the eyes of Bergeron, was its attitude towards the WFTU. He was deeply convinced that the CGT's affiliation would fundamentally change the very nature of the ETUC, a transformation that the majority of its members did not wish to occur.

During the course of these debates, a general problem appeared, namely that of the criteria on which the admission of a trade union should be based. It was therefore considered urgent to formulate general principles on this question.[105] This was done in 1979. An ETUC member, according to these principles, ought to possess a basic potential for reaching consensus with all the other affiliates. In particular, a trade-union organization would have had to be compatible with the 'free, democratic and independent trade-union action' of the ETUC. Geographically, the trade unions were to be situated in a country that was a member of one of the European intergovernmental organizations, the EEC, the EFTA or the Council of Europe. If several organizations from one country wished to be affiliated to the ETUC, they would have had to be capable of cooperating among themselves at the European level. Finally, particular attention would have to be given to the opinion of the ETUC affiliates regarding applications from organizations from their country.

In the case of the CGT, this last criterion gave rise to considerable difficulties. Whereas the French CFDT was ready to provide its good offices to obtain the CGT's entry into the European labour organization, the FO persistently maintained its opposition to such a step and actually threatened to leave the organization were the CGT to be admitted.[106]

In January 1980, the CGT repeated its request for another meeting to discuss its affiliation to the ETUC.[107] During the ensuing encounter the ETUC delegation insisted mainly on the incompatibility between CGT membership of the WFTU and its eventual affiliation with the ETUC. When the issue finally came to a vote within the ETUC, no organization voted in favour of the CGT's affiliation. Even the trade unions which had previously spoken out in favour of the CGT (the Belgian CFDT, the Italian confederations including the CGIL, and the French CFDT) abstained.[108] The ETUC's official explanation for this negative result centred mainly around the view that the CGT held fundamentally different conceptual views about a democratic society and the role of trade unions therein. In particular, the CGT's close relationship with the FCP and its international affiliation were considered incompatible with the ETUC's concepts of a trade union's political independence from party and government. The affiliation of the CGT would thus not reinforce the political impact of the ETUC within the Common Market, but would, on the contrary, gravely endanger its internal cohesion.[109]

Why did the CGT lose the support of organizations that originally backed its entry into the ETUC? What were the new developments that effected such an attitude? The first element was undoubtedly the domestic situation in France. The continuously firm opposition of the French FO could not be ignored, even by such CGT supporters as the British TUC. The FO, as a founding member of the ICFTU and the ETUC and as one of those organizations that had over the years maintained an active pro-European stand, could not be offended by the admission a French trade union to which it was opposed. Also, the 'Common Front' on the trade-union level between the CGT and the CFDT had collapsed closely following the breakdown of the 'Common Front' of their political counterparts in 1977. The relationship between the two-trade union confederations further degenerated after the defeat of the FCP during the March 1978 elections, while the dependence of the CGT on the FCP appeared to be constantly growing. These internal developments in France contributed strongly to the weakening of CFDT support for the CGT's entry into the ETUC.

The second element was the reinforced nationalistic attitude the CGT took towards the EEC. During 1979—the year of direct elections to the European Parliament which had been a major demand voiced by the European trade-union organization—the CGT accused the ETUC of promoting supra-nationality on the European level. This, in its view, was directed against the national interests of France and the French trade unions. Furthermore, the CGT sharply criticized the German DGB as the prototype of a 'reformist' trade-union confederation attempting to place the ETUC under 'social-democratic hegemony'. Moreover, it was criticized about the candidacy to the European Parliament of three major DGB leaders, among them its president, H. O. Vetter.[110] This negative attitude against direct elections to the European Parliament as such, and against the ETUC's and some of its affiliates' involvement in the election campaign, collided with the views of one of the major supporters of the Italian CGIL, which was one of the most active campaigners for the directly elected European Parliament.

Finally, the CGT's attitude towards the Soviet invasion of Afghanistan—which corresponded to the position of the FCP—also contributed to the ETUC decision to bar the entry of the CGT into the organization. In fact, this was viewed as a sign of the CGT's renewed *rapprochement* towards the WFTU and its international policy positions which were totally aligned to those of the Soviet Union.[111]

The Spanish communist trade unions (Commisiones Obreras-CCOO)

Adhering to the principle of European trade-union unity and encouraged by the CGIL's admission to the ETUC, the Spanish communist trade unions also showed interest in affiliation. This was even evident while they were operating clandestinely.[112] However, the question was pursued actively after the legalization of trade unions in Spain in 1978. At the first CCOO Congress in Madrid in July 1978, the question of the trade-union attitude towards the European Community and the ETUC was amply discussed. There appeared to exist a general agreement with a statement made by the leader of the French communist trade union, George Seguy, to the effect that the ETUC would not be able to represent workers probably in Southern Europe unless and until it admitted the French CGT, the Portuguese 'Intersindical' and the Spanish CCOO to its ranks.[113] Accordingly, the congress decided to request its admission to the ETUC officially.[114]

The same major questions relating to the admission of a communist trade union into the ETUC were again reiterated in the context of the CCOO request. The first deal with the international affiliation of the organization; the second with its attitude towards the Common Market and basic ETUC principles and policies; and the third asked about its relations with the other Spanish trade-union organizations already affiliated to the ETUC.

International affiliation did not raise any major difficulties since the CCOO was not a member of any trade-union International, though it maintained friendly relations with the WFTU with which it had signed a cooperation agreement in 1979.[115] The CCOO's attitude towards the Common Market and the ETUC basically appeared to be positive. Its second Congress came out in favour of strengthening European integration and cooperation between EEC and EFTA.

However, and notwithstanding such a positive approach, considerable differences surfaced on the question of the CCOO's links with the Spanish Communist Party. The UGT's attitude on the CCOO's admission had evolved from cautious reservation to that of firm disapproval.[116] A series of domestic events had contributed to this evolution. Historically, the UGT, being a socialist-orientated trade union, had lived through a series of differences and contradictions with the Spanish communist workers' organizations. This was closely related to the general political and ideological evolution within the international socialist and communist movements.

Rivalry between the two organizations was further aggravated after the legalization of trade unions in Spain in 1978, when the trade-union elections in Spain had attributed 45 per cent of the total union membership to the CCOO and 30 per cent to the UGT.[117] Resenting any political gains that the CCOO might possibly obtain from a membership in the ETUC, the UGT became even more opposed to its admission.[118]

This became even more acute on the occasion of the 1st of May activities when the UGT accused the CCOO of harassing UGT member organizations, of disturbing UGT manifestations and of hindering a 'Solidarnosc' representative speaking to the workers assembled on Independence Plaza in Madrid.[119] Its most important criticism, however, was directed against CCOO's relationship with the Spanish Communist Party, with whom close organizational ties had been established during the Franco regime and which remained significant in post-Franco Spain.

In the UGT's view, the situation became even more difficult after the Fifth Congress of the Communist Party of Catalonia (PSUC—Partido Socialista Unificado de Cataluña) at which the 'eurocommunist' tendency was replaced by a coalition of Leninist and pro-Soviet factions.

These developments and the close relationship between the Communist Party and trade unions thus led the UGT to firmly oppose the CCOO's affiliation to the ETUC. Moreover, in the UGT's view, the second CCOO Congress had clearly demonstrated a regression of the democratic positions, particularly those of the 'euro-communist' tendencies, within the CCOO. The election to the CCOO national Executive Committee, it argued, had given 26 per cent of the votes to the pro-Soviet faction. Also the representation of Leninist and other non-democratic tendencies had been strengthened. In the view of the UGT, these results pointed to the resurgence of anti-democratic and anti-eurocommunist forces within the CCOO.

On the domestic scene, the UGT feared that the Communist Party of Spain—having obtained only 10 per cent of the votes in the general election—would use the CCOO as its major instrument to exercise political pressures. Furthermore, and contrary to claims made by the CCOO, the UGT did not see any prospects of united action among the two labour organizations, given their basic strategic and ideological differences. Whatever agreements had been concluded between the two trade unions, they were basically *ad hoc* and were geared to short-term practical political issues.[120]

However, what is interesting and even paradoxical is that notwithstanding the strengthening of pro-Soviet elements within the Catalonian communist movement the CCOO of this region during its Congress clearly came out in favour of its organization's entry into the ETUC. This decision was based upon the argument that one of the causes of the economic crisis was the internationalization of capital, the establishment of organizations with supranational character, such as the EEC, and especially the increasingly powerful multinational corporations. The ideological division between trade unions, considered basically a residue of the cold war, should therefore be overcome by the establishment of regional cooperation between communist trade unions in the Mediterranean area, and by affiliating to the ETUC along with the French CGT and the Portuguese Intersindical.[121]

During the Congress of the SCP as a whole, which took place shortly thereafter, significant pro-Soviet tendencies became again apparent. Thirteen persons, representing the orthodox communist line, were elected to the national committee. Though compared to the thirty-six 'eurocommunists', also elected to the Committee, this represented a minority, it was nevertheless a sign of a reinforcement of the pro-Soviet line.[122]

On the European scene, the UGT feared that the CCOO's admission might change the very nature of the ETUC. In its view, the latter's affiliation would open the doors to the French CGT and the Portuguese Intersindical, a situation that might lead to a bloc position by the Mediterranean communist trade unions against the majority of the ETUC members, thereby splitting the organization which up to then had been able to function by consensus.[123]

Within the ETUC Executive Committee, the problems of the CCOO's affiliation gave rise to major disputes, as had already been the case during debates on affiliation of other communist trade unions. The Committee was again divided. On the one hand, there were British and Italian trade unions who desired the ETUC to be open to all ideological trends within the European trade-union movements; on the other, there were the DGB and the FO, who feared the disintegration of ETUC's political unity and the weakening of its efficiency as a body representing workers' interests within the European communities.

To avoid a split within the ETUC on this issue, the ETUC president proposed the postponement of any decision until the next CCOO Congress, due to be held in June 1981. An examination of the Congress's decision might enable the Committee to clarify its views on the admission or rejection of the CCOO.[124]

It was decided at the ETUC Executive Committee to dispatch a delegation to this Congress to observe its proceedings and political discussions. Since the international policy resolutions passed on this occasion favoured the CCOO's affiliation to the ETUC, and supported the integration of Spain into the Common Market,[125] the ETUC delegation drafted a favourable report.[126]

However, since a firm coalition had been established between the Spanish trade-union centres and some other ETUC member organizations, including the DGB, against the admission of the CCOO, the DGB contested the ETUC Secretariat report saying that it had received different information regarding the proceedings and contents of the Congress. It persisted in its belief in the communist domination of CCOO and threatened to leave the ETUC should the CCOO be admitted.

Nevertheless, since an important majority of the ETUC affiliates appeared to favour the CCOO's membership, the Dutch ETUC president, Wim Kok, being on excellent terms with the German trade union, made a special effort to persuade the DGB Central Committee to adopt a more flexible stand on the issue and, in particular, to reconsider its threat to leave the ETUC should CCOO be admitted.[127] The Spanish organizations were again asked to examine the possibilities of cooperation with the CCOO.

The ETUC's Finance and General Purposes Committee—where supporters and opponents of the CCOO's admission were represented—tried to reach a compromise. It recommended that the Spanish organization should again attempt to cooperate with the CCOO on the domestic level, and that the CCOO's point of view should be heared by the Executive Committee during its next session in December 1981. A vote on this recommendation yielded a favourable majority, the two Spanish organizations, the German DGB, the French FO and LO Denmark opted against it.

Disappointed by the results of this meeting, the CCOO leadership[128] reiterated that the CCOO had, in fact, fulfilled all the criteria for admission officially required by the ETUC. It had shown the representative nature of its organization through elections,[129] it demonstrated its independence on the national and international level and had frequently affirmed its acceptance of the statutes, objectives and orientations of the ETUC. It also pointed out that its national aim remained common action with the UGT with whom it had already reached agreement on two major issues: a 'national employment agreement', and resolutions on the 'consolidation of democracy against terrorism and against military coups'.[130]

The reactions of the two Spanish ETUC organizations, however, remained negative. Both refused to respond positively to the CCOO's request for a meeting.[131] In their view, the latter's affirmation of political independence was incorrect, since forty out of forty-three members of its Secretariat were also members of the SCP and since its principal leaders (Camacho, Sartorius, Ariza, etc.) belonged to the SCP's Executive and Central Committees, and in their political action, they showed an absolute dependence on SCP policy. Regarding their international independence, the UGT argued that even though there was no formal affiliation to the WFTU, privileged relations did exist and did play an important role in the CCOO's foreign affairs.

In spite of this refusal to cooperate by the Spanish trade unions, the CCOO was invited to defend its point of view in front of the ETUC Executive Committee.[132] During the same session, their admission request was put to a vote where it obtained a majority but not the required two-thirds necessary to enter the organization. According to ETUC statutes in such circumstances, the issue is kept on the agenda.[133]

The CCOO strongly criticized the result of this vote, labelling in particular the UGT opposition as purely 'electoralist' and that of the DGB as purely ideological. Nevertheless, it continued to reaffirm the necessity of 'unity of action' on the national and European levels and its willingness to seek affiliation in due course.[134]

Notes

1. CESL–EFTA/TUC, press release: 'Déclaration des représentants syndicaux européens réunis à Oslo les 5 et 6 novembre 1971', *ETUC Archives*.
2. *The Financial Times*, 1 January 1973, interview with Victor Feather on TUC participation in the EEC.
3. 'Bericht über TUC Kongress', 17 March 1972, *ETUC Archives*.
4. Peter Coldrick, 'The Likely Development of TUC Attitudes Towards the EEC', March 1972, *ETUC Archives*.
5. TUC, 'The Economic Review', 1972.
6. *The Bulletin*, Brussels, 21 January 1972; see also Victor Feather, 'Multinational Companies: The British Experience', *Free Labour World*, Brussels, May 1972.
7. 'Notes of ECFTU Secretariat on meeting of Trade Union leaders of Western Europe', Luxembourg, 4 October 1972; 'Report of the working group ECFTU–EFTA-TUC for the extension of European trade union cooperation', Brussels, 19 April 1972. *ETUC Archives*.
8. Kaare San de Gren (Secretary of EFTA-TUC), 'Points on Future Trade Union cooperation in Europe', 8 December 1971, pp. 1–3. *ETUC Archives*.
9. 'Report of the Working Group ECFTU–EFTA-TUC for the extension of European trade union cooperation to the meeting of Western Europe trade union leaders in Geneva, 6 June 1972', *ETUC Archives*.
10. 'Notes of Meeting of Trade Union Leaders in Geneva, 6 June 1972', *ETUC Archives*.
11. Volken Jung, 'Neuer Europäischer Gewerkschaftsbund', *Gewerkschaftliche Monatshefte*, April 1973, pp. 213, 213.
12. CESL–EFTA-TUC Working Group on Extended European Trade Union Cooperation, note, 'Summary of the Discussions in the CESL–EFTA-TUC Working Group, Comments on Points of Divergence, and Proposals on a Statute for a European Trade Union Organization', Brussels, 19 April 1972, p. 5, *ETUC Archives*.
13. ECFTU-EFTA-TUC, 'Verbatim Record', Meeting of West European Trade Union Leaders in Geneva, 6 June 1972, *ETUC Archives*.

14. There would be ten confederations from EEC states and six from non-EEC states, of which two would be from Finland. Membership from EEC states would amount to 23,400,000 and from the others to 5,300,000. Note by ECFTU Secretariat, Brussels, June 1973, *ETUC Archives*.
15. ICFTU 10th World Congress, London, July 1972, 'Extraits de discours concernant l'organisation syndicale européenne' (mimeographed), pp. 2–4, 7, 9, 10, 13, 14.
16. ECFTU, 'Notes for the meeting of 16 European national trade union confederations, 4 October 1972, in Luxembourg', Brussels, notes by ETUC Secretary General on Luxembourg meeting, 4 October 1972, *ETUC Archives*.
17. Within the DGB, differences of opinion on this issue existed between the Confederation and its President, H. O. Vetter and the leaders of its two most powerful affiliated trade unions, E. Loderer (IG–Metall) and E. Klunker (ÖTV). H. O. Vetter, who was also the President of ETUC at this time, was more open to arguments other than those of his own organization and was therefore more flexible in his approval to certain compromises. Interview with H. O. Vetter, Brussels, March 1981.
18. ECFTU note on Luxembourg meeting, op. cit.
19. Note by Secretary-General, ECFTU, on Luxembourg conference, 30 November–1 December 1972, Brussels, 8 December 1972, *ETUC Archives*.
20. Statement by H. O. Vetter to Luxembourg conference, 30 November 1972, *ETUC Archives*.
21. ECFTU–EFTA–TUC, 'Note: Problems in connection with Future Trade Union Cooperation in Europe', Luxembourg, 30 November–1 December 1972, Annex 1, *ETUC Archives*. By the end of the 1970s, the geographical dimension was further tested by an increasing number of applications from other European countries. The 1979 Congress, for example, was faced with the task of deciding on fifteen admission requests. Since this issue had become considerably time-consuming, it was decided not to discuss it but to empower the Executive Committee to decide on the matter. While rejecting eight requests, the Committee admitted two small organizations from Malta and Iceland, two Cypriot organizations and the Portuguese UGT. Admission requests by Turkish organizations remained pending during 1983 and were to be reconsidered only after clarification of a highly confusing and uncertain political situation.
22. ECFTU Secretariat, 'Notes on the Luxembourg conference, 30 November–1 December 1972', statements by André Bergeron, (French FO), H. O. Vetter, (German DGB), O. Kersten (ICFTUC), G. Nielson, (Danish LO), *ETUC Archives*; see also Jung, op. cit., p. 21.
23. Heinz O. Vetter, 'Die Europäischen Gewerkschaften 1972', *Die Neue Gessellschaft*, January 1972, p. 41; Heinz O. Vetter, 'Zwanzig Jahre Gewerkschaftspolitik', *Gewerkschaftliche Monatshefte*, April 1973, p. 202.
24. George Lefranc, op. cit., pp. 36–50; M. Bouvard, op. cit., pp. 78–82; 'Quarante ans de la confédération internationale des syndicats chrétiens', *Labour*, March 1960, p. 105.
25. 'La CMT: unité dans la diversité', *Labour*, March–April 1970, p. 67; Europäische Dokumentation 1970, *Die Europäische Organisation des Weltverbandes der Arbeitnehmer* (WVA), Brussels, 1970. Member organizations in the European countries were: CFDT, France; CSC, Belgium; NKV, Netherlands; LCGB, Luxembourg; ACLI, Italy; (extraordinary members) CHG and SVEA, Switzerland; CMTU, Malta; CGB, Germany; three Spanish organizations.
26. 'Résolution concernant l'intégration européenne', *Labour*, Bouvard, op. cit., pp. 80–2.
27. Perez-Calvo, op. cit., pp. 13, 97, 116, 130–8.

28. Europäische Dokumentation, 'Die Europäische Organisation . . .', op. cit., pp. 1–3. Perez-Calvo, op. cit., p. 163; August Cool, 'L'orientation des structures et de l'action du mouvement syndical dans une dimension européenne', *Rapport à la IVe Conférence Européenne des Syndicats Chrétiens, Amsterdam, 6–8 Octobre, 1966*, Brussels, OE–WCL, October 1966, pp. 18, 19.
29. 'La CMT . . .', op. cit., pp. 58, 59, 68, 70; Perez-Calvo, op. cit., pp. 13, 163–5.
30. EO–WCL Congress, 7–9 May 1969, *Résolution Générale*, ECFTU, Comité Exécutif du 5 juillet 1959, 'Procès Verbal', Point IV.3, *ETUC Archives*.
31. CESL–OE–CMT, 'Suggestions sur le renforcement de la collaboration entre la CES et l'OE–CMT suite à la recontre commune du 21 octobre 1970', Brussels, 24 April, 1971, *ETUC Archives*.
32. *Second Congress of the EO–WCL*, Luxembourg, 16–19 May, 1972, 'Résolution concernant le syndicalisme européen', pp. 1 and 2; Perez-Calvo, op. cit., p. 164; 'La CISL s'organise pour dialoguer avec la CMT d'une nouvelle coopération syndicale européenne', *La Cité*, 8 June 1972.
33. CESL–OE–CMT, 'Note sur la réunion des représentants CESL–OE–CMT à la Haye, le 5 février 1972', Brussels, 8 February 1972; CESL, Comité Exécutif du 17 février 1972, 'Procès Verbal', Brussels, *ETUC Archives*.
34. CESL, Comité Exécutif du 17 février 1972, 'Procès Verbal', CESL, Comité Exécutif du 30 novembre et 1er décembre 1972, 'Procès Verbal', Brussels, *ETUC Archives*.
35. CISL, Comité Exécutif, 6 juin 1972, 'Procès Verbal', Geneva, p. 2, *ETUC Archives*.
36. *La Libre Belgique*, 10–11 February 1973; Europe, 1973 and 24 January 1973; OE–CMT, Comité Exécutif du 22 et 23 mars 1973, communiqué de presse; letter to Victor Feather, Theo Rasschaert, 23 March 1973, *ETUC Archives*; ETUC, extract from the minutes of the executive committee meeting of 4 May 1973, Brussels, 28 June 1973, p. 3, *ETUC Archives*. This was the position of the German DGB, the French FO, the Scandinavian Confederations and the Swiss Confederation SGB.
37. ETUC, Executive Committee meeting, 28 September 1973, 'Agenda Item 4—Report and Conclusions of the ETUC–EO–WCL Meeting of 12 July 1973', p. 6, *ETUC Archives*; *Le Peuple*, 23 January 1974. FGTB Press, Brussels, 22 January 1974. Besides the FTGB and FO, the Swiss SGB took up this point.
38. ETUC, Executive Committee, 4 May 1973, p. 6, *ETUC Archives*.
39. 'Note concernant les problèmes qui se posent dans la perspective de l'admission confédérations nationales membres de l'OE–CMT et la CES', Brussels, 3 April 1973, *ETUC Archives*.
40. 'Notes due Secrétariat de la CES sur la réunion entre une délégation de la CES et une délégation de l'OE–CMT, le 12 juillet 1973 à Bruxelles', pp. 2 and 3, *ETUC Archives*.
41. Executive Committee, op. cit., 4 May 1973, pp. 3, 6.
42. Volker Jung, 'Erweiterung des Europäische Gewerkschaftsbundes', *Die Neue Gesellschaft*, September 1974, p. 634.
43. ETUC Executive Committee, 24–25 January 1974, *ETUC Archives*; *ETUC Press Release*, no. 16, Brussels, 28 January 1974.
44. OE–CMT Déclaration du Comité Exécutif, Brussels, 29 March 1974.
45. Donald L. Blackmer, *Unity in Diversity*: Italian Communism and the Communist World, Cambridge, Mass., The MIT Press, 1968, pp. 305–29. ICFTU, 'Extracts from Proceedings at the Sixty-first Executive Board Meeting', Brussels, 31 May 1974, *ICFTU Archives*. See also ETUC, 'Procès-Verbal, Réunion du Comité Exécutif, Brussels, 28 septembre 1973', *ETUC Archives*.
46. Donald L. Blackmer, Annie Kriegel, *The International Role of the Communist Parties of Italy and France*, Cambridge, Centre for International Studies, Harvard University Press, 1973.

47. Donald L. Blackmer, *Unity...*, op. cit., pp. 265–6; Peter Weitz, 'The CGIL and the PCI', in Donald L. Blackmer and Sidney Tarrow, *Communism in Italy and France*, Princeton, N.J., Princeton University Press, 1975, p. 548; Gilles Martinet, *Sept Syndicalismes* (L'Histoire Immédiate), Paris, Editions du Seuil, 1979, pp. 106–8.
48. Blackmer, *Unity ...* op. cit., p. 267.
49. *L'Unità*, 20 July 1957.
50. Blackmer, *Unity...* op. cit., p. 277.
51. 'Programmation nationale et progammation communautaire dans les pays de la CEE'. Texte de l'intervention prononcée par A. Novella, Secrétaire Général de la CGIL à la conférence organisée par le Conseil National de l'Economie et du Travail (CNEL), 2 December 1962, *ETUC Archives*.
52. Besides the CGIL (Italy), WFTU affiliates from these countries were CGT (France) and FLA (Luxembourg).
53. 'Précisions de la CGIL sur les buts de sa politique européene', *Bulletin d'Information de la CGIL*, no. 17, Rome, January 1964; 'Thèmes pour le VIᵉ Congrès de la CGIL (Italie): politique syndicale internationale', Bologne, 31 March–4 April 1965, pp. 30–3.
54. Umberto Scalia, 'Current Problems of the Trade Unions Movement in the Common Market Countries', *World Marxist View*, 6, 9 September 1963, p. 40.
55. Martinez, op. cit., pp. 112–16.
56. Peter Weitz, op. cit., pp. 553–59, 560.
57. *Le Monde*, 30 October 1978; 'Vers l'unité syndicale en Italie: la réunion des trois conseils généraux de la CGIL, de la CISL, et de l'UIL', CEE, *Informations Syndicales et Ouvrières*, no. 29, October 1970.
58. 'Thèmes pour le VIᵉ Congrès de la CGIL (Italie)', op. cit., pp. 35–8, 40; Eighth CGIL Congress, *Political Resolution: International Relations*, Bari, 7 July 1973.
59. Sergio Lama, 'Basic Policy Statement', Bari, July 1973; ibid., 'Resolution on International Relations'.
60. CGIL letter to Victor Feather, President of the ETUC, 30 July 1973, *ETUC Archives*.
61. 'Note sur l'entretien entre délégations de la CES et CGIL, London 20 November 1973; CES, 4 December 1973; 'Report on the Second meeting between a delegation from the ETUC and a delegation from the CGIL', ETUC, 3 March 1974; CES Comité Exécutif, Brussels, 9 May 1974, 'Rapport sur la troisième rencontre entre une délégation de la CES et une délégation de la CGIL, Brussels, 10 April 1974, *ETUC Archives*.
62. Quoted in Blackmer, *Unity...*, op. cit., p. 241.
63. ETUC, 'Report on the second meeting', op. cit.
64. ETUC Executive Committee, 9 May 1974, 'Report on the third meeting between a delegation of the ETUC and a delegation of the CGIL, Brussels, 10 April 1974, op. cit.
65. Letter from the CISL and the UIL to the ICFTU, 29 April 1974, *ETUC Archives*.
66. ETUC, 'Procès-Verbal', Réunion du Comité Exécutif de la CES, Brussels, 24–25 January 1974, item 6 of the agenda, *ETUC Archives*.
67. 'CGIL Declaration to the Second Regional European Conference of the ILO, 19 January 1974'. *ETUC Archives*.
68. ETUC, 'Procès-Verbal', Réunion du Comité Exécutif de la CES, Brussels, 24–25 January 1974, point 6, *ETUC Archives*.
69. ETUC, 'Procès-Verbal', Réunion du Comité Exécutif, Brussels, 9 July 1974, *ETUC Archives*; see also Alfred Ströer, *Solidarität International*, Der ÖGB und die internationale Gewerkschaftsbewegung, Vienna, Verlag des Österreichischen Gewerkschaftsbundes, 1977, p. 170–1.
70. ETUC Comité Exécutif, Brussels, 24–25 January 1974, op. cit.
71. ETUC, 'Procès-Verbal' du Comité Exécutif, Brussels, 24–25 January 1974, op. cit;

ETUC, Executive Committee, Brussels, 9 July 1974, op. cit; Letter from H. O. Vetter, 3 July 1974, to members of the ETUC Executive Board concerning decision of 2 July 1974 by the DGB Federation Executive Committee that the debate about admission of the CGIL should be adjourned until the question of affiliation to WFTU had been cleared, *ETUC Archives*.

72. ETUC Executive Board, 9 May 1974, item 6 of the agenda, 'Report on the third meeting between ETUC and CGIL delegations in Brussels, 10 April 1974.' *ETUC Archives*.

73. ICFTU, 'Extract from proceedings ...', op. cit.

74. Then head of the Soviet trade unions.

75. ICFTU, 'Extract from proceedings ...', op. cit.

76. ETUC, Executive Committee, 'Prices Verbal', Brussels, 9 July 1974. Voting against the admission of CGIL into the ETUC were the DGB—Germany (3 votes), the FO—France (1 vote), the LCGB—Luxembourg (1 vote), the CNG—Switzerland (1 vote), the CSC—Belgium (1 vote), *ETUC Archives*; 'Italiens CGIL Wurde Mitglied', *Die Quelle*, Heft, September 1974, p. 355.

77. Europäische Gemeinschaften, *Gewerkschaftsinformationen*, 'Die CGIL benedet ihre Mitgliedschaft im Weltgewerkschaftsbund', Brussels, **2**, 1978, p. 19.

78. Communautés Européennes, *Informations Syndicales*, Comité Exécutif de la CGIL sur la politique internationale', **6**, June 1975, p. 14; Europäische Gemeinschaften, *Gewerkschaftsinformationen*, 'Der neunte Kongress der CGIL (6–11 Juni 1977) in Rimini. Die internationale Politik und die Probleme der Mitbestimmung.' **6**, 1977, pp. 15–16.

79. Bouvard, op. cit., p. 92; Blackmer, *Communism* ..., op. cit., p. 509; Deppe, op. cit., p. 279; A. Lacrois, 'La CGT et la Plan Marshall', *Cahiers de l'Institut Maurice Thorez*, April 1974, pp. 25-7; A. Barjonet, 'Le Marché Commun, c'est l'europe allemande', *Le Peuple*, **528**, 1957, pp. 6-7.

80. Deppe, op. cit., pp. 280-2; J. Duma, 'Le PCF et l'europe', *Cahiers de l'Institut Maurice Thorez*, April 1974, p. 105.

81. *Cahiers du Communisme*, June–July 1979, p. 521.

82. Deppe, op. cit., p. 283; CGT, *Europa der Monopole ist nicht das Europa der Arbeiter*, Paris, 1973.

83. Blackmer, 'Unity ...', op. cit., pp. 322-8; see also, 'Die Kommunisten und der Gemeinsame Markt', *Europäische Schriften des Bildungswerks Europapolitik*, **18**, Cologne, Europa Union Verlag, 1968, p. 44.

84. 'Sur la rencontre de Moscou', *Cahiers du Communisme*, XXXIX, **1-2**, January–February 1963, p. 30; *France Nouvelle*, **905**, 26 February 1963, pp. 11–24.

85. Wolfgang Leonhard, *Eurokommunismus*, Munich, Bertelsmann, 1978, p. 216; Martinet, op. cit., p. 147; *Euro-Communism: Myth or Reality*, F. Della Torre, F. Martimer and J. Story (eds.), Penguin Books, Harmondsworth, 1979, p. 119.

86. 'Die Kommunisten und der Gemeinsame Markt', op. cit., p. 47; Europäische Gemeinschaften, 'Ständiger Ausschuss CGT-CGIL', *Europäische Dokumentation*, 1971, p. 1.

87. Letter from the CGT to the President of ETUC, 29 August 1974, *ETUC Archives*.

88. CGT, Thirty-ninth Congress, Le Bourget, 22-7 June 1975, 'Report by G. Seguy', Paris, 1975, pp. 28-31.

89. *Le Peuple*, 15–30 June 1976, p. 23.

90. Extraordinary meeting of the WFTU Council, Berlin, 28-9 January 1975. (German version): 'Die Verschärfung der Krise der Kapitalistischen Welt', pp. 5, 10–14, *ETUC Archives*.

91. 'Développer notre action unitaire en europe', report presented by Johannes Galland, *Le Peuple*, 15–30 June 1976, p. 25.

92. 'Développer notre action . . .', op. cit., p. 25; Letter from G. Seguy to H. O. Vetter, 29 August 1974, ETUC Archives.
93. *Le Peuple*, 15–30 June 1976, p. 22.
94. ETUC, Finance and General Purposes Committee, Minutes, Geneva, 30 September 1976, *ETUC Archives*.
95. Letters from the CGT to the ETUC, 21 January 1974 and 23 August 1974, *ETUC Archives*.
96. ETUC, Executive Committee, 'Minutes', Brussels, 6 February 1975, *ETUC Archives*.
97. *Le Peuple*, op. cit., p. 22.
98. ETUC, Executive Committee, 'Minutes', Brussels, 30 November–1 December 1975, *ETUC Archives*.
99. ETUC, Executive Committee, 'Minutes', 1 October 1976; Letter from ETUC General Secretary to General Secretary of CGT, 4 October 1976, *ETUC Archives*.
100. ETUC, 'Report on Meeting between CGT and ETUC delegations, 5 November 1976, in Brussels'. *ETUC Archives*.
101. ETUC, Executive Committee, 'Minutes', Brussels, 9–10 December 1976; ETUC, Executive Committee, 'Minutes', Brusels, 20 September 1978, *ETUC Archives*.
102. Letter from George Seguy to M. Hinterscheid, Secretary-General of the ETUC, 28 September 1978, *ETUC Archives*.
103. Interview with René Duhamel, CGT Secretary, in *L'Humanité*, 'La Richèsse du débat fraternel', 28 November 1978.
104. Speech by G. Seguy at the CGT meeting for the preparation of the 40th Congress in Grenoble from 26 November to 7 December 1978, in *CGT* Press Release, no. 30, October–December 1978, p. 5.
105. Letter from André Bergeron to all ETUC affiliates, 10 January 1979, *ETUC Archives*; ETUC, *Third Statutory Congress*, 'Report of Proceedings', Munich, 14–18 May 1979, p. 208.
106. ETUC, Executive Committee, 'Minutes', Brussels, 29 and 30 November 1979, *ETUC Archives*.
107. Letter from the CGT to the ETUC, 16 January 1980, *ETUC Archives*.
108. ETUC, Executive Committee, 'Minutes', Geneva, 12–13 June 1980, *ETUC Archives*.
109. Letter from the ETUC to the CGT, 23 June 1980, *ETUC Archives*.
110. *Le Monde*, 31 July 1980.
111. ETUC, Executive Committee, 'Minutes', Geneva, 12–13 June 1980, op. cit. *Le Matin*, 16 June 1980; *Le Monde*, 15–16 June 1980.
112. Letters from the CCOO to Victor Feather, president of ETUC, 20 Febraury 1973 and to H. O. Vetter, president of ETUC, 30 May 1975, *ETUC Archives*.
113. *El Pais*, 22 June 1978.
114. Letters from Marcelino Camacho, Secretary-General and Serafino Aliaga, International Relations Secretary of CCOO to the ETUC Executive Committee, 4 July 1978, *ETUC Archives*.
115. *El Pais*, July 1 1976, July 13 1978.
116. ETUC, 'Memorandum on Admission Requests', Brussels, 18 February 1980, *ETUC Archives*.
117. *The Financial Times*, 16 January 1980.
118. letter of UGT to all ETUC affiliates, 15 September 1981, *ETUC Archives*.
119. Letter from UGT to ETUC Secretariat, 5 May 1982, *ETUC Archives; El Diario*, 4 May 1982.
120. Letter from UGT to all ETUC affiliates, 15 September 1981, *ETUC Archives*.
121. CCOO Catalonia, *Second Regional Congress*, 'Resolution on International Affairs', Barcelona, February 1981.
122. *El Pais*, 22 June 1981 and 23 June 1981.

123. ETUC, Executive Committee, 'Minutes', Brussels, 2–3 April 1981, *ETUC Archives*.
124. Ibid.
125. CCOO Congress, 'Resolution on CCOO Affiliation to the ETUC and on the Common Market', Barcelona, 21 June 1981.
126. 'Report by the ETUC Secretariat', Brussels, 31 August 1981, *ETUC Archives*.
127. ETUC, Executive Committee Meeting, 'Minutes', Brussels, 8–9 October 1981, *ETUC Archives*; *DGB Press Release*, 7 October 1981.
128. Letter from CCOO to all CES affiliates, Madrid, 9 September 1981; Letter from CCOO to UGT and STV, Madrid, 26 October 1981; in CCOO, *International Informations*, Madrid, December 1981; *Special: El Pais*, 10 October 1981.
129. *Institute of Mediation, Consiliation and Arbitrage* (IMAC), Spain, 'Election Results', 23 January 1980: CCOO 30.76 per cent; UGT 29.22 per cent.
130. *El Pais*, 10 October 1981.
131. Letter from UGT to CCOO, Madrid, 10 October 1981; Letter from STV to CCOO, Madrid, 17 November 1981, *ETUC Archives*; *El Pais*, 10 October 1981.
132. ETUC, Executive Committee, 'Minutes', 17 December 1981, *ETUC Archives*.
133. ETUC Statutes, Art. 20.
134. CCOO, *Informations Internationales*, Madrid, January–February 1982, no. 7, p. 3. Besides the Spanish case, the issue of the Portuguese Intersindical was also discussed. This organization—though hesitant about Portugal's entry into the Common Market—had nevertheless expressed the desire to affiliate to the ETUC. Without much debate, this request was put to the vote by the Executive Committee and rejected.

Chapter 3

ETUC: objectives and organizational framework

Objectives

The constituent assembly of the ETUC which met in Brussels on 8 and 9 February 1973 defined the objectives of the ETUC in a very general manner. It decided that the organization should 'represent and advance the social, economic and cultural interests of the workers on the European level in general and towards the European institutions in particular—including the European Communities and the European Free Trade Association'.[1]

This self-image as an interest group seemed to be far removed from the idealistic concept of promoting political integration within the Community. Opinions within the ETUC on this question were so divided that a common attitude within the organization could not be achieved. While at one end of the spectrum some organizations—the German DGB and the French FO—insisted on emphasizing the need for political union in Europe, others—the British and Danish confederations—turned a deaf ear to the question.[2] Thus the ETUC was, for instance, unable to produce a statement on the Tindemans' Report on the European Union.

Under such circumstances, only a pragmatic approach could enable the ETUC to obtain general consensus within the organization. But even these less ambitious objectives could not be smoothly accomplished during the early stages of the ETUC's existence. The first 'Action Programme' drawn up by the 1974 Congress (23–24 May 1974 in Copenhagen), for example, was indeed a very general and vague resolution representing a catalogue of issues rather than a concrete programme of political activities. This lack of homogeneity in the approach of the European labour movement can undoubtedly be attributed to the wide differences that exist between the political, economic and social structures of their respective countries, and in which trade unions have evolved. Confronted with the necessity of having to formulate a consensus on different issues, they were initially unable to go beyond the proclamation of general statements and were unable to avoid the temptation to extrapolate their national concerns to the European level.[3]

The danger of such an attitude was highlighted by some of the trade-union leaders. They pointed out that national patterns of thought and behaviour, valuable as they might be, could not be efficiently applied to the European level, that the ETUC was in urgent need of proceeding with its own internal consolidation,[4] and that it should break away from its inability to progress 'from a European trade union movement whose role is one of discussing policies to a movement which takes action'.[5]

Some criticism about the incoherence within the ETUC was also clearly voiced during the Second Statutory Congress in London (22–23 April 1976).

Delegates held the view that economic and social problems could not any longer be faced at the national level alone, and expressed concern at the lack of cohesion within the organization which had prevented it, until this stage, from becoming a 'genuine European trade union movement'. Moreover, it was argued that the existence of diverging concepts on Europe should not stop the ETUC 'from facing up to the problems arising from the existence of the Common Market'.[6]

This self-criticism might have contributed to the fact that the Congress was finally able to reach a surprising degree of consensus on the objectives of the ETUC for the next few years. It was, however, the general dissatisfaction with rising unemployment and the lack of government policies in this field that undoubtedly acted as a major catalyst in generating an agreement among the ETUC affiliates. In fact, the Congress's discussions were widely dominated by two major issues: unemployment and industrial democracy. Although some differences on details persisted, widespread agreement was reached on the means of employment creation and the necessity to increase workers' participation in management decision-making processes.[7]

In addition to these two major issues, which were to remain focal areas of discussion for years to come, the Congress also discussed a seven-point programme dealing with the following issues:

— Energy policies: it proposed the establishment and the implementation of a common European energy policy under the direction of public authorities invested with sufficient power to safeguard the interests of the Community over private interests in the energy sector.
— Working environment: it demanded Community regulations ensuring the right to work in an environment in which the worker would be free from 'psychological, physical and chemical risks'. National legislation in this field should be harmonized on the highest possible level, and strict control about safety at work should be exercised by government authorities and trade unions.
— Equal rights and equal opportunities for workers: the Congress pointed out that numerous instances of inequality existed among workers which tended to affect such specific categories as women, young people, migrant, handicapped and older workers, and which tended to occur in certain areas more than in others. To remove such inequalities, consolidated trade-union action would be needed at national and regional levels.
— The Lomé Convention: while strongly approving the agreement, the Congress requested close association of the trade unions in the implementation of the provisions on industrial cooperation contained in the Convention.
— Migrant workers: while expressing concern about the close linkage existing between jobs for migrant workers and the variations in the business cycle, the Congress demanded an effective and concerted employment and migration policy at the European level, in the elaboration of which the European trade unions should actively participate. In its view, a regional policy should be elaborated which would aim at reducing the role of the poorer regions as a labour reserve for those which were wealthy.

Finally, two political resolutions were passed demanding democracy and freedom of coalition in Spain and Greece, and supporting *détente* and security policy in Europe.[8]

The trend towards stronger cohesion of political concepts and positions, which was set into motion during this Congress, was gradually reinforced, and the areas in which a consensus could be reached were continuously broadened. The two following Congresses held in Munich (14–18 May 1979) and in The Hague (19–23 April 1982) continued to be largely dominated by the unemployment issue. Proposals dealing with possible solutions for the increasingly difficult situation took up a large part of the deliberations and resolutions.

The issue of 'economic democracy', permitting workers to have a greater say in management's decision-making process, was also extensively discussed. The Congress formulated a wide spectrum of political conceptions on issues such as agricultural policies, consumer policies, quality of life, trade-union participation in the EEC's developmental policies, migrant workers, regional policy, etc.[9]

Organizational framework

The affiliates of the ETUC are national trade-union confederations and European industry committees.

Trade-union confederations

At the national level, trade-union confederations are themselves composed of individual trade unions of varying numbers and strength, ranging from well over one hundred industrial and craft unions, represented by the British Trade Union Congress, to sixteen industrial unions organized within the German DGB. While in some European countries there is only one trade-union centre, in others several such centres may be found, frequently representing different ideological or religious inclinations.

Within the ETUC itself, membership in terms of affiliated organizations as well as the number of workers represented has been constantly increasing since the foundation of the European Confederation.

Originally in 1973 membership had been limited to only seventeen West European affiliates of the ICFTU. This was extended to twelve Christian organizations in May 1974, and to the Italian communist trade-union confederation in October 1976. Additional admissions brought the total number to thirty-four in 1983, representing altogether over 40 million workers (see Tables 3.1–3.3). Membership figures are based on data provided by the affiliated organizations for budgetary calculations. Such data are usually deflated by about 10 per cent, so that the total ETUC membership should be closer to 45 million.

It should be noted that trade unions from three countries—Great Britain, the Federal Republic of Germany and Italy—account for more than 50 per cent of the total membership. Also, membership within each confederation varies from 10,000 to 10 million affiliates. Internationally about 80 per cent of the ETUC organizations are also affiliated to the ICFTU, 6 per cent to the WCL and 14 per cent do not belong to any International.[10]

Industry committees

Industry committees function as regional—European—federations of individual trade unions, established on an industry basis. Representing specific categories of industrial workers, they establish a direct link between the industrial base and the community. They are associated in a variety of relationships and with different degrees of autonomy with the International Trade Secretariats (ITS) which group industrial unions on a world-wide basis. The committees with the longest history and the highest degree of cooperation at the European level exist at the metal and mining industries—the two sectors forming the ECSC.

Since the geographical and the ideological extension of the ETUC did not automatically extend to the industry committees, it injected a series of contradictions in the composition of European trade-union structures. In many cases, the committees wre faced with the problem of changing their membership rules to open up to those Christian and communist unions interested in joining them. But as the committees were largely dependent upon the views of the ITS on these matters, they did not always follow the general policy of the ETUC, nor did their member organizations conform to the policy of their national confederations, which had accepted the widening process of European trade-union structures. Instead they remained attached to their traditional structures and composition.

The structural scenery of European industry committees thus remains a very varied one. Geographically, some organizations remain within the EEC framework, others within the one provided by the ETUC, still others in between the two; and finally, one of the most important committees, the EUROFIET even goes beyond ETUC limits and includes organizations from Monaco, Israel and Lebanon.[11] Ideologically also, a number of differences remain. While some organizations exclude Christian and CGIL organizations, others accept the CGIL organization but exclude some of the Christians. Finally, the degree of autonomy from the corresponding International Trade Secretariats varies considerably from one organization to the other.

In order to meet the problems created by this structural diversity, the ETUC Executive Committee established a few criteria with which an industry committee had to comply in order to be acceptable. In particular, it should have a certain degree of autonomy from its International Trade Secretariat with independent organizational and budgetary structures. Geographically, it should cover the same countries as those covered by the ETUC and should cluster organizations of the ETUC affiliates.[12]

The criteria for recognition which seemed to have created serious difficulties, pertained to the requirement that the committee should not exclude any trade union belonging to a confederation which was itself a member of the ETUC.

Table 3.1 ETUC membership in 1973

Founding members	Workers represented	Country
Fédération Générale de Travail de Belgique (FGTB)	900,000	Belgium
Deutscher Gewerkschaftsbund (DGB)	6,800,000	Federal Republic of Germany
Landsorganisationen i Danmark (LO Denmark)	873,600	Denmark
Union General de Trabajadores de España (UGT)	—	Spain
Confédération Générale du Travail-Force Ouvrière (CGT-FO)	1,000,000	France
Trades Union Congress (TUC)	9,774,000	Great Britain
Althydusamband Islands (ASI)	35,000	Iceland
Confederazione Italiana Sindicati Lavoratori (CISL)	2,000,000	Italy
Unione Italiana del Lavoro (UIL)	800,000	Italy
Confédération Générale du Travail-Luxembourg (CGT, Lux.)	30,000	Luxembourg
Nederlands Verbond van Verkverenigingen (NVV)	674,000	Netherlands
Landesorganisasjionen i Norge (LO Norway)	580,000	Norway
Schweizerisches Gewerkschaftsbund SGB	446,000	Switzerland
Toimihenkilo-Ja Virkavriesjärjastöjen Keskusliitto (TVK)	182,000	Finland
Landsorganisationen i Sverige (LO Sweden)	1,617,000	Sweden
Tjänstemännens Centralorganisation (TCO)	821,000	Sweden
Österreichischer Gewerkschaftsbund (OGB)	1,526,264	Austria
Total (including founding members)	36,158,600	

Sources: ETUC *Report on Activities, 1973–1975*, Brussels, April 1976, p. 6; ETUC *Report on Activities, 1976–1978*, p. 4.

However, in the early years of the ETUC, committees were admitted that excluded CGIL member organizations, since they were composed exclusively of socialist-orientated ICFTU affiliates. This applied to four out of eight recognized industry committees, namely the EUROFIET, which refused to affiliate two CGIL organizations, FIDAL and FILDA with 63,000 and 118,000 members respectively; the European Trade Union Committees for the Public Sector, the Postal Telegraph and Telephone Committee, and the European Secretariat of Entertainment Unions.[13]

Table 3.2 ETUC membership in 1976

Founding members, plus:	Workers represented	Country
Confédération des Syndicats Chrétiens (CSC)	1,100,000	Belgium
Fällesrädet for Danske Tjenestemandsog Funktionärsorganisationier (FTF)	210,000	Denmark
Solidaridad de Trabajadores Vascos (STV-ELA)	–	Spain
Confédération Française Démocratique du Travail (CFDT)	777,000	France
Irish Congress of Trade Unions (ICTU)	547,000	Ireland
Letzbuerger Chrëstleche Gewerkschaftsbond (LCGB)	15,000	Luxembourg
General Workers Union (GWU)	25,680	Malta
Nederlands Katholiek Vakverbond (NKV)	339,621	Netherlands
Christelijk Nationaal Vakverbond (CNV)	210,489	Netherlands
Christlichnationaler Gewerkschaftsbund der Schweiz (CGS)	97,816	Switzerland
Schwiezerischer Verband Evangelischer Arbetsnehmer (SVEA)	13,000	Switzerland
Suomen Ämmattiliittojen Keskusjärjesto (SAK)	720,000	Finland
Confederazione Generale Italiana del Lavoro (CGIL)	3,800,000	Italy
Total (including founding members)	7,855,606	

Sources: ETUC *Report on Activities, 1973–1975*, Brussels, April 1976, p. 6; ETUC *Report on Activities, 1976–1978*, p. 4.

Similar problems existed with respect to some of the non-recognized industry committees. This was particularly so in the case of the textile workers' committee, which has not accepted the affiliation of the Italian CGIL member organization. Another case is that of the Chemical Workers' International which refuses to yield any significant degree of autonomy to its European regional organization. Once the industry committees are recognized by the ETUC, their status within the organization is regulated by the ETUC constitution which implies that, except for questions concerning ETUC statutes and finances, the industry committees have the right to vote in Congresses as well as the right to present proposals and to express opinions during Congress and Executive Committee meetings.[14]

Within ten years the number of recognized industry committees increased from six to ten.[15] Due to their close integration with their International Trade

Table 3.3 ETUC membership in 1983

Trade-union confederations	Workers represented	Country
Fédération Générale du Travail de Belgique (FGTB)	925,000	Belgium
Confédération des Syndicats Chrétiens (CSC)	1,140,000	Belgium
Cyprus Workers' Confederation (SEK)	41,000	Cyprus
Cyprus Turkish Trade Unions Federation (TURK–SEN)	10,000	Cyprus
Landsorganisationen i Danmark (LO)	1,270,000	Denmark
Fällesradet for Danske Tjenestemands-og Funktionärorganisationer (FTF)	303,000	Denmark
Deutscher Gewerkschaftsbund (DGB)	7,100,000	Federal Republic of Germany
Union General de Trabajadores de España (UGT)	251,000	Spain
Solidaridad de Trabajadores Vascos (STV–ELA)	110,000	Spain
Confédération Générale du Travail- Force Ouvrière (CGT–FO)	930,000	France
Confédération Française Démocratique du Travail (CFDT)	955,000	France
Trades Union Congress (TUC)	10,000,000	Great Britain
Greek General Confederation of Labour (GSEE)	300,000	Greece
Irish Congress of Trade Unions (ICTU)	640,000	Ireland
Althydusamband Islands (ASI)	51,000	Iceland
Bandalag Starfsmanna Rikis og Baeja (BSRB)	17,000	Iceland
Confederazione Italiana Sindacati Lavoratori (CISL)	2,800,000	Italy
Confederazione Generale Italiana del Lavoro (CGIL)	4,350,000	Italy
Unione Italiana del Lavoro (UIL)	1,151,000	Italy
Confédération Générale du Travail de Luxembourg (CGT-Lux.)	39,000	Luxembourg
Letzbuerger Chrëstleche Gewerkschafts- bond (LCBG)	15,000	Luxembourg
General Workers Union (GWU)	29,000	Malta
Confederation of Maltesian Trade Unions (CMTU)	11,000	Malta
Federatie Nederlandse Vakbeweging (FNV)	966,000	Netherlands
Christelijk National Vakverbond (CNV)	263,000	Netherlands
Landsorganisasjonen i Norge (LO)	650,000	Norway
Österreichischer Gewerkschaftsbund (ÖGB)	1,673,000	Austria
Schweizerischer Gewerkschaftsbund (SGB)	459,000	Switzerland

Table 3.3 (*Cont.*)

Trade-union confederations	Workers represented	Country
Christlichnationaler Gewerkschaftsbund (CNG), including		
Schweizerischer Verband Evangelischer Arbeitnehmer (SVEA)	110,000	Switzerland
Toimihenkilö-ja Virkamiesjärjestöjen Keskusliitto (TVK)	310,000	Finland
Suomen Ammattiliittojen Keskusjärjestö (SAK)	950,000	Finland
Lansorganisationen i Sverige (LO)	1,910,000	Sweden
Tjänstemännens Centralorganisation (TCO)	990,000	Sweden
Uniâo Geral de Trabalhadores (UGT)	251,000	Portugal
34 trade-union confederations	41 million members	20 countries

Source: ETUC Secretariat, June 1983.

Secretariat, three committees—having never applied for recognition—remain outside the ETUC system.[16]

ETUC organs

The ETUC has four organs: the Congress, the Executive Committee, the Finance and General Purposes Committee and the Secretariat.

The Congress meets at least once every three years and is composed of representatives of national trade-union confederations and recognized industry committees. Each confederation may be represented by four delegates per country, plus one additional representative for every 500,000 members. At the

Table 3.4 Industry Committees recognized immediately after the establishment of the ETUC

The European Metalworkers Federation (EMF)

The European Federation of Agricultural Workers' Unions in the Community (EFA)

The Postal, Telegraph and Telephone International (PTTI) European Committee

The Metalworkers' and Miners' Inter-Trade Committee (ICFTU-ECSC)

The European Committee of the International Secretariat of Entertainment Trade Unions

The European Regional Organization of the International Federation of Commercial Clerical and Technical Employees (EUROFIET)

Table 3.5 Committees which had applied for recognition by 1976

European Trade Union Committee of Food and Allied Workers in the Community (ETUCF)

European Organization of the International Union of Food and Allied Workers (EO–IUF)

European Industry Committee for the Public Services (FSI)

European Organization of the International Federation of Employees in Public Services (EURO–FEDOP)

European Teachers' Trade Union Committee

World Confederation of Organizations of the Teaching Profession (WCOTP)

Committee of Transport Workers' Unions in the EEC

Source: ETUC 'Memorandum', Brussels, 5 November 1976; *ETUC Archives.*

1974 Congress, the British TUC, grouping 9.9 million members, for example, was entitled to twenty-three delegates, whereas the German DGB, with 6.8 million affiliates, was represented by seventeen delegates.

The Congress elects the Executive Committee on the basis of nominations from the affiliated confederations. Following the same procedure, it also appoints the president, the general secretary, and the deputy general secretary of the Secretariat. It has become customary to appoint the general secretary from an organization within the EEC, while the deputy general secretary, nominated by the EFTA group, comes from Scandinavia.

The Congress reviews the activities of the Secretariat, expresses its opinion on past activities, and decides on future programmes. Its decisions are reached by a two-thirds' majority. Under the ETUC constitution, the Executive Committee is composed of representatives from the national trade-union confederations, each of which may appoint one representative and one alternative representative. Furthermore, the representatives of recognized industry committees also participate in its meetings.

According to the rules of the organization, no single country—with the exception of the United Kingdom and the Federal Republic of Germany, where national centres represent more than five million members—may be represented by more than two representatives. The three Dutch, Swiss and Italian affiliates, therefore, are each represented by only two persons, but a rotational

Table 3.6 Committees which have not officially applied for recognition

---

European Federation of Building and Woodworkers in the EEC

Committee of Chemical and General Workers' Unions in the EEC (ICF)

European Committee of Textile, Garment and Leather Workers' Unions

---

Source: ETUC 'Memorandum', Brussels, 5 November 1976; *ETUC Archives.*

Table 3.7 Industry Committees recognized by December 1983

Name of Committee	Number of affiliated organizations	Countries	Membership
The European Metalworkers' Federation (EMF)	31	15	7,000,000
The European Federation of Agricultural Workers' Unions in the Community (EFA)	16	9	1,300,000
The Postal, Telegraph and Telephone International (PTTI) European Committee	60	21	1,500,000
The European Regional Organisation of the International Federation of Commercial, Clerical and Technical Employees (EURO-FIET)	70	24	4,205,000
The Metalworkers' and Miners' Inter Trade Committee (ICFTU-ECSC)	18	9	3,600,000
The European Committee of the International Secretariat of Entertainment Trade Unions (EC of ISETU)	30	7	60,000
European Liaison Committee of Transport Workers' Unions	68	10	2,500,000
European Committee of Food, Catering and Allied Workers within the IUF (ECF-IUF)	65	19	1,400,000
European Public Service Committee	79	20	3,700,000
European Trade Union Committee for Education	54	18	2,200,000

Source: ETUC Secretariat, Note, Brussels, December 1983, *ETUC Archives*.

system permits all three organizations to send representatives successively to the Executive Committee.[17] The two largest organizations, the British TUC and the German DGB, are the only ones entitled to three full and three alternate members.

The Executive Committee has the responsibility for representing the ETUC at European institutions. It meets at least six times a year. One of these meetings is devoted to the examination of the trade-union situation and its future prospects in each member country. The Committee also proposes and implements the resolutions and action programmes decided by the Congress. To prepare its work, it relies heavily on the Secretariat and various working groups, drawing on national experts for the topics under discussion.[18]

The Executive Committee appoints the other members of the Secretariat and elects seven vice-presidents from its ranks. Together with the president and the Secretary General, they constitute the Finance and General Purposes Committee which—according to the constitution—deals primarily with financial matters. In fact, its role has evolved beyond budgetary and financial matters. The Committee has become instrumental in preparing the most difficult dossiers for consideration of the Executive Committee.[19]

It has become normal practice for the Executive Committee to reach decisions by a general consensus. However, if such a consensus cannot be obtained and a vote becomes necessary, decisions are taken by two-thirds' majority. If proposals submitted to the Executive Committee only obtain a simple majority, they are kept on the agenda and are referred back to the Secretariat for further examination.[20] It should also be noted that problems dealing specifically with EEC or EFTA issues can be voted on only by member organizations of the area. Finally, the recognized industry committees have the right to submit proposals to the Executive Committee and to participate in its discussions on an advisory basis.[21]

The Secretariat

The Secretariat—with headquarters in Brussels—is composed of the secretary-general, the deputy secretary-general, and four secretaries, entrusted with the daily business of the organization. They are assisted by a staff of twenty-four. Each secretary has to cover a vast area of responsibility,[22] and represent a considerable workload for each secretary who has to deal with them almost single-handedly.

The major tasks of the Secretariat are the coordination of all ETUC activities and the preparation of all ETUC meetings, in particular those of the Executive Committee, the permanent committees and working groups of the ETUC and the EEC institutions. They also represent the ETUC in meetings and consultations of the various European institutions.[23]

The Secretariat has been headed since April 1976 by Mathias Hinterscheid, a Luxembourg trade unionist. He replaced Théo Rasschart of Belgium, who had served in that capacity since the establishment of the ETUC in 1973.

The Secretariat—through its continuous work of consultation and coordination with the national trade-union centres—is instrumental in seeking a consensus within the ETUC. Moreover, as a liaison body between the Executive Committee and the European institutions, its task is equally important in the often painstaking process of reaching compromises at the European level.

ETUC working parties and committees

In order to carry out its different tasks, the Secretariat establishes working parties and committees which function either on a permanent or an *ad hoc* basis. They are composed of experts from ETUC affiliates. If problems

Table 3.8 Distribution of duties in the Secretariat

Secretary-General
  General Secretariat
  ETUC budget
  Coordination of all sectors
  Finance and General Purposes Committee
  Executive Committee
  Relations with the affiliated confederations and the international trade-union
    organizations
  Industry committees
  General representation and public relations
  European Trade Union Institute

Deputy Secretary-General
  Assists the general-secretary in some of his duties and deputizes for him in his
    absence
  Energy policy
  Women
  Youth
  Labour market policy
  External relations–peace and disarmament
  TUAC–OECD (coordination)
  Cooperation between European institutions

Secretary I
  Economic, monetary and trade policy (European and world context)
  Global industrial policy
  Agricultural policy
  Industrial research (new technologies)
  EFTA (Consultative Committee and coordination)
  Community budget

Secretary II
  Migration
  Mediterranean policy
  Consumers
  Information division and Social Partners' Office
  Development policy (Lomé Convention—conventions or agreements between the
    European institutions and third world countries or regions)
  Coordination of funds
  Regional policy and the environment
  Liaison work with the industry committees in the field of industrial policy
    (collaborating with secretary I)

Secretary III
  Democratization of the economy and of institutions
  Workers' rights and company law
  Multinational undertakings
  European Social Fund

Vocational training (CEDEFOP—Berlin)
Education and training
Inter-regional trade union councils
Economic and Social Committee (coordination)
Social security

Secretary IV
Working conditions and organization of work (Dublin Foundation)
Working time
Hygiene, health and safety at work and ACHS in Luxembourg
Radio protection
Standing Employment Committee (coordination)
Collective bargaining
Council of Europe (Social Charter and coordination)
European Parliament (coordination)

Source: ETUC Secretariat, May 1982.

concerning the EEC are under consideration, only organizations from the European Community are represented. Six permanent committees have been established.

The committee on collective bargaining

This committee, which meets twice a year, was created to gather information on collective bargaining at the national level as well as to familiarize itself with the socio-economic situation in the member states. The basic aim is to obtain an alignment—at the European level—of collective bargaining procedures and priorities, an area which is deeply embedded in historical traditions and national socio-economic conditions. In addition to this task, it was decided in 1976 to give special priority to a number of specific subjects:

- the international comparison of wage costs,
- the role of wage increases in the inflationary process,
- methods of safeguarding purchasing power,
- incomes policy and free collective bargaining,
- collective bargaining and employment (job security agreements).

The committee on democratization of the economy

This Committee meets at least six times a year and deals with all problems related to company law—in particular the representation of employees in factories and enterprises—and the rights of employees and their trade unions. An area of high importance is multinational companies and questions of economic democracy in such enterprises.

The standing committee on migrant workers

This committee was established by decision of the 1976 Congress. originally its task was to deal with problems related to the free migration of workers within the EEC. Since the problem of migrant workers has also extra-European aspects, the Committee meets with the ICFTU and the WCL on a regular basis to coordinate their policies in this field.[24]

Within the framework of EEC institutions, joint meetings with the EEC Advisory Committee on freedom of movement for workers and the EEC Advisory Committee for Social Security for Migrant Workers are held in order to inform the EEC institutions about ETUC views on these questions.

The standing committee was also instrumental in November 1978 in the organization of a Euro-Mediterranean colloquium between ETUC affiliates and trade-union organizations of the Mediterranean basin to consult about the problems of migrant workers during recessionary periods in industrialized countries. Finally, the standing committee increasingly participates in meetings on the problems of migrant workers organized by the European Parliament, the European Centre for the Development of Vocational Training and the Council of Europe. A series of problems have been considered at these meetings such as illegal immigration and the protection of migrants against abuse, the status of migrant workers, their participation in the European elections, the problems of frontier workers, etc.[25]

Energy group

Established in the aftermath of the 1973 oil crises, this working group has the task of following up energy policies established by the European governments, with the aim of developing concepts on such policies which can be accepted by all members of the ETUC and in particular by the trade unions operating in the energy sector.

The core of this working committee has been formed by professional unions whose activities lie in the industrial sector related to gas, electricity and nuclear energy rather than by miners or petroleum trade unionists. Their major field of interest concerns the prospects of future energy supplies, alternative sources of energy, radiological protection and the preparation of policy proposals on these subjects.

Working party of women trade-union leaders

This working party developed out of the advisory committee on women workers established by the ETUC Executive Committee in 1973. It meets to discuss problems affecting women workers in the EEC and has brought out a 'White Paper' on women at work. It has been following closely the application of the EEC directives on equal pay and on equal treatment of men and women in the social security field.

ETUC youth group

After some sporadic meetings in the early stages of the ETUC, the youth group became firmly established as a permanent ETUC committee in 1976. Ever since, it has been functioning in coordination with the European Youth Centre of the Council of Europe and the European Youth Forum, which is a Community institution, and has considerably increased its activities. Its primary concerns are youth employment and vocational training. Among its major activities are seminars and courses on various topics related to trade-union activities and European politics and institutions.[26]

Ad hoc groups

Besides the permanent working groups and committees, the Executive Committee can establish working groups meeting for fixed periods to discuss specific topics or policies.

In the period 1976–8, for example, the following ad hoc groups were in operation:

- economic and monetary policy
- regional policy
- working conditions
- fiscal harmonization
- consumers
- environment and quality of life
- industrial safety and hygiene
- better EC/EFTA coordination
- agriculture[27]

The purpose of all these working groups is to seek a consensus among the participants which, in turn, is submitted to the Executive Committee for its approval in the form of a policy statement or position paper on topics related to EEC or EFTA policies. An increasingly large number of these position papers deal with proposals by the EEC Commission on a wide array of subjects.

Thus an important field of activity for the ETUC working committees— frequently dealing with highly technical aspects of social policies—is the representation of the ETUC's position on the Advisory Committees established by the EEC Commission to discuss specific issues and proposals. Moreover, considerable work on the preparation of the various meetings of the following EEC institutions was carried out by the ETUC representatives on the

- Management Board of the Foundation for the Improvement of Living and Working Conditions (Dublin)

- Management Board of the European Centre for the Development of Vocational Training (Berlin)
- Group II of the Economic and Social Committee of the EEC.[28]

Finances

The ETUC is financed by its affiliated organizations. Membership fees are calculated on the basis of the number of workers in each organization. In 1974, they amounted to 600 BF per thousand members. On the basis of membership, figures of close to 36 million for 1974–5, the budget for 1975 would have totalled roughly US$540,000.

By 1983, the fees had increased to a rate varying between 1,015 BF and 1.816 BF per thousand members. Varying rates were established in 1977 upon request of the TUC; they are mainly a consequence of the practice of paying membership dues in national currencies, so that the contributors—though not the ETUC—would remain unaffected by changes in the exchange rate. This arrangement has, however, not been detrimental to the ETUC.

In 1983, the annual budget amounted to roughly US$1 million. This relatively modest amount is only sufficient to cover the costs of running the Secretariat. Travel and personal expenses for the Executive Committee are met by the participants themselves. In addition, valuable infrastructural assistance is provided by the Commission. Furthermore, the Community meets all expenses incurred by ETUC representatives—as well as by all other participants—in preparatory meetings and in consultative sessions with the various EEC institutions.[29]

Related institutions

The European Trade Union Institute (ETUI)

The decision to establish a European Trade Union Institute goes back to the Social Action Programme of 1973, decided by the EEC summit meeting in Paris in 1972. Its purpose is the amelioration and strengthening of the role of the social partners, in particular the trade unions, within the EC. Frequently, lack of relevant data and information had been considered a major impediment to the effective functioning of trade unions at the European level. This situation had been perceived as a major disadvantage in comparison to employers' organizations whose flow of information—due to greater financial resources— was far superior to anything the trade unions could hope to attain in this respect. It was therefore considered useful to establish a trade-union institute within the EEC which would be able to fill the gap in research and information.

In this connection, the Council of Ministers decided, in January 1974, to give its full support to the establishment of such an institute whose task would be to assist the ETUC and to set up educational and information facilities on European matters.[30]

It took a number of years before this decision was implemented. After considerable pressure by the ETUC on the Commission, the Council and on sympathetic governments, the ETUI was finally founded in 1978. While it is financed—with the exception of a token ETUC contribution—entirely by the EEC Commission, it is supervised and directed by the ETUC Executive Committee through a Governing Body which is in fact identical to the ETUC Finance and General Purposes Committee, plus a representative of the Nordic trade unions. Other organs of the ETUI are the General Assembly, composed of representatives of thirty-three ETUC member organizations. Generally, trade-union representatives from organizations such as the ICFTU, the TUAC, the WCL, the Nordic trade-union council and representatives from the EEC Commission participate in its meetings without, however, exercising a right to vote.

While the Governing Body is the main decision-making organ of the ETUI, a group of experts advises on the formulation and execution of ETUI projects.

The three basic tasks of the ETUI are (a) to provide policy-orientated research, (b) to act as an information and documentation centre on European political, economic, social and trade-union matters and (c) to give active support to trade-union educational activities in the European context.[31]

The Institute's research activities are basically orientated towards practical issues. They enable the ETUC to formulate solidly based policy positions with respect to matters debated within the framework of the EEC and other European institutions. The priority areas are:

— economic and structural industrial policy
— employment policy, especially regional problems and migrant workers
— collective bargaining policies, in particular the upholding of purchasing power of workers, shortening of working hours, effects of rationalization and automation, etc.

A series of research reports have already been published, the most important of which are:

The Economic Situation in Western Europe;
Reduction of Working Hours in Western Europe, Parts One and Two;
"The Impact of Microelectronics on Employment in Western Europe in the 1980s";
"The European Economy 1980–1985: An Indicative Full Employment Plan".

The ETUI has also established a documentation centre that collects all information relevant to the European trade-union movement, acts as a central archive for documents on trade-union congresses and conferences as well as all types of special trade-union documents particularly publications, newsletters and press declarations of national trade-union centres and their affiliates.[32]

Interregional Trade Union Councils (ITUC)

These councils are not ETUC institutions as such, but regional trans-border associations among trade unions in certain areas covering parts of two or three

Figure 3.1 Inter-regional trade union councils within the ETUC (founded in)

1 Saar–Lorraine–Luxembourg (1976)
2 Hasselt/Liège–Aachen–Maastricht (1978)
3 Weser/Ems–Noord-Nederland (1979)
4 Alsace–Basel–Sud-Baden (1980)
5 Rijn–Ijsel–Ems (1980)
6 Nord/Pas de Calais–Hainaut/West–Vlaanderen (1981)
7 Lombardy–Tessin (1982)
8 Pyrenees–Mediterranean (1983)

adjoining states. Although formally and practically independent from the ETUC, they nevertheless function under its auspices and within its general policy framework. Moreover, they are an example of transnational regional trade-union cooperation representing one of the most interesting attempts to solve common regional problems on practical and political levels.

Trade unions in these regions perceived the existence of certain socio-economic entities in areas often artificially divided by national frontiers. By setting up trans-border trade-union organizations, they focused their attention on their common problems. The first ITUC was established in the area Saar–Lorraine–Luxembourg in 1976. By 1983, another seven such councils had been established in the following regions:

— the Maas–Rhein region, covering the areas around Aachen–Liège–Maastrich;
— the Rhein–Ijsel–Ems region, covering parts of Germany and the Netherlands;
— the Weser–Ems Noord-Nederland region, which covers an important Dutch-German coastal area of the North Sea;
— the Basel–Southern Baden–Southern Alsace region, with parts of France, Germany and Switzerland;
— the region of North of France–Pas de Calais–Hainant Province–West Flanders Province, establishing a Franco-Belgian council;
— the Lombardia–Tessin region, between Italian and Swiss trade unions,
— The Pyrenees–Mediterranean region, between France and Spain.[33]

Trade-union cooperation in these regions is concerned principally with practical problems facing the workers in a given area and with finding cross-frontier solutions whenever appropriate. Although the problems of the frontier regions, as well as their structures and forms of cooperation vary from one to the other, there are, nevertheless, some basic areas of common concern:

— unemployment in the region and cross-frontier employment policies;
— varied problems of frontier workers, such as taxation, social security, etc.;
— vocational training, particularly for working women and young people;
— area management, for example, cross-frontier infrastructure, and environmental planning, for example, sites for power stations in the vicinity of national frontiers;
— participation in socio-cultural relations.

To carry out their activities, the ITUCs set up working groups, operating in several languages if necessary. Their activities are directed by a permanent bureau and supervised by general assemblies.

These initiatives are strongly supported by the national trade-union centres of which the regional organizations are a part. The ETUC also has shown great interest in the activities of the ITUCs and has organized regular meetings between them and representatives of the EEC institutions.[34] It has also acted as a coordinator between the ITUCs, promoting regular exchange of information on all topics of mutual interest. In particular, all questions pertaining to frontier workers are regularly discussed.[35] In the view of the ETUC, this type of regional cooperation promotes the finding of European solutions—albeit on a small-scale basis—for a series of practical problems.[36]

Notes

1. ETUC, *Constitution* Preamble, Brussels, 1973.
2. ETUC, *Report of the Proceedings of the Second Statutory Congress*, London, 22, 23 & 24 April 1976, pp. 29, 44.
3. ETUC, *Report 1973-75*, op. cit., pp. 4, 40, 41. ETUC, *Supplement to the Report on Activities*, 1973-75, Brussels, 1976.
4. Tenth Federal Congress of DGB, *Resolutions*, Düsseldorf, 1976, pp. 47-50.,
5. 'Free Labour World Interviews George Debunne', *Free Labour World*, June 1975, p. 4. (Debunne was Secretary-General of the Fédération Générale du Travail de Belgique (FGTB) and Vice President of the ETUC.); ETUC, *Report of the Proceedings of the Second Statutory Congress*, Brussels, 1976, p. 28.
6. ETUC, *Report of the Proceedings of the Second Statutory Congress*, Brussels, 1976, pp. 28, 29, 34-50.
7. ETUC, *Reports on Activities, 1976-78* and *1979-81; Supplements to the Reports on Activities, 1976-78* and *1979-81; General Resolution and Specific Resolutions, 1982-85; Action Programme, 1979-82*.
8. ETUC, *Objectives, 1976-79*, Brussels, April 1976.
9. ETUC, *Action Programme, General Resolution and Specific Resolutions, 1979-82*, Brussels, 1979; ETUC, *Action Programme, General Resolution and Specific Resolutions, 1982-85*, Brussels, 1982.
10. Ernst Piehl, 'International Arbeit: Westeuropa und die Welt', in Michael Kittner, ed., *Gewerkschaftsjahrbuch 1984*—Daten—Fakten—Analysen, Cologne, Bund Verlag, 1984, p. 550.
11. ETUC file on Industry Committees, January 1984, *ETUC Archives*.
12. ETUC, Executive Committee Meeting, Rome, 18 June 1973, Item 3 on Agenda: 'Acceptance of the Industry Committees', *ETUC Archives*.
13. ETUC, 'Memorandum of 13 March 1981 to Finance and General Purposes Committee', *ETUC Archives*.
14. ETUC *Constitution*, Brussels, May 1974, Article 4.
15. See Tables 3.4 and 3.5.
16. See Table 3.6.
17. ETUC *Constitution*, op. cit., Art. 6-11.
18. ETUC *Reports*, op. cit.
19. Piehl, op. cit., p. 549.
20. ETUC, *Constitution*, op. cit., Art. 20. It is this provision that prolongs the decision-making process on membership applications.
21. Ibid.
22. See Table 3.8.
23. Piehl, op. cit., p. 553.
24. ETUC, *Report*, 1973-5, op. cit., pp. 18-26; *Transnational 15*, p. 64. ETUC, *Report*, 1976-8, op. cit., pp. 52, 62.
25. ETUC, *Supplement to Report on Activities 1976-78*: Statement on Euro-Mediterranean Colloquium, November 1978, Brussels 1979, p. 51. ETUC, *Report*, 1976-78, op. cit., pp. 52-3.
26. Ibid., pp. 36, 57, 58, 61.
27. Ibid., p. 10. Two *ad hoc* groups—ECC/EFTA coordination and fiscal harmonisation—were abolished by 1984, (ETUC, *Report on Activities, 1982-84*), but three more

committees—the economic committee, the working party on inter-regional trade-union councils, and the working party on industrial research and development—had taken up their work.

28. Ibid., pp. 54, 11.
29. Piehl, op. cit., p. 526.
30. Günter Koepke, 'Vorbereitung von gewerkschaftlichen Entscheidungen: Das Europäische Gewerkschaftsinstitut (EGI)', *Transnational 15*, pp. 65-6; Günter Koepke, 'Aufgaben und Tätigkeit des EGU', *Gewerkschaftliche Monatshefte*, May 1979, pp. 30-40.
31. ETUI, *Report on Activities*, 1976-8, op. cit., pp. 14, 15, 3-12.
32. ETUI, *Report on Activities*, 1979-82, op. cit.
33. ETUC, Executive Committee, 'Communication of the Secretariat', Brussels, 9-10 December 1982, *ETUC Archives*. ETUC press release, 27/82; 'Information on the 'Inter-Regional Trade Union Councils' (ITUC) in the ETUC', Brussels, 15, 16 December 1983, *ETUC Archives*; See also Fig. 3.1.
34. Ernst Piehl, 'Europäische Gewerkschaften arbeiten immer mehr in Grenzregionen zusammen', mimeographed, Brussels, October 1982.
35. ETUC, 'Memorandum on frontier workers', Brussels, 1981, *ETUC Archives*.
36. ETUC, 'Guidelines for past and future cooperation among the ITUCs, the confederations concerned, and the ETUC Executive Committee'. Brussels, 15 and 16 December 1983, *ETUC Archives*.

Chapter 4
Channels of influence

As stipulated in its preamble and basic objectives, the ETUC is an all-European organization representing workers' interests in European institutions, but the focal point of its attention, is directed at the European Community and its institutions, where it carries out most of its activities.

The representation of workers' interests in the Community operates at three different levels: one is at the topical level, another is at the regional level and the third is at the national level. At the topical level, the ETUC attempts either to impress its views upon the Community decision-makers on issues under debate, or to attract the attention of the EEC institutions to topics it considers particularly important and on which it desires legislation. It also attempts to influence the decision-making process of the different institutions by voicing its views during all stages through which the proposals have to pass before reaching their final form.[1]

At the regional level, the ETUC's policies are frequently aimed at improving the functioning of the Community institutions to increase trade-union influence within them. By voicing serious reservations about some of the Community advisory structures, the trade unions have been particularly able to promote the establishment and the strengthening of tripartite structures as a basis for consultation with governments and employers. Also, they have favoured the extension of the dialogue—beyond the one established with the ministers of labour and social affairs—to the ministers of finance and economics. In their view, the increasingly difficult employment situation in the Community could not be dealt with by the ministers of labour alone, but also required effective economic and financial measures.

At the national level the ETUC operates through two channels. It uses the national confederation of trade unions to impress its point of view on the respective governments on issues of direct concern. It has also through the years, institutionalized direct meetings with the heads of government of the country that has the rotational presidency of the Council.

Since the three levels are interconnected and there is really no neat compartmentalization, in this chapter it is proposed to mix them while analyzing the ETUC's interaction with European institutions, and while surveying the ETUC's stance on major European issues in the subsequent chapter.

The Commission

The ETUC has always attributed high priority to its relations with the Commission. By virtue of its status as the main organ that formulates legislative proposals for the Community, the Commission is obviously viewed as the most

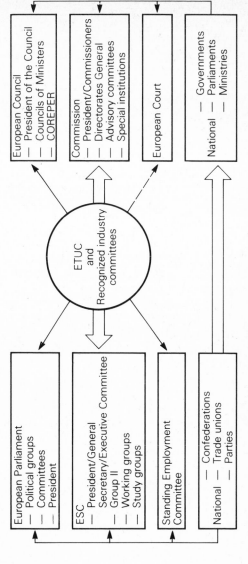

Figure 4.1 Interest representation at EEC institutions
Source: Ernst PIEHL: with permission of the author

crucial institution with which a continuous interaction is fundamental. To influence the orientation of legislation in a particular direction, the ETUC considers that it is vital to cooperate actively at a very early stage with the Commission in the elaboration of policies.[2]

The Commission, too, realizes the vital importance of maintaining a continuous interaction with the ETUC, since it represents a very large majority of the EEC's labour force, whose cooperation would be obviously essential for the effective designing and implementation of social legislation. In this connection, it is important to note that the Commission has established a wide spectrum of meetings, consultations, contacts, etc., which it uses with considerable frequency.[3] Contacts between the Commission and the ETUC take place both at the formal and at the informal level. Formal contacts usually occur at high level. Originally they were simply declaratory, but with the deterioration of the overall economic situation within the Community, they have become more and more substantive.[4]

At the informal level, continuous but non-institutionalized contacts are maintained between the EEC officials of all levels and the ETUC Secretariat. Though they are not easily traceable, they are of considerable importance, and their significance within the overall decision-making process in the Community cannot be underestimated.[5]

At the Commissioners' level, consultations with trade unions were originally concentrated on the Commissioner of Social Affairs. But with the arrival of Roy Jenkins as the Head of the Commission in January 1977, contacts with the Commission as a whole have become more frequent. In the early stages of his presidency, for example, he invited the ETUC for discussions with him and his colleagues, regarding the Commission's political priorities and its programme of work. Since then such meetings have become more institutionalized and now seem to take place about twice a year.[6]

The increasing frequency of such high level contacts did not, however, prevent the occurrence of differences between the two institutions. During the July 1979 meeting, that was convened to explore the different economic measures to meet the oil crisis and its ensuing negative consequences on the labour market, wide divergences emerged between the representatives of the two institutions. While the ETUC—echoing decisions taken at the Munich Congress in May 1979—called for the stimulation of consumption as a motor for growth, and proposed the creation of employment through the reduction of working time, the Commission favoured deflationary policies and refused to deal with the issue of working time, considering it as a matter for direct negotiations between employers and trade unions.

When the Commission—after some discussion—finally conceded and agreed to submit a proposal on working time to the Council, the ETUC not only considered it unsatisfactory, but actually perceived it as contrary to its basic interests. The relations between the Commission and the ETUC thereafter became increasingly strained and were virtually broken off.

Finally, the dialogue was reopened in January 1981 with the installation of the new Commission led by Gaston Thorn.[7] While the differences persisted—and were aggravated by many of the Council's decisions to follow a monetarist and deflationary policy—a *modus vivendi* was established that allowed for the continuation of working relations.

ETUC's interaction with the individual Commissioners is also important. In many ways it is even more significant than the general meetings, since most of the basic groundwork is carried out within each department. Clearly, the Commissioner for Social Affairs is ETUC's prime interlocutor; for it is in this department that most of the work pertaining to the trade unions is conducted. This became particularly evident after the 1972 Council meeting in Paris agreed to lay stronger emphasis on social aspects of integration. The final declaration of the summit even went so far as to reject the previous subordination of social to economic policies, emphasizing that it attached as much importance to vigorous action in the social field as to the achievement of economic and monetary union.

To this end, the Commission submitted proposals for a social action programme that was adopted by the Council in January 1974 and which contained three major objectives: 'the attainment of full and better employment, the improvement and upward harmonization of living and working conditions, and the increased involvement of management and labour in economic and social decisions of the Community and of workers in the life of their firms'.[8]

In this connection, a number of advisory committees were established under the jurisdiction of the Commissioner whose task was to focus attention on three aspects of social policy:

— hygiene and safety at the place of work;
— social security for migrant workers;
— free movement of workers.[9]

The importance of the social affairs' department can also be gauged from the fact that two tripartite institutions dealing with specialized aspects of social policy were established under the auspices of the Commissioner for Social Affairs. The first was the European Centre for the Development of Vocational Training (CEDEFOP) with headquarters in Berlin, and the second was the Foundation for the Improvement of Living and Working Conditions with its central office in Dublin.[10]

Though fully aware of the vital importance of social affairs in its dealings with the Commission, the ETUC has nevertheless avoided concentrating its relations with this one department. Convinced of the inter-relatedness between social issues and other activities of the Community, it has tried to forge relations with other Commissioners as well. But since the success of such initiatives is largely contingent on the subject matter in question and on the personal disposition of the Commissioner, the ETUC experience has not been uniformly positive. While in such areas as energy policy and the EEC's relations with the Third World, direct cooperation between the Commissioner concerned and the ETUC has increased considerably, it has been less satisfactory in other areas, particularly in the field of the Community's economic policy.[11]

Below the Commissioner level, the ETUC generally maintains good relations with the director-general and his staff. The flow of information between them and the ETUC Secretariat is considered quite satisfactory. Real working relations based on daily contacts between the staff of the two institutions has been established and are perceived as a guarantee for an intensive interaction, particularly during the preparatory stages of the Commission's deliberations.

If one were to generalize and summarize the pattern of the decision-making process which is followed before a proposal appears in its final form, it could be stated that it has to go through certain stages:

First of all, if a proposal emanates from the ETUC itself, it has already gone through a process of internal consensus finding. Normally, a ETUC working group, manned by experts from national trade-union centres and the ETUC secretariat—frequently in preconsultation with the Commission—establishes a position paper for the consideration of the ETUC Executive Committee. After amendment or acceptance by this body, the proposal is forwarded to the Commission's relevant directorate. At the same time, it is sent to the European Parliament and the Economic and Social Committee. During the period of intense discussions in these institutions, the ETUC lobbies in favour of the proposal while, at the same time, it participates in *ad hoc* expert consultations called by the Commission.

In the light of the opinions expressed by the European Parliament and the Economic and Social Committee on the proposal, the Commission makes the appropriate revisions and submits it to the European Council. The Council, in turn, sends it to its Working Party on Social Questions, composed of the representatives of the member states. After consideration by this group, the text goes to the Committee of Permanent Representatives (COREPER) at the EEC, which, in turn, remits it to the Council after proposing the amendments it deems appropriate.

There are many pitfalls in this procedure. The dangers of diluting the original ETUC initiative are indeed very great. The employers' organizations, for example, may strongly lobby against it. The Economic and Social Committee may not necessarily render a favourable opinion, if a coalition between the employers' group and other interest groups can be forged. The European Parliament with its centre/right majority may not necessarily look positively upon a trade-union proposal. In the view of the ETUC, it is, however, the Council Working Party on Social Questions which has often shown the greatest reluctance to retain ETUC-initiated proposals in the form adopted by the Commission, and it is this group which, together with COREPER, is particularly unreceptive to trade-union influence.[12]

The European Council

Whereas relations between the ETUC and the Commission have become increasingly complex and increasingly interactive over the years, they have remained rather static and formalistic with the European Council.

Since the meeting of the Heads of States and Governments in Brussels in July 1975, it has become customary for the acting President of the Council to receive—on the eve of their meeting—a ETUC delegation, which is usually composed of the ETUC president, its general-secretary and a trade-union representative from the country holding the Council's presidency. These rather formal encounters have been used to present ETUC positions and demands to the Council.[13]

In view of the recessionary situation, the major issues raised by the ETUC at these meetings pertain to unemployment. But such other questions as direct elections to the European Parliament (July 1976; December 1977); the coordination of the Community's financial resources (November 1976); the reform of the Economic and Social Committee (April 1978), and of European monetary reform (all of the meetings in 1978) have also been brought up.[14]

Recently, the ETUC has begun to contact governments even before they take over the presidency. The objectives of these encounters are to discuss the government's political and economic programmes during the six months of its presidency. In most cases, these representations have yielded only limited results.

An additional effort to press the employment issue upon the government was made by the ETUC before the 1983 summit meeting in Stuttgart (Germany), and the ETUC employment conference in Strasbourg in June 1984. Before these meetings, a ETUC delegation visited all Heads of State of the EEC and EFTA states individually, in order to present its views for a possible solution to the unemployment problem, and, in particular, urged the governments towards an increased coordination of economic, social and fiscal policies in order to come to grips with the unemployment problem.[15]

The ETUC has attempted to establish working relations with the Council's administrative organs. Between its different working groups, its Secretariat, the Committee of Permanent Representatives (COREPER) and the ETUC, no working relations have, however, been established. Although a few meetings between the ETUC and COREPER have taken place since 1978, they have been confined—due to COREPER's reluctance to discuss substantial issues—to a mere exchange of information.[16]

The ETUC also attempted to establish direct contacts with the various Councils of Ministers. They are already institutionalized within the framework of such existing tripartite structures, such as the Standing Employment Committee and the European Social Fund where Ministers of Labour and Social Affairs are represented. Beyond this ETUC attempts to establish a viable relationship with the Council of Ministers have remained largely unsuccessful.[17]

Trade Unions can influence the Council through national channels. Since practically all the ETUC positions are based on a compromise, there is no guarantee that its affiliates will always represent and defend the common positions at the national level. With respect to the Tindemans' Report, for example, the Danish LO supported its government's reservations concerning direct elections to the European Parliament. On the other hand, it was an initiative of the German DGB towards the Willy Brandt government that led the 1972 summit to decide the amelioration of the 'social symmetry' within the Community thus implying an increased role of trade unions and employers in the Community decision-making process.[18]

The European Parliament

The quest for a directly elected European Parliament had been an intrinsic part of the European labour movement's earlier conceptions of a unified Europe. Over the years, the trade unions repeatedly called for an accelerated democratization of the European institutions, a process which in their view could not be successfully achieved without holding the direct elections provided for by the Treaty of Rome.[19] They consistently supported the European Parliament's attempts during the 1960s to implement the Rome Treaty's stipulations. But these attempts were blocked by the Council of Ministers; the European Parliament, exasperated by the delays, even considered the idea of taking legal action against the Council.[20]

With the enlargement of the EEC in 1973, the problem was reconsidered. The EP's political affairs committee drafted a new proposal that was submitted to the summit meeting of the European Council on 9 and 10 December 1974 in Paris. On this occasion the meeting decided, in principle, to hold direct elections in 1978.[21]

Although this decision was confirmed by the 1975 Rome summit meeting—where trade union pressures were once again exercised in favour of the elections—a series of issues remained unsettled. At the national level, for example, Britain expressed the need for further internal consultations, and at the European level problems arose regarding the nature of the electoral system to be established for this occasion. The provisions of the Rome Treaty requiring a 'uniform procedure'[22] for the elections were not very clear, and were, therefore, subject to different interpretations. Some argued that a unique electoral system should be established for the elections in all the countries. It was quickly recognized that such a interpretation of the Rome Treaty would imply the solution of numerous complex problems on the national level.

The requirement for a uniform procedure was therefore defined in such broad terms as respecting 'basic democratic principles' and assuring that the elections would be 'equal, free, universal, direct, and secret' while leaving the decision regarding the nature of the electoral system to the member states.

The most difficult problem was the number of seats the Parliament should have and the manner in which they should be distributed among the member states. Myriad proposals were discussed for a number of months until a compromise was finally reached.[23] The trade unions kept themselves away from these discussions on the ground that these interstate exchanges on such detailed issues did not concern them directly.

The Council's decision to proceed with the direct elections was greeted with moderate enthusiasm, if not with some scepticism by the ETUC Executive Committee. Although it considered the direct universal suffrage 'to be an important step inasmuch as it will bring about a more extensive and fundamental democratization process, which the ETUC, moreover, has been demanding for some time', it expressed concern as to 'whether the extension of the Community powers of decision would not also bring the consolidations of Community bureaucracy'. Also, it expressed the belief that 'the extension of parliamentary powers will not alone suffice to establish real institutional democracy', and that they should be combined with a 'real Community economic and monetary policy' and should be accompanied by the reform of such other Community institutions as the Economic and Social Committee and the Standing Committee of Employment.[24]

Notwithstanding the introduction of these issues to the debate on direct elections, the ETUC realized that it could not avoid formulating a specific electoral strategy. In fact, it was concerned with two major issues: one was the role the ETUC should play during the election campaign and the second pertained to the voting right of migrant workers.

As an organization that was independent from political parties, the ETUC could not possibly support any party or a group of parties, despite the socialist character of many of its member organizations. At the same time, it could not possibly exclude itself from what was undoubtedly a major event in the ongoing process of European integration. It therefore came to the conclusion that its major task, under the circumstances, should be to provide information to trade-union members about the political significance of the elections, and to mobilize them for a maximum participation in the polls. Although it would not campaign in favour of any particular party, the ETUC decided to increase trade unions' and their members' sensitivity to certain party programmes which would represent trade-union conceptions on political, social and economic issues.[25]

The second issue concerned the problem of the voting rights of migrant workers from member states. The September 1976 governmental agreement on the direct elections did not contain any provisions on voting rights for migrant workers who were citizens of one EEC member state but resident in another. In the ETUC view, migrant workers were precisely the group 'most directly involved in the development of Community policy'.[26] The problem became particularly pressing in those EEC countries where the right to vote was linked to both citizenship and residency. Thus it was estimated that in the case of a strict application of the national electoral systems, several million workers would be deprived of their voting right in direct elections. The most efficient solution to this problem, in the ETUC view, would be to allow all nationals of member states, residing in one of the states, to vote in the elections. It was, however, not clear whether such citizens would have the right to vote for candidates in their country of residence—thus allowing, for example, a French communist worker in Germany to increase the chances of a German communist candidate, highly undesirable in the eyes of the DGB—or whether they should vote for candidates from their countries of origin.[27]

The strict linkage of the European Parliamentary election to national electoral systems made it extremely difficult for the ETUC to come up with a Community solution to the problem. If a country allowed voting by proxy or by mail, workers were encouraged to use these means to participate in the election. In other cases, special arrangements were made on the national level to allow workers to return to their home country for the occasion.[28] Thus, during the period preceding the elections, the ETUC concentrated increasingly on its self-imposed task of informing workers about the European realities and the Community's objectives. The aim was to increase workers' awareness of their specific problems and to stimulate them into maximum participation in the elections.[29] In this task, the ETUC was assisted by the European Community, and—in varying degrees of commitment and nationalistic colouring—by its member organizations.

The British TUC, however, flatly refused to have anything to do with the election campaign, and the Danish LO expressed serious reservations about participation in any activities the ETUC might envisage. The other organizations—while pointing out certain difficulties they might encounter at the national level or projecting their own visions of Europe—were generally willing to contribute manpower and organizational facilities to the campaign.[30]

The Commission's contribution was primarily financial. It had allocated one million Units of Account for the purpose of diffusing information about the European elections and supporting information programmes organized by movements particularly interested in European integration. Out of this special budget, the Commission showed willingness to allocate a certain sum for ETUC activities concerning direct elections.[31]

The ETUC decided that its actions regarding direct elections would take place in two phases. During the first phase, meetings with journalists would be held to inform the trade union press on the situation in the Community, and on decisions taken by the Executive Committee regarding the elections. During the second phase, a series of documentary papers would be drawn up covering the ETUC positions on a number of subjects.[32] Such papers were established in the form of brochures and translated into the Community languages. They covered the following topics:

1. The prime aim of economic policy
2. Migrant workers' problems
3. Energy policy
4. ETUC youth group
5. Lomé Convention
6. The European Social Fund
7. The common agricultural policy
8. Developments in the Harmonization of provisions of company law in the European Communities
9. Multinationals
10. Women at work
11. Working conditions—environment
12. Consumer policy
13. Regional policy as structural employment policy
14. Democratization of Community Instruments[33]

Among the fourteen topics listed, only one dealt directly with the European elections, while the others contained ETUC positions on various problems arising within the European Community.

The ETUC stance on the elections basically reflected the earlier discussions within the Executive Committee. Since there were no prospects for any increase in the political powers of the Parliament, the elections were expected to be 'primarily of symbolic importance' in the sense that they would be 'a political affirmation at supranational level'. Nevertheless, ran the argument, it would be an important step in the direction of a 'more extensive and more fundamental democratisation ...' The ETUC reiterated its concern that 'the extension of parliamentary powers alone will not suffice to establish true institutional democracy.' They had to be supplemented by reforms of such other Community institutions as the Economic and Social Committee, the Standing Committee on Employment, the advisory committees and the tripartite conferences.

Furthermore, the ETUC stressed that

the democratisation process advocated by the trade unions will only acquire its full value if it helps to meet the socio-economic aspirations of the workers. The trade unions will therefore also use this campaign to increase pressure for more effective measures to combat unemployment, improve the living standards and working conditions of working people, and to guarantee workers' spending power and the purchasing power of social benefits.

The ETUC also pointed out that in spite of reservations on behalf of some of its members,

the great majority of the trade unions in the countries of the European Community are in favour of true European union based on real parliamentary democracy. On condition, however, that the main objective of this Community is the well-being of workers and their families, that it is open to its immediate neighbours and avoids anything which could lead to a barrier between the Community and the other industrialised countries throughout the world, and that it never forgets its duties of solidarity with the third and fourth world.[34]

At the national level, while some trade unions became actively involved in encouraging maximum participation, particularly of trade-union members, others continued to express scepticism about the effectiveness of the new parliament, given the fact that its political status would remain basically unchanged. The German DGB and the Italian trade unions, for example, were the most ardent advocates of the Parliament. The former expressed concern about what its president had termed 'Europamüdiketi' (weariness of Europe), and sought to revive the European idea in a vast colloquy organized for local trade-union officials with the participation of the EC Commission, the ETUC Secretariat, ETUC affiliated trade unions from EEC member countries, German politicians from all political parties and representatives from the academic world particularly involved with European problems.[35] Furthermore, in collaboration with the Italian trade unions, it established a programme allowing foreign workers in Germany (this was particularly relevant for Italians) to return to their country of origin on the election day in order to cast their votes.[36]

The final result of all this interest was the election of a number of high-ranking Italian and German trade unionists of differing political orientations to the directly elected parliament. Among them were the president of the German trade union confederation, H. O. Vetter, who—after his retirement from the

DGB presidency in 1982—became one of the most active members of the Parliament, and the presidents of the two major German trade unions, Eugen Loderer, from the metalworkers' union and Karl Hauenschild from the chemical workers' union. All three had campaigned on the Social Democratic ticket. On the Italian side, where a dual role in trade unions and parliaments is prohibited by trade-union statutes, some trade-union members resigned in order to campaign for the European Parliament. Among them were Luigi Macario, former president of the CISL, running on the Christian Democrat ticket; Mario Dido, former member of the CGIL Executive Board, running on the Socialist Party's ticket; Aldo Bonnacini, also a former member of the CGIL Executive Board, campaigning on the Communist list; and Fabrizia Badnel Glorioso of the Economic and Social Committee of the EEC.[37]

Though the ETUC already had established informal contacts with the Parliament and its various working committees, they were intensified after the direct elections. Its Secretariat increasingly adopted the role of a lobby aiming at influencing the Parliament to pass legislation corresponding to ETUC positions, particularly for proposals dealing with industrial policies and the so-called Vredeling initiative, as well as programmes for working conditions, research and development, migrant workers, part-time work, etc.

Contacts between the ETUC and the Parliament took place on a regular basis and at different levels. Regular discussions were sought with members of parliamentary groups of experts in order to make known and defend ETUC views on the subjects under discussion. At least three times a year, discussions took place between the ETUC and the different parties represented in the Parliament. The ETUC president and the Secretary-General attended all plenary meetings as observers; the ETUC Secretaries followed all committee sessions on specific themes in which they were interested. They also maintained close contacts with committee chairmen and individual committee members on issues of particular concern and participated, whenever possible, in parliamentary hearings to present their views.

The ETUC Secretariat considered that trade union influence on the European Parliament was fairly limited. While they often found socialist and communist deputies fairly receptive to their views, their influence with the centre-right groups was practically non-existent. The ETUC attempted to institutionalize their activities by proposing the establishment of a trade-union group within the European Parliament that might act as a catalyst for trade-union views within the EP, but the group did not appear sufficiently coherent to act as a viable and efficient intermediary between the ETUC and the Parliament.[38]

On balance, the performance of the Parliament—from the trade-union view—was rather disappointing. While it was recognized that the Parliament had become a unique forum for voicing ETUC positions on a wide spectrum of issues, it was clear that the implementation of trade-union policies was much less successful. One of the major reasons for this was the indifference of the centre-right majority within the EP to many of the ETUC views and political positions.[39]

An air of resignation had developed within the ETUC which could be noted during the preparatory stages for the second direct elections. Not only did the British and the Danish scepticism about the usefulness of the EP appear to have gained some justification, but even the supporters of the European Parliament seemed to be less enthusiastic during the campaign. Moreover, since the Commission did not provide funds for the campaign, the ETUC was largely unable to mobilize its membership for active participation.

Consequently, the ETUC was unable to make a major contribution to the 1984 election campaign. It did, however, use the occasion to propagate its major concern—the unemployment problem. A 'manifesto' signalling the existence of thirteen million unemployed, a considerable decrease in workers' spending power, increasing curtailment of achievements of social security systems and a series of economic policy failures was widely distributed for this purpose.[40] An appeal was made to the voters to support these candidates favouring the ETUC's revendications.[41]

The Economic and Social Committee (ESC)

The traditional consultative organ of the Council and the Commission is the Economic and Social Committee, where trade unions, employers and 'various interest groups' are represented. According to the Rome Treaty, members are nominated by national governments, but appointed by the Council of Ministers for a four-year term.[42] In most cases the governments' role in the nomination is purely formal since they select the persons proposed by the groups represented in the ESC.

The selection process of trade-union representatives, however, does not conform entirely to ETUC wishes, who would like to be the sole organization qualified to nominate trade-union representatives. But this is not the case, since out of fifty-seven trade-union members of the ESC, only forty-eight are ETUC affiliates, the others being members of the French CGT, or the German employees' trade union (DAG), or other associations considered by their respective governments as workers' representatives.[43]

Since trade union representatives to the ESC are nominated at the national level, the ETUC Secretariat, as such, is not represented there. Attempts by the Secretariat to obtain one national seat for one of its political Secretaries—which would considerably improve its effectiveness regarding ESC activities—have not, as yet, succeeded.[44]

According to the Treaty stipulations, the Committee has to be consulted by the Commission and the Council on a variety of subjects.[45] Since its very beginning, however, the ESC has been generally viewed as an institution with a limited role, and the trade unions, in particular, have been clamouring for a series of reforms to render the Committee more efficient, and labour's influence more significant.

The first issue taken up by the Committee dealt with its right to express opinions on its own initiative, not merely when it was called upon to do so by the Council and the Commission.[46] Centering the first discussion on this issue was perhaps understandable since the Consultative and Social Councils within member states on which the ESC was modelled were invested with the right to take initiatives any time and on any issue that fell within their competence. The question, was discussed at some length during the negotiations for the establishment of the Common Market.[47] But most participating governments were against the extension of too many rights to the social groups at the Community level. The German government—lacking any consultative institutions internally—was one of the most fervent partisans of such a stand. It was argued, in particular, that, since the European Parliament did not have the prerogative to develop its own initiatives, there was no reason that such a right should be accorded to the ESC.[48]

At the very first meeting of the Committee in May 1958, it became clear that its members—all high-ranking officials of their respective national organizations—were not prepared to accept the limited role given to the Committee by the founding members. They did not consider themselves, and did not wish to be considered as some sort of a 'council of superior experts', but saw themselves as 'an economic assembly' entitled to treat all subjects that were of interest to them.[49] Their opposition became all the more tenacious when it became increasingly evident that they were to be consulted only on technical matters, and not on problems of political interest regarding the integration of Europe.

Meeting with continuous opposition from the Council, the Committee successfully introduced a 'disguised' form of initiative by proposing to the Council and the Commission certain subjects on which they wished to be consulted. This practice was, thereafter, increasingly used and, by 1965, the president of the ESC—in order to establish a well-structured working programme—indicated to the president of the Commission, area by area, the questions on which the ESC wanted to express its opinion.

This arrangement was, not considered to be entirely satisfactory. All the groups of the Committee therefore continued to reiterate their right to take initiatives as a means of increasing the influence of the socio-economic forces within the Community and of improving the EC's economic and social legislation.[50]

It was, only in the late 60s that the Council began to take a more positive attitude on this question. Heavy social unrest in Italy and France in 1968–9 had persuaded their governments to take a more positive approach to their domestic trade unions and to give greater weight to their socio-political concepts.[51] But it was principally the change of governments in France and Germany which led to a more open view on Community matters. In France, De Gaulle's government was replaced by George Pompidou who had a less critical stand on the EEC than his predecessor and had different views on economic and social matters at the Community level. In Germany the new government of Willy Brandt was dominated by new socio-economic concepts.[52] In fact, the previous German governments had been the principal opponents to any attempts to give greater importance to the socio-economic forces within the Community. Under Erhard, first as Minister of Economics, and then as Chancellor (from 1948 to 1966), any such notion was considered contrary to the rules of market economy.[53] But during the recession in Germany in 1966–7, a certain planning of economic and social policies had to be introduced. This new approach, adopted by the 'great coalition', led to the establishment of the 'law for the encouragement of economic stability and growth' that favoured a 'concerted action' by the state, the trade unions and employers' associations to attain these goals. It was recognized that the social partners were directly concerned with such essential economic issues as salaries, prices, employment and investments, and should therefore be drawn into the mainstream of the policy-making process of the government.

In this connection, it is important to note that the DGB, having developed concepts of consultation and co-determination during the same period, was an effective lobbyist for the allocation of a greater role to the social partners within the EEC, and particularly the ESC. The president of the ESC, A. Lappas, who was also vice president of the DGB, for example, intervened on several occasions with the Chancellery to insist that the ESC should finally be granted the right to take initiatives on its own.[54] Arguing along the same lines as the Council, which had in 1972 formally expressed its intentions to associate socio-economic categories with the forthcoming 'economic and monetary union', the DGB insisted that the Community's orientation towards an economic and monetary union should coincide with an increased participation of the economic and social forces in the life of the Community which, in turn would give new impetus to its policies.[55]

As a result of all these developments, Willy Brandt submitted a memorandum to the summit meeting in Paris, on 19–20 October 1972, suggesting a new approach to social policy in the Community, and proposing, in particular, the institution of the right of initiative within the ESC.[56]

The Council agreed. Although the decision became official only in February 1974, after the internal procedures had been changed accordingly, the Committee decided to interpret the Council decision in a broad sense and use this right immediately. Thus, before 1974, the ESC had issued five opinions on issues such as the GATT, industrial policies and technology, the economic and monetary union and agricultural policies.

The right of initiative was not the only preoccupation of the trade unions in the ESC. A series of other issues—aimed at the improvement of the ESC's role and efficiency, and the strengthening of labour's influence within the Committee—were repeatedly pressed upon the Commission and the Council during the 1970s.

The enlargement of the Community and the ensuing increase in the membership of the ESC had resulted in the proliferation of complex issues, as a result of which the procedures and working methods of the ESC were no longer adequate for the effective functioning of the Committee. Its administrative set-up had become particularly insufficient. The trade unions, supported by other members of the Committee, demanded appropriate funds for the reorganization and the reinforcement of the administrative facilities of the Committee and its different groups. This was granted by the Council in 1974.[57]

The second concern pertained to trade-union representation on the Committee. In this respect, two major problems arose: the ETUC felt that, in comparison to the employers' group, it was seriously under-represented since a large number of members of the 'various interest groups' could—in their view—be considered as employers. It was not only with respect to the numerical representation that the ETUC felt discriminated against; it was also, and particularly, regarding its qualitative representation: ESC meetings were too frequent and too time-consuming. As many as 400 sessions had been convened, for example, in 1972, which required almost a weekly presence in Brussels. Many of the meetings were considered too technical by high level trade union leaders who were neither interested nor did they feel competent to advise on such matters. The time-consuming task of attending such technical meetings was increasingly problematic since more often than not it was at the expense of neglecting their national duties.

To remove some of the difficulties the trade unions proposed the appointment of deputies who could replace the representatives whenever necessary.[58] When this proposal was not favourably received by the Council, some of the trade unions—in order to assure a more efficient representation in the Committee—resorted to the appointment not only of top trade-union leaders, but also of some of their staff members as full members of the ESC. Although this solution was not considered entirely satisfactory, it was increasingly adhered to during the late seventies.[59]

The employers, on the other hand, did not have the same problem. Their representatives on the Committee frequently were retirees and were outstandingly competent. Having retired from high-level domestic positions, they were completely free from other tasks, so that they were able to use their full weight and devote all their time to their work on the Committee. The ETUC, however, having refused a similar solution for themselves, argued that since the retired persons were no longer active at the domestic level, they could not be considered truly representative. It suggested that an age limit be introduced for Committee members.[60]

A third concern was the publication of dissenting opinions expressed in the ESC. This demand was strongly reiterated, as the continuously deteriorating economic situation made it more and more difficult for the trade unions to reach agreement with other groups. Under the circumstances, the trade unions preferred to see a clear record of their dissenting views rather than seeing them diluted in general compromises. This attempt to reform the internal regulations of the Committee was also firmly blocked by employers and other groups within the ESC.

In view of the generally negative response to its demands, the ETUC decided to exercise increased pressure to obtain satisfaction on at least some of its revendications. First of all, it aired the issues at the national levels with a request to its affiliates to take up these matters with their respective governments. The Danish, German, and Belgian rotating presidents of the Council were approached. In April 1978, the issues were taken up by the ETUC president with the European Council at its meeting in Copenhagen. Pressures were also increased at the Committee level. The ETUC was particularly fortunate in having an Italian trade-union leader as the president of the Committee from 1978 to 1980, who was naturally responsive to ETUC demands.[61]

All these efforts finally bore fruit. Some of the reforms proposed by the ETUC were finally introduced in 1980. It was, for example, agreed that

Committee members could be represented by their deputies, and that assistants could accompany them to the Committee meetings; also it was agreed that dissenting opinions could be published as an annex to the Committee opinions.[62]

Aside from the problems arising within the ESC, the trade-union members were also faced with a problem of internal coordination. The frequency with which ESC meetings took place made it increasingly difficult for ETUC members to participate regularly in the preparatory meetings that were supposed to develop coordinated positions. To facilitate attendance at these meetings, it was suggested that the topics under discussion should be classified into two categories: those of general interest to the Community, and those of technical character. Since it would be the first type that would require most preparation and coordination, preparatory meetings should be restricted only to those.[63]

An additional problem was that the ETUC Secretariat, though in charge of coordination between Group II and the ETUC, is not represented in the ESC. To obtain ETUC Secretariat presence in the ESC meetings, it was proposed to admit 'observers' from the European non-governmental organizations such as the ETUC and UNICE, which might improve the coordination within the different groups. But this proposition would be problematic for the ETUC. For while it would welcome an observer status for its own secretariat and for the employers' association, UNICE, it would find it difficult to accept observers from other groups such as COPA, COGECA, EUROCCOP, etc., an unavoidable development if the proposition were implemented.[64]

In recent years, the coordination within the Group II and its cooperation with the ETUC Secretariat appears to have improved considerably. The Group has also become more active in elaborating a series of opinions on topics of direct interest to the labour movement such as unemployment, income distribution, new technologies, regional policies, ACP-EEC cooperation, and the like.[65]

In spite of these improvements and reforms, the problem of over-representation of the employers still remains unresolved. The ETUC continues to maintain serious reservations regarding the various interest groups, which, in its view, contribute considerably to this situation. Moreover, many representatives of the different interests cannot make—due to their limited approach—a significant contribution to the increasingly difficult discussions on overall economic and social problems in the Community. They thus tend to hamper rather than improve the proceedings of the Committee.

Since this issue seemed intractable and there did not appear to exist any palpable hope for a solution in the near future, the ETUC—while recognizing the Committee's importance as a consultative organ—did not wish to upgrade it further. It argued that the Committee should remain a consultative body and should not be overly involved in any negotiations or in any decision-making. This, in its view, should be reserved for such tripartite bodies as the Standing Committee for Employment or for other tripartite conferences that might take place in the future.[66]

This should not imply that the ETUC does not favour any more reforms of the ESC; for it does, as can be ascertained from its proposal that the Council and the Committee should justify any occasions when the ESC's recommendations are not taken into account; or from its continuous insistence for better cooperation and better coordination between the ESC and other EEC institutions, particularly the European Parliament. On the latter point, it is interesting to note that the ESC has already established wide-ranging contacts with the directly-elected European Parliament, including frequent talks with different Parliamentary committees on a series of topics of mutual interest.[67]

The European Social Fund (ESF)

The European Social Fund was the only institution stipulated by the Treaty of Rome to deal specifically with employment problems. It was established 'to increase the opportunities of employment for workers in the Common Market, and to contribute thereby to the rising standard of living'.[68] The aim was to provide a mechanism for compensating persons whose employment was threatened by any structural changes that the establishment of the Common Market might unavoidably generate.

The Fund was to be administered by the Commission with the assistance of a consultative committee composed of representatives of governments, workers and employers.[69] Each group was to send two representatives from each member state to the Committee.[70]

Initially, the Fund was considered as the most important social component of the Treaty, and was perceived as the 'cornerstone in the edifice of social security', and as the 'first supra-national guarantee for those living in the European Community'.[71] However, this initial enthusiastic evaluation did not correspond to reality. For one thing, the scope of aid the Fund was entitled to provide was basically limited to the training and to resettlement of workers who had lost their employment through structural industrial changes.[72] For another, the Council did not show any deep interest in rapidly implementing even the limited social provisions of the Treaty, and dragged its feet for some time before establishing regulations which would permit the activation of the Fund. In fact, it was only after considerable pressures were exercised by the trade unions that the necessary administrative rules for its operation were provided in 1960.[73]

Under these rules, the Fund's main function was to re-emburse 50 per cent of the expenses incurred by the Community's member states for the retraining and the resettlement of workers. Under the circumstances, it could hardly become a stimulus for national or Community manpower policies as had been expected by the trade unions; and even in its limited capacity as an organ for refunding expenses it was hampered by a wide array of complicated and cumbersome procedures.

Since the functioning of the Fund was generally considered unsatisfactory, proposals for reform were put forward to the Council by the Commission in 1965, and again in 1969, after the first ones had remained in abeyance on the Council's agenda for three years. Finally, when the Council did act (July 1970), the scope of the Fund's activities was somewhat increased, in so far as it was allowed to act in some cases even before redundancies occurred.[74]

In spite of this revision, the ETUC did not consider it a reliable instrument for employment policies during the 1970s and became even more critical and even more dissatisfied with the Fund's activities as unemployment increased in the Community. The trade unions were particularly dissatisfied with the cumbersomeness and the opacity of its administration. Also, they complained about the malfunctioning of the Fund's consultative committee, which in their view met only infrequently and did not permit effective and regular consultation with social partners.

The financial resources of the Fund (about 1.7 billion ECU for 1983) were also considered insufficient to meet the growing demands for retraining, and should—in accordance with the recommendations of the European Parliament, strongly supported by the ETUC—be increased to cover 10 per cent of the Community's total budget. It was estimated that the Fund's budget should be in the vicinity of about 22 billion ECU in 1983.[75]

These financial resources, furthermore, should—in view of the ETUC—be closely controlled through a more efficient participation of the social partners in the management of the Fund. To achieve this, the Commission should provide complete information about the planned and effective allocation of the Fund's resources to the social partners, and consult them regularly regarding its activities and its projects. Besides its administrative shortcomings, its activities should also be streamlined.

The Social Fund—in the ETUC's view—is not equipped to become an instrument of employment policy. Therefore, while financial resources for the creation of employment should be sought from such financial institutions as the Regional Fund and the European Investment Bank, the Fund should focus its attention essentially on vocational training and devise innovative policies in this sector. It should particularly contribute to the solution of employment problems of the most adversely affected groups, i.e. young workers, women and migrant workers. Since employment opportunities of these groups were considerably affected during the late seventies and early eighties, they were in urgent need of professional orientation and vocational training adapted to the requirements of the labour market.

Generally speaking, the effectiveness of the Social Fund is largely contingent upon the effective coordination of its work with the other financial institutions of the Community, as well as with the national organs involved in vocational training activities. Moreover, in the view of the ETUC, the closest possible consultations with trade unions at the European and national levels would also contribute to a better functioning of this institution and its programmes.[76]

The Standing Committee on Employment (SCE)

For many years since its establishment, the EEC neglected issues pertaining to the European labour force, its structure and degrees of training, the labour market and employment conditions. Unprecedented economic growth had created favourable employment conditions leading most governments to assume that free movement of labour would be a sufficient corrective for any imbalances that might occur in the labour market. The only social policy instrument stipulated in the Treaty of Rome, the Social Fund, proved to be inadequate. It played only a marginal role in the field of employment policies.[77]

It was only during the mid-1960s that a surge in the unemployment rate prompted the Council to pay greater attention to labour problems. The labour market situation at the time had become rather complex. While, on the one hand, unemployment was unequally distributed, with France and Italy bearing the heaviest burden, there was, on the other hand, a labour shortage that created severe bottlenecks in economically expanding sectors. This unbalanced situation was aggravated by unemployment in the agricultural sector where rampant mechanization was increasingly rendering a segment of the labour force superfluous.

The Community institutions were thus obliged to interest themselves more in labour-market issues. The Commission became involved in doing some basic studies on the decline in agricultural employment, on the rates of its increase in other sectors, and on regional employment disparities. Also, it carried out studies dealing with individual industries such as textiles, shipbuilding, etc. Its reports on the manpower situation repeatedly drew attention to the need for vocational training, to the importance of installing firms in areas where labour was available and to problems involved with labour mobility and the employment of foreign labour.[78]

Though more reluctantly, the Council also began to show some interest in labour-market problems. The decline of the hitherto booming economic situation resulted in the abandonment of some of its free market ideology and in the acceptance of some cautious economic planning, the most important manifestation of which was the establishment of a medium-term economic programme in 1967.[79] This programme formally recognized manpower as an element of economic development.[80] The Council, furthermore, became more attentive to labour/management relations at the national level, and approved a plan to improve collaboration on employment policies between member governments through the more effective utilization of joint discussions with social partners.[81]

When the social partners—particularly the trade unions—dissatisfied with the Economic and Social Committee's functioning, proposed that a new body should be established where employment could be discussed at a tripartite level, and that for the establishment of such an institution, a tripartite conference should be convened, the proposal was well received by the EEC institutions.[82]

The Commission, for example, reacted to this request by calling a bilateral meeting between its staff and the trade unions in Luxembourg, in November 1969, where the issue of such a conference was discussed. During the same month, it also expented formal recognition to the French and Italian communist trade unions, allowing them to participate in Community affairs—an act which was not to the liking of the labour confederations already established in the Common Market.[83]

The Council became really attentive to social problems during The Hague summit in December 1969. On this occasion, unprecedented attention was given to social matters within the overall development of more efficient economic and monetary cooperation within the Common Market. This meeting also emphasized the need for a more effective employment policy, leading to an increase in employment services, for more vocational guidance and occupational training and for a greater variety of aid to the unemployed.[84] It agreed to convene a tripartite conference which should provide a forum for discussing such issues. The conference was finally convened in Luxembourg on 27 and 28 April 1970. It inaugurated a new type of consultation which gained momentum during the following decade.

The main conclusion drawn by the conference was the need to introduce a policy that aimed at full and better employment through the optimal usage of the existing labour reserves. It was recognized, in particular, that information at the Community level, on national labour markets, on the structure of unemployment, on the effects of free movement of workers and a whole series of related questions remained precarious; and the statistical data, wherever available, on these issues could not be effectively compared due to the lack of any uniformity in gathering and processing techniques. It was, therefore, agreed that before any efficient employment policy could be devised thorough groundwork would have to be carried out on statistical data and basic policies, both at the national and Community levels. Since such initiatives, as well as the formulation of a Community employment policy, would require permanent consultation and conceptual harmonization, a Standing Committee on Employment was proposed that would be invested with necessary authority to carry out such tasks. The Luxembourg conference also proposed that the Standing Committee should be charged with the task of elaborating proposals for the reform of the EEC Social Fund.[85]

Acting promptly on the recommendations of the Luxembourg conference, the Council, shortly thereafter, decided in favour of the establishment of the proposed Standing Committee, whose principal task would be to ensure 'close contact at Community level . . . with the representatives of the employers' and workers' organizations in order to facilitate coordination by the member states of their employment policies in harmony with the objectives of the Community.'[86] Closely following the recommendations of the Conference, the Council, as a priority, mandated the Committee to undertake an inventory and to rationalize the information about earlier developments, the current situation and the future prospects of the labour market in the EEC; to obtain information regarding vocational and professional training in the member states with a view to coordinating existing and future policies; and to examine closely the question of the free movement of labour in the Community with its effects on national labour-market policies. The Council also formally decided to reform the European Social Fund and assigned the task of elaborating relevant proposals to the SCE.[87]

The Standing Committee was endowed with some innovative features in comparison with other consultative institutions. So far it is the only permanent body where consultation and dialogue take place between the Council, the

Commission, the workers and employers. It is presided over by the labour minister of the country holding the Council presidency, who, in cooperation with all other Committee members, prepares and convenes the meetings, to which any member can propose items for discussion. The Commission's task is to assemble all the elements that are necessary for the work of the Committee. Since it is a consultative body with no decision-making authority, the President summarizes the contents of the debates at the end of each meeting.[88]

While the trade unions were in agreement with the structural framework and the tasks allocated to the Committee, they had, from the very beginning, expressed strong reservations regarding the composition of the worker's group.[89] The Council had decided to restrict the composition of the workers' and employers' groups to the organizations that had participated in the tripartite conference in Luxembourg. According to this precedent, of the eighteen seats allocated to trade-union representatives, nine were given to the ECFTU, four to the EO/WCL, two to the CGT/CGIL and one each to the Confédération Internationale des Cadres (CIC), to the French CGTC and to the German DAG.[90] Both the ECFTU and the EO/WCL strongly objected to the allocation of seats to the last four organizations. For ideological reasons, already mentioned above, the presence at the EEC level of the French and Italian communist trade unions was strongly resented by the majority of the Socialist and Christian trade unions; the other three were not considered trade-union organizations in the usual sense of the term.

Apart from these political considerations, a more formal objection was raised against the presence of these organizations on the Committee: they were, it was argued, national organizations without a transnational structure at the Community level, which rendered them unrepresentative.[91] Despite these objections, the Council nevertheless decided to retain its original proposal regarding the allocation of seats. The trade unions thereupon declared that this situation was unacceptable.[92] The deadlock that ensued was further accentuated with the enlargement of the Community and the creation of the ETUC. The latter simply refused to participate in any further meetings of the SCE unless a compromise on this issue could be reached. Finally, the Council gave in. It changed the composition of the workers' group in January 1975, the ETUC was allocated seventeen out of eighteen seats, and the French CGT and CFTC and CGC were alternately to occupy one seat.[93]

The differences between the Council and the trade unions were not only institutional issues. They also disagreed over substantive problems faced by the workers. While agreeing with the Committee's mandate to reform the Social Fund, to encourage the mobility of labour and to collect information on employment situations and its future prospects,[94] the trade unions were concerned about the orientation imposed on the Committee by the majority of its members, in particular the government representatives and parts of the Commission. The Committee, in their view, tended to treat most social problems narrowly, focusing its attention essentially on labour-market issues, and making no serious attempt to deal with unemployment problems in spite of the fact that it had reached serious proportions following the 1973 oil crisis.

From 1973 to 1975, the ETUC followed a two-pronged contradictory policy with respect to the SCE. On the one hand it boycotted the SCE and searched for other means of consultation on employment issues; on the other, it attempted to strengthen the Committee by continuously demanding a broadening of its role.[95]

While the Committee remained dormant and the harmful effects of the 1973 oil crisis on employment became increasingly evident, the ETUC pushed for a 'Tripartite Conference on European Social Policy'. The conference was expected to open another forum of discussion on the increasingly pressing unemployment problem and, at the same time, to activate the SCE. Though the Committee did resume its sessions shortly after the tripartite conference, its role remained limited during the following years (1975–8). The ETUC preferred its subordination to the tripartite conferences and favoured its involvement in the preparations for and in the follow-up of social matters decided by the conferences. Convened under the new impulse given to the participation of the social partners in the Community policy-making process,[96] the tripartite conferences already had become a preferred forum for the ETUC. This was due to their composition on the government side, where, besides the ministers for labour and social affairs, the economic and finance ministers were also represented, thus allowing for a broader approach and a more efficient mix of policy measures against unemployment.

Since an impasse was reached regarding measures to fight inflation and unemployment at the November 1978 tripartite conference, it is interesting to note that the ETUC turned again to the SCE with renewed interest, in the hope that it would be used more intensively and that its operations would be generally improved.[97] However, with the continuously deteriorating employment situation, the Committee's work became increasingly difficult. The employers and the trade unions did not see eye to eye on the causes of the necessary remedies for the unemployment problem.[98]

One of the major points of controversy centered around the question of the 'adaptation of working time'. While the ETUC had emphasized the importance of this step as a means of reducing unemployment,[99] the employers had firmly rejected any possibility of finding a solution on the matter at the European level.[100] The Council proposed a conciliatory compromise on the subject which was rejected as inadequate by the ETUC.[101] In sum, the ETUC viewed the Committee's record as unimpressive. Undoubtedly, the increasingly serious economic and social situation of the late seventies and early eighties clearly did not facilitate its task. The Committee's ineffectiveness—ran the argument—was mainly due to its very nature, which prevents it from using all the necessary economic and financial policy instruments to combat unemployment and remains restricted to labour-market policies. Though some reforms were carried out during the last few years, they were essentially technical in nature, pertaining to the Committee's working methods.[102]

While the Committee was not very successful in finding solutions to substantive problems, it did produce some positive results in technical areas such as temporary and part-time work, flexible retirement, etc. A limited consensus between the social partners was even reached in the complex area dealing with the impact of modern technology, in particular microelectronics, on employment. The Committee favoured the introduction of new technology in order to foster competitiveness of the Community. It pointed out, however, that the social changes and increased employment problems resulting from such a policy need to be carefully considered and require thorough discussion between governments and social partners.[103] While the trade unions requested that such consultations should take place before decisions on the introduction of new technologies were taken,[104] the employers emphasized the need for freedom in their investment decisions.[105] A deadlock on this question was at least temporarily avoided by the Commission's proposal to establish a European Pool of Studies and Analyses (EPOS) to study the impact of new technologies on employment.[106]

The tripartite conferences

During the mid-1970s, it became increasingly apparent to the trade unions that the Community's existing consultative structure did not yield the desired results. While the ESC's efficiency was largely hampered by the inclusion of the 'various interests' group', the Standing Committee on Employment—the only institution where governments, trade unions and employers were represented— dealt only with some of the many aspects of employment policies. Besides, these and other committees were only consultative and their impact on the Council's decisions was marginal. The ETUC therefore sought to find more efficient ways for consultations. In its view, regular tripartite conferences on economic and social questions would be the ideal forum where concerted and politically binding decisions could be taken.

In April 1970 and in December 1974, social conferences—attended by the Ministers of Labour, the employers, and the labour unions—had already taken place, but were considered insufficient as a framework for discussion. In the ETUC's view, social and employment questions could not be dissociated from the overall economic situation; and a meaningful dialogue for overcoming the economic crisis was not possible without the presence and the active participation of the Ministers of Finance and Economy.[107]

Some intense lobbying at the national and Community levels was, however, necessary by the trade unions before such a proposal could gain acceptability. At the July 1975 meeting of the Council, the ETUC president, Vetter, for example, strongly reiterated the ETUC's desire to enlarge the usual forums of consultations from the social to the economic and financial domains. In his view, it could only be in such a framework that strong initiatives for the recovery of the economy and the control of unemployment could be agreed upon.[108] It was during this meeting that the resistance of some governments and parts of the Commission was finally overcome, and a conference as proposed by the ETUC was decided upon.[109]

The first Tripartite Conference finally took place on 18 November 1975 in Brussels. During this meeting, considerable consensus emerged regarding the nature of the economic situation of the mid-1970s, and its structural and short-term causes. However, substantial divergencies surfaced between the different groups regarding the measures to be taken to overcome the problem. The Commission recommended cautious and selective reflationary measures, and the expansion of certain public investments catering to the priority needs of the economy. Aid for private investment should be directed to firms which create additional and stable employment. While a moderation in the rate of increase of earnings should be a key to growth, the burden, it argued, should not be borne by the salaried employees alone, but should be compensated by a redistribution of taxes, by an equitable distribution of income and wealth, by an increased level of public services and by an active employment policy. Such policy should not attempt to maintain the status quo on the pretext of safeguarding jobs, but should be aimed at supporting changes while ensuring that the burden of such transformations would not be borne by the workers alone.[110] The employers advocated a series of fiscal and monetary measures to stimulate private investments, decrease the rate of growth of salaries and the burden of social security payments incumbent on the enterprises.[111]

The ETUC, while recognizing the necessity to control inflation, favoured a coordinated and selective revival policy. It refused to accept that salary increase is the principal factor behind price increases and argued that control of monopoly and essential commodity prices was a more effective means for obtaining price stability. Employment should be protected by the redistribution and the reduction of working time and by the imposition of strict measures against the rapidly rising trend of hiring illegal labour. Additional employment should be created through the increase of public investment in communal and infrastructural projects and by supporting measures for those private investment sectors which were effectively creating employment. In order to assess investment projects, a clear definition of Community objectives would be necessary, and prior notification of investment projects should become mandatory. A special Community institution should be established to that effect.[112]

There was, however, no unanimity within the ETUC on all the points presented in the official statement. First of all, disagreements arose regarding investment control. The Chairman of the German trade unions, who was also the ETUC president, could not wholeheartedly endorse the concept of investment control, which had been rejected as unrealistic by its organization.[113] The second difference of opinion related to the problem of protectionism. Although the ETUC refused to endorse a concept of protectionism regarding inter-Community trade, the British government representative and the TUC president both came out in favour of eventually imposing import controls to protect employment. This idea was strongly rejected by the Danish and German government representatives. The TUC also spoke up in favour of the 'locomotive theory', requiring those countries with a positive balance of payments to act as leaders in the reflationary process. This was aimed particularly at Germany which, during that period, had relatively low rates of inflation and a consistently positive balance of payments. This proposal was rigorously rejected by the German trade unions.

Although the conference did not lead to any concrete results, it was generally agreed that this type of meeting was valuable in so far as it permitted an exchange of views on highly complex matters. Another such meeting would be desirable, and should be prepared during the months to come and should take place not latter than spring of 1976.[117]

The preparations for this conference lasted longer than expected. In March 1976, the ETUC president reminded the presidents of the Council and the Commission that the Commission had been instructed by the 1975 Tripartite Conference to produce a working paper based on the discussions at the meeting to serve as a preparatory document for the next conference. At the following Council meeting he conveyed the ETUC's dissatisfaction with the 'evident lethargy' of the Community institutions regarding economic and employment problems and requested thorough preparatory work for a tripartite conference to be held soon.[118] Shortly thereafter, when the Commission brought out a document,[119] extensive consultations were carried out with the social partners. A broad agreement on the basic orientations presented by the Commission was reached even before the Conference. In particular, it was admitted that the simultaneous restoration of full employment and price stability could be achieved, and should be given priority; that this required concerted action at the Community level; and that all those playing decisive roles in the Community's economic and social life should jointly act to promote growth, employment and price stability.[120]

Despite this basic understanding, differences persisted due to the different interests that were represented. While the ETUC wanted governments to acknowledge that restoration of full employment should be their prime political target determining their economic and financial measures,[121] the employers favoured the curbing of additional labour costs and the limitation of government intervention in economic matters.[122]

Most of the governments were favourably inclined towards the orientation proposed by the Commission. However, due to the disparity in the economic performance of the different member states, the less advanced countries (Italy and Ireland) regarded the full employment and stability targets as highly ambitious, and would need considerable Community aid in order to approach EC averages in these areas. France, on the other hand, remained sceptical with regard to the concept of tripartite conferences at the EC level, since it had consistently rejected similar approaches within its own national framework.[123]

The Conference convened on 24 June 1976 in Luxembourg, under the chairmanship of Denis Healey, made some visible progress. It ended with a consensus on quantified targets for employment creation and for the achievement of greater price stability in the Community. This was recorded in a joint declaration which stipulated that the rate of inflation should be gradually reduced and should reach 4 to 5 per cent by 1980. By that year, full employment should also be restored that in turn would require for the Community as a whole the achievement of an average annual growth rate of approximately 5 per cent over the period from 1976 to 1980.

Not only did the Conference agree on economic targets, it also decided that the dialogue between the participants should continue. For this purpose it suggested that 'a further Conference could be convened in due course to review developments in the situation and to take stock of the results achieved by the joint efforts of all parties. Until then, informal contacts will be maintained between the representatives of the institutions and of employers and labour whenever this appears necessary to one of these parties.'[124]

This declaration was a novelty in the history of the Community. For the first time the trade unions, employers, governments and the Commission were able to establish an economic programme jointly. Though it was not legally binding, there is no denying the fact that it carried a certain political weight, at least for a short period. That the programme was unrealistic can be gauged from the fact that unemployment has been continuously increasing and that inflation rates have remained disparate among the member countries. Nevertheless, they were included as the Community's medium-term economic policy programme and were reiterated in its Annual Report on the EEC's economic situation.[125]

Considerable importance was attached to the 'follow-up' of the conference, for which a 'steering-group', composed of representatives of trade unions, employers, the Commission and the Council presidency was appointed. This group was to be kept small enough to allow flexibility and informality so that meetings could take place whenever necessary. The role of the Standing Committee on Employment was to be reinforced to enable it to contribute to the amelioration of the unemployment situation; and the Economic Policy Committee[126] was expected to begin discussions on economic issues with the social partners.[127]

By the end of 1976, it had already become apparent that the Community's economic situation would not permit the attainment of the targets. The ETUC was thus to accuse governments, employers and the Commission for not following the decisions of the conference, and declared that it 'will not be party to a strategy which replaces action by talking.'[128] It decided to seek a meeting with the president of the Commission to express its concern about the deteriorating situation and the lack of adequate government policies. It asked its affiliates to approach their governments and urge them to conform to the Luxembourg decisions, and proposed to the steering committee to request that governments and the Commission should give an account of the policies that had been pursued at the national and European levels and the measures they proposed to take.[129]

The trade unions, it argued, had made a significant contribution to stability by restraining their wage demands, as a result of which salaries increased only moderately, whereas enterprises had become increasingly profitable in many industrial sectors, without making any significant contribution to employment-creating investments.

In order to review the economic situation more closely and to 'take stock', as was decided by the Luxembourg Conference, some ETUC members favoured the convening of another tripartite confrence during the first half of 1977. But there were others who had serious reservations on the matter. Since the participants to previous conferences had not honoured their commitments and were not likely to do so in the foreseeable future, another conference might only end up with empty words instead of yielding concrete results.[130]

The latter group was supported by the European Parliament, which had also come to the conclusion that tripartite meetings had only led to verbal consensus and not to the realization of targets, particularly in the reduction of unemployment. Therefore should another conference be held, it must reach binding decisions on Community employment policies.[131]

But the first tendency prevailed. The consultations that were made possible by the tripartite conferences were considered important in themselves irrespective of their success. If governments were ready to give account to the social partners of their past and future policies this was, ran the argument, already a valuable exercise in itself. Although the three targets established by the Luxembourg conference were far from being achieved, an increasingly substantial dialogue at the tripartite level had occurred during the follow-up to the conference. It was feared that should there be no conference in the foreseeable future, this type of contact could be considerably reduced.

Within the ETUC, the preparatory discussions dealt not only with the contents of the statements to the proposed conference, but also with the attitude to be adopted during the conference. Should there be dialogue or confrontation? Under the influence of the German ETUC president, with his long experience of meetings with representatives of industry and government within the framework of the German 'concerted action', dialogue was favoured over confrontation.[132]

The next tripartite conference was thus convened in June 1977. Its objectives were to report on economic developments since the last conference, to jointly consider the economic and social problems facing the Community and to reach a consensus about the policy measures that were necessary to reach the previously determined targets.

It was recognized that the Community's economic situation—influenced by the world recession as well as by an increasing amount of obsolete and inflexible industrial structures—had worsened.[133] Also, it became apparent that the position of the social partners had basically remained unchanged.[134] Most governments, far from 'taking stock' of their contributions to overcome the crisis, took no clear position on either stand but insisted on cooperation between all actors on the economic scene.

The previously established targets were not revised, nor were concrete policy measures taken for reaching them. The conference ended with a summary given by Denis Healey, its president, who pointed out that the participants should cooperate on the examination of the following subjects:

— the redistribution of work;
— the creation of employment in the service sector;
— the reconsideration of investment and employment models in the light of the international economic situation;
— employment-creating investments.

These questions were referred to the Standing Committee on Employment and to the Economic Policy Committee for examination.[135]

The results of this conference were considered rather disappointing. The trade unions, who had requested the meeting with the aim of asking governments to explain their inability to meet the targets they had agreed to, had received only general and vague answers. It was also generally deplored that the poor results of the conference had diluted the concept of cooperation.[136] During the follow-up, increasing disparities of opinion between the trade unions and the employers also became apparent. While the employers insisted more and more on the importance of facilitating private investments through the reduction of financial and labour costs, the trade unions believed that growth should be stimulated through increases in private consumption, and that employment should be created through the redistribution of work.[137]

Interaction with the governments also became problematic. The ETUC was, for example, increasingly disappointed with its meetings with the Economic Policy Committee during which government representatives remained completely silent: the only active participation of that group was a general résumé by the chairman at the end of the meetings.[138]

The situation improved slightly during the German presidency in 1978 which also favoured the convening of another tripartite conference. But the ETUC reacted cautiously. In its view, the Commission had produced a few positive concepts regarding investment policies, the tertiary sector and the reduction of working time. But there was no indication of the governments' position on these matters. If the governments or the Council were unable or unwilling to come to the conference with satisfactory answers to a number of pressing questions, it was pointless to continue to maintain the illusion of concerted action.[139]

The conference (9 November 1948, in Brussels), in the view of the ETUC, failed to reach any meaningful conclusions. The governments, while making increasingly bold statements on the necessity for coordination of policies, in fact, did not cooperate. The employers refused to negotiate with the trade unions at the Community level on matters that were of direct concern to both parties.[140] If anything, the conferences were used by the governments as 'listening posts' rather than as a forum for real and meaningful discussion.[141] The ETUC therefore decided not to participate in any further conferences organized on the same lines.[142]

In spite of an intervention by the German Chancellor Schmidt with the ETUC President Vetter, and of the Commission with the ETUC Secretariat to reconsider this decision,[143] the ETUC remained firm on this issue.[144] The Commission and the Council thereupon presented proposals for the improvement of the conferences' working procedures,[145] which were, however, considered insufficient by the ETUC. In their view, such proposals would merely foster dialogue between the social partners and the Commission while the Council looked on. The ETUC believed that contacts with the employers and the Commission did not constitute a problem; it wanted to develop direct access to the Council as the Community's major decision-making organ. Tripartite Conferences were intended to provide such an opportunity and, at the same time, involve the social partners more closely in the economic and social decision-making process. But, since this was not achieved, it would be preferable to improve and enlarge the activities of the Standing Committee for Employment.[146]

Notes

1. ETUC, *Report on Activities*, 1979–82, op. cit., p. 24; see also Fig. 4.1 'Interest Representation at EC Institutions', p. 152.
2. Ibid., p. 24, 25.
3. EEC Commission, *Reports on Social Developments, 1973–83*.
4. Interview with ETUC Secretary-General, Mathias Hinterscheid, Brussels, December 1984.
5. Interview with François Staedelin, Political Secretary of the ETUC, Brussels, June 1983, and with M. Hinterscheid, December 1984.
6. Ibid., and ETUC, *Report on Activities*, op. cit., p. 26. It should be noted, though, that rarely all of the commissioners are present on that occasion.
7. ETUC, *Report on Activities*, op. cit., p. 27; ETUC *Information CP02/81*, 'ETUC Meeting with Thorn', Brussels, 26 January 1981.
8. European Documentation, *The Social Policy of the European Community*, Periodical, 5/1983, p. 22.
9. ETUC, *Report on Activities*, op. cit.
10. *Official Journal* of the European Communities, no. L 39, 13 February 1975 and no. L 139, 30 May 1975.
11. Interview with M. Hinterscheid.
12. Interview with F. Staedelin.
13. EEC *Trade Union Information*, No. 8, 1975.
14. ETUC, *Report of Activities*, 1976–8, p. 14 and ibid., 1979–81, pp. 36, 37.
15. Interview with M. Hinterscheid.
16. ETUC *Report of Activities*, 1976–8, op. cit., p. 16.
17. Interview with François Staedelin.
18. Heinz Kramer, *Ziele und Verhalten der Sozialpartner in Westeuropa als Faktoren für die Gemeinschaftsbildung*, Forschunginstitut für International Politik, Ebenhausen, 1977, pp. 8, 55.
19. Treaty of Rome Art. 183 (3).
20. European Parliament, Directorate General for Information and Public Relations, *Direct Elections*, 1978.
21. Meeting of the Heads of States and Governments, Paris, 9, 10 December 1975, *Communiqué*.
22. Treaty of Rome, Art. 138 (3).
23. European Parliament, op. cit., pp. 5, 7, 8.
24. ETUC Executive Committee, *Statement on the Election of the European Parliament by Direct Universal Suffrage*, Brussels, April 1977.
25. ETUC Executive Committee, 'Verbatim Record', Brussels, 21 January 1977, *ETUC Archives*.
26. ETUC Executive Committee, 'Verbatim Record', Brussels, 21, 22 April 1977, *ETUC Archives*.
27. ETUC, 'Proposals on Voting Rights for Migrant Workers', Brussels, 4 April 1977, *ETUC Archives*.
28. See p. 75.
29. ETUC Executive Committee, 21, 22 April 1977, op. cit.
30. ETUC, Executive Committee, 21, 22 April 1977, op. cit.
31. Commission of the European Communities, *Le programme de la Commission pour les élections directs du parlement européen*, Brussels, march 1977, p. 27.

32. 'Summary of the internal discussions held at the meeting of the trade union press group', Luxembourg, 3 and 4 November 1977, *ETUC Archives*.
33. ETUC, *Information Documents*, 'Election of the European Parliament by direct universal suffrage'.
34. ETUC, 'Election of the European Parliament by Direct Universal Suffrage: Democratization of Community Instruments'.
35. *Das Europäische Gespräch*, June 1977, Cologne, Bund Verlag, 1979.
36. Interview with H. O. Vetter, president of DGB, Brussels, March 1978.
37. *Le Monde*, Dossiers et Documents, 'Les premières élections européennes, (juin 1979): La campagne et les résultats, les institutions et le bilan de la CEE. Supplément aux dossiers et documents du Monde', June 1979.
38. Interview with F. Staedelin, January 1985.
39. Erwin Kristoffersen, 'Das Europa der Gewerkschaften', *Gewerkschaftliche Monatshefte*, May 1984, pp. 261-7.
40. ETUC, 'For a Europe of Working People'. (Pamphlet).
41. Interview with M. Hinterscheid, January 1985.
42. Rome Treaty, Articles 193-5.
43. Non ETUC members of the workers' group are: General Confederation of Liberal Trade Unions (Belgium); Federation of Civil Servants and Salaried Employees' Organization (FTF, Denmark); Employees' Trade Union (DAG, Germany); General Council of the Civil Servants' Association (Greece); Confederation of Executive Staffs (CGC, France); Communist Workers' Confederation (CGT, France); Italian Confederation of Business Managers (CIDA, Italy). ESC *Annual Report*, 1982, Annex A.
44. Interview with F. Staedelin, January 1985.
45. Treaty of Rome, Article 198.
46. Comité Economique et Social des Communautés Européennes, Secrétariat Général, *Le Droit d'initiative du comité economique et social des Communautés européennes*, 2nd edition, Brussels, Editions Delta, 1981, pp. 1-5.
47. S. Neri and H. Sperl, *Travaux préparatoirs, déclarations, interprétatives des six gouvernements, documents parlementaires*, Edité par la Cour de Justice des Communautés européennes, Luxembourg, 1962. Art. 165: Historique.
48. Declaration of W. Hallstein to the ESC, 19 May 1958, Doc. CES/4F/58, Annex 4.
49. Gerda Zellentin, *Formen der . . .*, op. cit., p. 105; 'Le Droit d'Initiative', op. cit.
50. *Le Droit d'initiative*, op. cit.
51. Martinet, *Les Sept Syndicalismes*, op. cit., pp. 114, 140.
52. Jean Lecerf, *La Communauté en péril*, histoire de l'unité européenne 2, Paris, Gallimard (Collection Idées), pp. 117, 127, 128.
53. *Le Droit d'initiative*, op. cit., pp. 53-60.
54. Interview with Helmut Ries, then Chef de Cabinet of the ESC President Lappas, Brussels, June 1982.
55. Alfons Lappas, 'Die Gesellschaftsgruppen brauchen Kontrollfunktionen', *Europa-Union*, November 1972, p. 5; Alfons Lappas, 'Uber Höhen und Tiefen—vorwärts und rückwärts', *Die Quelle*, (official DGB publication), Heft 9/1974, pp. 343-5.
56. Memorandum by Chancellor Willy Brandt, 'Deutsche Initiative für Massnahmen zur Veröffentlichung einer europäischen Sozial—und Gesellschaftspolitik', *EC Bulletin*, 20 October 1972, pp. 1757-60.
57. *Le Droit d'initiative*, op. cit., pp. 64-6.
58. ETUC, *Comité Economique et Social: Le fonctionnement et la participation*, Brussels, 27 February 1973.
59. ESC, *Annual Reports*, 1977-80.

60. ETUC, 'Rapport Debunne au Groupe II du Comité Economique et Social', 3 January 1974, *ETUC Archives*.
61. ETUC, *Report on Activities*, 1976–8, op. cit., p. 19–20.
62. ESC, *Amendments to the Rule of Procedure*. Text adopted by the ESC at its 180th Plenary Session, Brussels, 2–3 July 1980.
63. ETUC, 'Projet complémentaire à la déclaration du Comité Exécutif de la CES pour une réforme du Comité Economique et Social', Brussels, 9 September 1977, *ETUC Archives*.
64. Document de travail pour la réunion extraordinaire du groupe II, 16 December 1980. DI 131/80 (gr. II).
65. ETUC *Report on Activities*, 1979–81, p. 28.
66. ETUC Statement, op. cit., April 1977; Wirtschafts- und Sozialausschuss, *Die Europäischen Interessenverbände und ihre Beziehungen zum Wirtschafts- und Socialusschuss*, Eine Dokumentation, Baden-Baden, NOMOS Verlagsgesellschaft, 1980, pp. 199–201.
67. ESC, *Annual Reports*, 1980–3.
68. Treaty of Rome, Art. 123.
69. Ibid., Art. 124.
70. Ernst Piehl, *Die Reform des Europäischen Sozialfonds*, Mimeographed, Brussels, 1983.
71. EEC Commission, 2nd *General Report*, paragraph 170 and EEC Commission, 3rd *General Report*, paragraph 291.
72. Treaty of Rome, Art. 127.
73. Bouvard, op. cit., p. 214; Collins, op. cit., p. 70.
74. EEC Commission, *The European Social Fund*, European File 2/84, Brussels, January 1984, p. 6.
75. ETUC Executive Committee, Geneva, 10 November 1982, Point 7 of the Agenda: 'ETUC Position on the Reform of the European Social Fund'. *ETUC Archives*.
76. Ibid; See also Piehl, *Die Reform*, op. cit., pp. 3–4.
77. EC Commission, *The European Social Fund*, op. cit., pp. 5–6.
78. EC Commission, *General Reports*, No. 2, para. 181; No;. 3, para. 304; No. 5, para. 145; No. 7, para. 277; No. 8, para. 240; No. 10, paras. 232, 236.
79. The Council of the European Communities, *Economic programme for the 1960s*, Brussels, 1967.
80. EC Commission, *Les problèmes de main d'oeuvre dans la Communauté en 1968*, Brussels, 1968.
81. Collins, op. cit.
82. Letter from the CESL, OE/CMT and UNICE to the president of the Council, Brussels, 9 May 1968; Letter from the EO/CMT and the CESL to the president of the Council, Brussels, 18 October 1968, *ETUC Archives*.
83. Collins, op. cit., p. 46; See also Chapter 2.
84. EC Commission, *3rd General Report on the Activities of the Communities, 1969*, Brussels, 1970.
85. EC Commission, *4th General Report on the Activities of the Communities, 1970*, Brussels, 1970.
86. Décision du Conseil du 14 décembre 1970, JO, No. L273/25.
87. Conseil des Communautés européennes, press release, Brussels, 26 November 1970, Annex II.
88. Décision du Conseil, 14 décembre 1970., op. cit., Art. 2, paras. 2, 3.
89. CESL/OE-CMT Aide Mémoire, 'An den Ministerrat für soziale Angelegenheiten gerichtetes Aide-Mémoire des EBFG und der EO-WVA über die Errichtung eines europäischen Rates für die Beschäftigung vom 25. und 26. Mai 1970'. *ETUC Archives*.

90. Le Conseil des Communautés Européennes, 3 December 1970, 2252/70 (CON-FESOC 43).
91. CESL/OE-CMT Aide Mémoire, op. cit.
92. Letter by T. Rasschaert, ETUC Secretary-General, to the president of the Council of Ministers, Brussels, 7 January 1971.
93. Décision du Conseil du 20 janvier 1975, JO No. L 21/17.
94. *Memorandum*, 'Improved working methods of the Standing Committee on Employment: problems and prospects', Brussels, 1983, *ETUC archives*.
95. ETUC *Pressemitteilung*: 'Erklärung zur Frage eines sozialen Aktionsprogrammes der Europäischen Gemeinschaft und damit zusammenhängende Breiche', Brussels, 15 October 1973.
96. Commission of the European Communities. *Social Action Programme*, Brussels, 24 October 1973.
97. ETUC 'Statement on the Revival of the Standing Committee on Employment and the Improvement of its Operation', Brussels, September 1977; 'The Twelve Points put forward by the ETUC–Standing Committee on Employment', Brussels, 9 October 1979, *ETUC Archives*.
98. *Memorandum*, op. cit., pp. 18–22.
99. ETUC, *Report of Activities*, 1979–81, pp. 36, 52–4; ETUC, Statement of ETUC Executive Committee, 28 September 1979, Annex: 'Working Document on Employment, Economic Development and Energy', *ETUC Archives*.
100. *Memorandum*, op. cit., p. 22; CLE (Comité de liaison d'employeurs), *Observations du Comité de liaison d'employeurs sur le mémorandum sur la réduction et la réorganisation du temps de travail*, Brussels, 21 March 1983.
101. ETUC, 'Resolution on the conclusions of the Council of Ministers of Social Affairs on the reorganization of working time', Brussels, November 1979. *ETUC Archives*.
102. ETUC, *Reform of the Community Institutions*, Brussels, 9 August 1983.
103. *Memorandum*, op. cit.
104. ETUC's '8 Points on Employment and the New Microelectronic Technology' (ETUC Statement to the Standing Committee on Employment—February 1980); *Supplement to the Report on Activities, 1979–1981*, pp. 45–7.
105. *Arbeitgeber*, Jahresbericht der Bundesvereinigung der Deutschen Arbeitgeber-verbände, 1980, p. 147.
106. EC Commission, *Employment and new Microelectronics*, Brussels, 1980.
107. ETUC, *Report on Activities*, op. cit., 1973–5, p. 49.
108. Letter from the ETUC general secretary to the members of the ETUC Executive Committee, 18 July 1975, *ETUC Archives*.
109. Communautés Européennes: Le Conseil, note: Objet: *Conférence réunissant les Ministres des Affaires économiques, les Ministres du Travail, la Commission et les Partenaire sociaux*', Brussels, 1 October 1975.
110. EC Commission, *Tripartite Conference*, Economic and Social Situation in the Community and Outlook. Brussels, 22 October 1975.
111. UNICE, *Conférence tripartite économique et sociale*, Brussels, 22 October 1975.
112. ETUC, *Secure employment—Guarantee Income*; Position of the European Trade Union Confederation, Tripartite Conference: Economic and Social Situation in the Community and Prospects, Brussels, 18 November 1975.
113. Heinz Kramer, 'Die Rolle der Sozialpartner in Entscheidungssytem der EG', *Aus Politik und Zeitgeschichte*, Beilage zur Wochenzeitung, Das Parlament, p. B 22.
114. *The Times*, 19 November 1975.
115. *The Daily Telegraph*, 20 November 1975.
116. *Süddeutsche Zeitung*, 20 November 1975; *Le Monde*, 20 November 1975.
117. ETUC, *Tripartite Economic and Social Conference*, Brussels, 19 November 1975.

118. ETUC, *Objectif premier de la CES: Le plein emploi*, press release, Brussels, 1 April 1976; Letter from H. O. Vetter to François-Xavier Ortoli, 3 March 1976, and to Gaston Thorn, 3 March 1976, *ETUC Archives*.
119. EC Commission, *A Community Strategy for Full Employment and Stability*, Brussels, 2 April 1976.
120. EC Commission, *Restoring Full Employment in the Community*, Brussels, June 1976.
121. ETUC, *Statement of European Trade Union Confederation to Social and Economic Conference*, Luxembourg, 24 June 1976.
122. UNICE, *Tripartite Economic and Social Conference*, Brussels, 21 June 1976.
123. Eberhard Rhein, 'Europäische konzertierte Aktion, Ein Betrag zur gemeinschaftlichen Wirtschaftpolitik', *Europa-Archiv*, Folge 15/1976, p. 502. Heinz Kramer, *Ziele und . . .*, op. cit., p. 60.
124. Council of the European Communities, General Secretariat, 'Joint Statement by the Conference on the restoration of full employment and stability in the Community', *Press release*, Luxembourg, 24 June 1976.
125. EC Commission, Fourth Medium-term Economic Policy Programme, *Official Journal of the European Communities*, No. L 101, 25 April 1977; EC Commission, *Annual Report on the Economic Situation in the Community*, Brussels, 29 December 1976.
126. The Economic Policy Committee of the Community is composed of high-ranking civil servants from national governments and representatives of central banks.
127. 'Joint Declaration . . .', op. cit., p. 4. EC Commission, *Suites de la Conférence tripartite*, Brussels, 24 November 1976.
128. ETUC Statement by the ETUC Executive Committee on the Current Economic Situation, December 1976, p. 1.
129. ETUC Executive Committee, 'Verbatum Record', Brussels, 9, 10 December 1976, *ETUC Archives*.
130. ETUC press release, Brussels, 8 March 1977. ETUC Executive Committee, 'Verbatim Record', Brussels, 10, 11 February 1977, *ETUC Archives*.
131. Parlement Européen, Session 1977–8, *Résolution sur la prochaine conférence communautaire tripartite*, 13 juin 1977.
132. Peter Coldrick, (ETUC political secretary), 'European Tripartite Conferences', Brussels, 14 March 1977, *ETUC Archives*; ETUC, Executive Committee, op. cit.
133. EC Commission, *Tripartite Conference*, 27 June 1977, 'Growth, Stability and Employment: Stock-Taking and Prospects', Brussels, 23 May 1977, p. 1.
134. UNICE, *Tripartite Economic and Social Conference*, 27 June, 1977, Brussels, 23 June 1977; ETUC, *Tripartite Conference*, on 'Growth, Stability and Employment Stocktaking and Prospects', Brussels, 21 June 1977.
135. Council of the European Communities, press release, Luxembourg, 27 June 1977.
136. Interview with Mathias Hinterscheid, *Tageblatt* 25 June 1977; see also, *Tageblatt*, 28 June 1977; *Le Peuple*, 29 June 1977; *Frankfurter Rundschau*, 28 June 1977.
137. Communautés Européennes, Secrétariat du Comité de politique économique, *Résumé de l'échange de vues, Comité de politique économique—Partenaires sociaux, Bruxelles, 11 janvier 1978*, Brussels, 17 January 1978; see also, Economic Policy Committee, *Conclusion from the Chairman*, Brussels, 2 June 1978.
138. ETUC Executive Committee, 'Report on the Meeting with the Economic Policy Committee on 11 January 1978', Brussels, 9 and 10 February 1978, *ETUC Archives*.
139. Letter from M. Hinterscheid to H. O. Vetter, 11 October 1978, *ETUC Archives*.
140. Speech of the ETUC president to the conference, *ETUC Archives; press conference* by the ETUC Secretary-General, Brussels, 8 November 1978.
141. ETUC *Report on Activities, 1976–79*, op. cit., p. 58.
142. ETUC Statement to the press on *Results of 1978 Tripartite Conference*, Brussels, 13 November 1978.

143. Note du Secrétariat, 13 February 1979, *ETUC Archives*.

144. Letter to the president of the Commission from the ETUC general secretary, Brussels, 28 February 1979; Letter to Vice-President Vredeling of the Commission from the ETUC general Secretary, Brussels, 14 February 1978; *ETUC Archives*.

145. EC Commission, *Verbesserungen der Beziehungen zu den Sozialpartnern in Rahmen der Dreierkonferenzen*, (Mitteilung der Kommission an den Rat), Brussels, 26 April 1979; Letter from the general secretary of the Council to the ETUC general secretary, Brussels, 18 February 1980, Annex I: 'Improvement of relations with the two sides of industries in the context of the Tripartite Conferences', *ETUC Archives*.

146. Views of W. Kok (ETUC president) concerning the socio-economic consultations' structure on some main issues, Brussels, 5 July 1979, *ETUC Archives*.

Chapter 5

Issues and concerns: unemployment, multinational corporations and reform of the institutions

Having devoted time initially, to its consolidation as a viable regional trade-union organization, the ETUC has been increasingly involved in designing a policy on a wide array of issues. The growing awareness among its member organizations that important problems could no longer be solved at the national level alone but required solutions at the Community level generated an internal consensus within the ETUC on an increasing number of subjects. The dynamics of the Common Market and the myriad economic and social events that have occurred since its establishment have drawn the ETUC into more and more activities. In fact, so widespread has become its involvement in Community matters, it is impossible to cover the whole range of its activities regarding the different European issues on which it has taken a position.

Three issues have therefore been selected in order to evaluate the ETUC's stance on them and to discuss the pattern of its action at the Community level. The most important is the unemployment problem. Linked to it, in many ways, is the question of industrial policy and multinational corporations in the Community. Finally, the ETUC's position towards a European union and the reform of the Community institutions will be examined in order to ascertain the extent to which pragmatic concern with political realities has overshadowed longer-term visions of a united Europe which, after all, had been the historical basis for the European labour movement.

Unemployment

The problem of unemployment clearly is the most important and urgent issue that the ETUC has been facing for a number of years. Its earlier period of existence coincided with the emergence of an economic crisis of unprecedented proportions since the Second World War. This was also marked by the commencement of a steady and seemingly irreversible process of the expansion of unemployment.

In the early 1970s, the International Monetary System, established by the Bretton Woods Agreement of 1945, had virtually collapsed, giving way to uncontrolled currency fluctuations and to serious inflationary pressures. But the most important factor that generated this situation was clearly the first oil shock. It had a dual effect on the economies of the Community: one, it created cyclical developments of unprecedented similitude among the Common

Market countries; two, it resulted in a recessionary situation leading to a decrease in production and employment and in the accumulation of stocks.

By the end of 1975, the highest rate of unemployment since the Second World War (five million in the European countries) was registered by the OECD. It was recognized that the actual unemployment figure would have been even higher but was hidden by the tendency to employ as many workers as possible at considerably reduced working hours.

During this period, the Community members tended to tackle the inflationary situation rather than the employment problems although some governments introduced a series of fiscal measures to encourage investments in those sectors which were particularly affected by the crisis. In a few cases, the fiscal measures were supplemented by the application of new 'industrial strategies', the purpose of which was to facilitate adjustments to structural changes. A slight up-turn of the economy was consequently registered by the end of 1976, followed by a decrease in unemployment. This trend had reversed by the end of 1977. Unemployment rates continued to increase, reaching 16.3 million in the OECD (not counting Turkey and Portugal) notwithstanding intensified repatriation of migrant workers and an upward trend in employment registered in the United States.[1] To a large extent, this can be explained by the increase of the economically active population in the region.[2] Also, it became clear by this time that government measures—intended to stimulate employment-creating activities—had not succeeded. On the contrary, private investment appeared to be moving towards capital-intensive areas.

In a few cases, governments attempted to increase employment in the public sector. Some measures were also envisaged to reduce labour costs—mainly through the reduction of social security payments—of enterprises which offered additional employment possibilities. The labour markets were, furthermore, stimulated by the broadening and the strenghtening of employment and training services, by the development of early retirement systems and by the strengthening of regulations against any new immigration.[3]

By the end of 1978, a certain stability in the employment sector was achieved in Europe; in the United States and Japan, an increase was even registered. Once again the situation reversed itself and even became aggravated after 1979 as the impact of the second oil shock became increasingly severe. From 1979 to 1982, the global OECD unemployment rate rose spectacularly from 5.1 per cent to 8.2 per cent, bringing the number of unemployed up from nineteen million to thirty million. The bulk of this increase occurred in Western Europe—reaching an all-time high of 10.8 per cent in May 1984—while it continued to decrease in the United States and in Canada and remained at a stable low of 2.8 per cent in Japan. Between 1979 and 1982 unemployment almost doubled in Germany and more than doubled in Great Britain and in the Netherlands.[4] In the Community, as a whole, the number of unemployed increased from 6.1 million to 10.8 million during that period. Moreover, the proportion of long-term unemployment, i.e., lasting for more than one year, had reached alarming proportions of more than 40 per cent of total unemployment in Europe in 1983, varying between 25 per cent to 50 per cent in the Community countries.[5]

During this period, the discrepancy between supply and demand for labour had been continuously widening. While the economically active population had steadily increased owing to the growing numbers of young people and women entering the labour market, demand for labour had shown the reverse trend. Out of the three economic sectors—industry, agriculture and services—the first two were the most severely affected. Between 1960 and 1982, the agricultural population in the Community diminished by more than eleven million. This decrease was particularly rapid in the 1970s when 7,130,000 agricultural jobs disappeared. Since then, the rural exodus has taken on a much slower pace, particularly since employment possibilities in other sectors also decreased considerably.[6]

While a structural decrease of employment had been the general trend for some time in agriculture, it was the loss of industrial employment which was the most alarming. The decline in capital investments in most Western European countries became apparent in the mid-1970s, becoming even more accentuated after 1979, and accounting for a loss of five million jobs in seven of the major European OECD countries. In the United Kingdom, for example, 83 per cent of the employment lost between 1979 and 1983 was in the manu-facturing sectors.[7] Some parts of the industrial sector were particularly affected by the recession. Among the first to feel the pinch were the EEC consumer goods industries. During the first four years of the recession, more than one million jobs were lost in this area, particularly in the textile and clothing sector.[8] Other areas where the loss of employment was especially striking were the steel industry, the equipment goods industry, the building and construction sector and—in some countries—the motor vehicle industry.[9]

Industrial enterprises in the Community showed increasing reluctance to create new employment opportunities. It was generally argued that high labour costs relative to the cost of capital, the resulting squeeze in profitability of enterprises and the general rigidity of the labour markets were responsible for these developments. While in the United States labour cost in real terms had increased by 3 per cent from 1973 to 1981, it had risen by 20 per cent in Europe during the same period. Strict social legislation governing the process of hiring and firing have also contributed to the rise in labour costs which at the same time failed to be accompanied by corresponding productivity gains. As a direct result these were not only the increased marginalization of many enterprises but also the continuous expansion of 'underground' economic activity.[10]

In the late seventies and early eighties, a clear preference for investment in technological innovation rather than in labour-intensive activities had emerged. The widespread introduction of microelectronics into production processes had a strong potential for job displacement, particularly in such areas as telecommunications, calculating and business equipment and the fabrication of precision tools and watches.[11] The computerization of production methods in such areas as printing, steel rolling mills and assembly lines, for example, not only reduced employment in those areas radically, but also required quite different skills.

The only economic sector where employment has been created over the last decade was the service industry, where an additional 23.5 million jobs (at an annual average rate of 2 per cent) were created within the OECD between 1975 and 1982.[12] Service employment increased by 20 per cent in North America, by 16 per cent in Japan and by 12 per cent in Europe. At the Community level, a similar trend can be noted: some six million jobs were created in this sector during this period.[13] But even in this sector, increasing automation of many offices and of many functions in the banking and insurance sectors has already slowed down the growth in employment.[14] The potential for further computerization and even robotization of this sector has by no means been exhausted. There does indeed exist a real danger that gains in this sector may be reversed.

While all Community members are afflicted by unemployment problems, the degree varies from country to country. In 1983, the most affected countries were Ireland, the Netherlands, Denmark and Belgium with unemployment rates of 15.2 per cent, 15.2 per cent, 15.4 per cent and 16.2 per cent respectively. Italy and the United Kingdom with rates of 11 and 13.3 per cent lay in the middle of the strata, while Luxembourg, Germany and France were at the bottom with rates of 1.5 per cent, 7.5 per cent and 9 per cent respectively.[15]

Regional differences in unemployment levels also existed within the Community. Peripheral areas such as Brittany, Ireland, Wales and Southern Italy appear to be much more affected by high unemployment rates than more centrally located regions like l'Ile de France and southern Germany.

Since 1979, while practically all regions in Europe have known a considerable increase in unemployment (exceptions being l'Ile de France and some areas in central Italy), the most strongly affected areas have been large parts of England and Scotland and more centrally located areas like the Netherlands and Belgium. Unemployment has reached such proportions that it has spread out to more and more groups in society. Every category is affected by it: skilled workers as well as unskilled workers, manual labourers as well as office employees, young people leaving school or university, older workers, men and women alike. But the largest proportions of unemployed can be found among women of all ages and young people below the age of twenty-five.

In April 1984, women made up 41.1 per cent of all registered unemployed in the Community, with national figures ranging from 25 per cent to 53.4 per cent. Though statistics are incomplete, it has been estimated that 39.9 per cent of the unemployed in France are below twenty-five; the figures for Italy, Great Britain and the Netherlands are 46.6 per cent, 38.4 per cent and 37 per cent respectively.[16] This already alarming situation is further compounded by the increasing trend towards long-term unemployment in the EEC. While this tendency was rampant primarily among older workers in the beginning, more and more groups of unemployed, including young workers, are now coming to experience it.

Such a situation can severely affect the economic situation of persons who—after a certain period of prolonged unemployment—lose their unemployment benefits and are transferred to other forms of social assistance or take early retirement. Moreover, serious social and psychological consequences might be expected from such a situation. Analysing this, the OECD expressed the view that 'measurement problems beset any attempt to estimate the welfare loss from unrealized output, to which should be added the psychological costs, stress, ill health, crime and family disruption associated with unemployment'.[17]

In addition to the undesirable social, economic, and psychological consequences for those without work, unemployment generates high economic costs not only in terms of output losses but also in terms of public finances.

It has been estimated that the annual cost per unemployed person in the United Kingdom amounted to £4,500–£5,000, or to a total cost of £13 billion in the 1981-2 budget. Similar calculations for Germany have shown that the average cost per unemployed person amounted to DM 24,000 or the annual cost of DM 55 billion in 1983. In Denmark, expenditure for unemployment benefits and early retirement schemes amounted to DKR 24,43 billion or 5.8 per cent of the GDP in 1982. During the same year, costs related to unemployment in France amounted to 6.5 per cent of its GDP.[18]

The ETUC perception of inflation and unemployment

At an early stage, the ETUC recognized the dangers of rising unemployment linked with inflationary pressures. Rejecting the suggestion that inflation might be caused essentially by increasing production costs in which labour costs have an important share, by the mid-1970s, it began to argue that profound structural changes had become apparent in Western economies. The most striking examples of these changes were represented by the emergence and the strengthening of trusts and monopolies, the multinational corporations, which were operating more and more on an international scale and were thus increasingly escaping from national regulations and controls.[19] The result of all this has been the progressive disappearance of free market mechanisms for the establishment of price levels. Multinational corporations have extensive control over their own price policies which they determine according to global and regional considerations and as part of their overall plans and strategies. Moreover, as 'price leaders', they are imitated by the smaller firms in the establishment of price levels.[20]

Another cause for inflation was attributed to the international monetary disturbances after the collapse of the Bretton Woods system, and the failure of countries with a positive balance of payments to share the responsibility of making structural adjustments to achieve balance of payments' equilibrium. Moreover, capital movements, particularly in the Euro-money markets, having remained erratic and uncontrolled, generated speculative pressures forcing parity changes which may contribute to an increase in price levels.

Under those circumstances government policies, usually aimed at controlling inflation by demand management, were severely criticized by the trade unions. Traditional methods of demand management could no longer be considered an efficient instrument for inflation control. Besides, they provoked a decrease in global demand leading to increased unemployment, while remaining incapable of avoiding decreases in wage earners' real incomes. In spite of the fact that the problem of inflation control dominated government policies over the 1970s, little was done to check monopoly pricing and the instability of the international monetary markets.[21]

While accepting the importance of dealing with inflation, trade unions insisted that the removal of unemployment should become the major goal of government policies. In their view, 'the only sustainable solution to inflation must be found against a background of growth and high employment, not as an alternative to growth and full employment'.[22] Governments should radically change their hitherto inefficient anti-inflationary policies. Instead of trying to tackle inflation and balance of payments problems principally through restrictions of the general level of demand, they should adopt 'democratic planning' methods and try to reduce inflation through the following policies:

- Strengthening competition and anti-monopoly policies at national and European levels;
- Introducing and coordinating price surveillance systems, also at national and European levels;
- Negotiating world commodity agreements and establishing bufferstocks to ensure fair and more stable prices;
- Reforming agricultural price policies;
- Reforming the European and international monetary system to reduce inflation resulting from exchange rate movement and excessive international liquidity;
- Increasing production and thereby reducing unit costs;
- Removing bottlenecks with selective labour-market, industrial and regional policies;
- Promoting greater income and wealth equality to provide the basis for a better social consensus.[23]

The emphasis on the multinational corporations in the original ETUC analysis of the economic situation was somewhat reduced by the late 1970s; and more attention was directed instead towards government policies, which gave 'new responsibility' in some countries to the 'once bankrupt monetarist doctrines of the 1920s and 1930s' with disastrous consequences for growth and employment.[24] This tendency, according to the ETUC, has continued to prevail after the second oil shock, irrespective of its negative impact on employment. Not only have these policies been unable to prevent a decline in economic growth, they have, if anything, contributed to it.

Other causes for European unemployment increase during that period can be attributed to the substantial increase of young people in the labour market, the aggravation of trade problems with Japan and the growing monetary problems with the United States.[25] The accelerated introduction of new technologies was also a contributory element. While trade unions insist upon the promotion of economic growth through higher investments, they became increasingly aware of the negative effects on employment of technological innovations, and the danger of 'jobless growth' connected with it. In their view, growth should be selective and qualitative; it should respect the natural environment and lead to a balanced development of all regions.[26]

ETUC proposals for employment creation

During the last decade, the ETUC has given considerable thought to the unemployment problem and has developed a series of general and specific proposals to mitigate it. It has been increasingly emphasizing the necessity of coordinated policy measures within the framework of the Community and even beyond it. It views such a coordination as indispensable, as the economic inter-dependence among European countries has grown continuously over the last decades.

General studies have been made in recent years to investigate the impact of coordinated policies introduced in several countries at the same time. Running empirical tests based on the 'interlink system' established by the OECD,[27] the European Trade Union Institute has come to the conclusion that should ETUC programmes be implemented simultaneously in several countries, they would have a stronger effect on growth and employment.[28] Another study of the same type was carried out by the Nordic Trade Union Federation (NFS) and the German DGB. Quantifying the major trade-union programmes for economic expansion in Scandinavia, Germany, the Netherlands, the United Kingdom and the United States, it was calculated that after a period of two to three years following their implementation, employment would increase by some eight million jobs in the OECD.[29]

The measures that the ETUC considers indispensable for employment creation are:

increased public investment
the reduction of working time
a European industrial policy
policies towards the Third World
specific labour market policies
regional policies
specific measures to cope with technological change and rationalization.[30]

Public investment

One of the foremost areas suitable for an increase in employment, in the view of the ETUC, is the government sector. This is particularly relevant since the private sector, overloaded with record levels of spare capacities, cannot be counted upon to increase its investments before higher levels of capacity usage are reached.

The public sector already plays a major role in all European countries where public expenditure as a proportion of GNP is generally quite large, varying between 40 per cent and 60 per cent in the EEC member states.[31] And within this sector, governments still have a wide range of possibilities for implement-ing policies which are not necessarily determined by purely commercial interests. Public investments could thus be geared increasingly towards employment creation, and could be designed to overcome structural problems and to ensure competition, to reduce regional disparities and to meet people's needs for better living and working conditions.[32]

Since the mid-1970s, however, the governments have refused to follow such a line of action; if anything their policies have tended towards tighter financial controls. Their continuing preoccupation with budget deficits led them to decrease public expenditure, and a reduction in public investments proved to be the major target of most governments.

While cuts in government expenditures reduced budget deficits, they reduced employment and increased expenditures for unemployment financing. In the United Kingdom, for example, the budget was reduced in 1981, by 3.5 per cent of GNP; but during the same year, unemployment grew from 7 per cent to 10.6 per cent, increasing the budget deficit by 2.8 per cent due to unemployment compensation costs. The overall result thus was a decrease of the budget deficit by only 0.7 per cent, and a shift in the government expenditure pattern from productive services to unemployment financing. Notwithstanding this and other examples, the reduction of public investments has become a common policy within the EEC except in Ireland, where public investment has increased from 3.8 per cent in 1976 to 6.1 per cent in 1982 and in Belgium, where it has remained stable during the same period.[33]

The ETUI study on public investment points out that independently of employment considerations public investment in a number of areas in the Community has become a major necessity. There appears to be, for example, considerable scope for the improvement of housing in most countries. According to an estimate established by the European Federation of Building Workers, there are twenty million substandard dwellings in the EEC, of which one-third are beyond repair. If those were destroyed at a rate of 600,000 to 700,000 per year over the next ten years, this would establish between 1.2 million and 2 million jobs for construction workers in the EEC.[34]

Another area where investment is urgently needed is sewerage and water supply. In the United Kingdom, for example, the sewerage systems of its major cities were completed between 1860 and 1880, and are rapidly reaching the end of their usefulness. Sewer collapses increase yearly and other major problems such as blockages, leaks, rat infestation, etc., occur more and more frequently, involving continuously rising costs for repairs and the indirect cost of disruption. According to a report of the House of Lords Select Committee on Science and Technology, 'there is significant risk of decay in the sewerage system getting beyond the water authorities' control ... Too little has been spent on maintaining the system in the past and the industry, faced with the signs of accelerating failure rates, does not yet appear to be doing enough to contain the rate of decay'.[35] The TUC considers it vital to spend more than £1 billion over a period of five years to replace the sewerage systems; more than 25,000 jobs would be created in the process.

In other countries this particular problem might be less urgent. But there is considerable need to eliminate pollution in rivers and lakes, and to improve drinking water supplies. In Germany, for example, the DGB has expressed concern over the pollution of rivers such as the Rhine and the Elbe and has called for pollution prevention through legislation and some direct investment by both public and private sectors.

In several countries, runs the argument, the maintenance and development of transportation systems could also be considerably improved. In the United Kingdom there would be ample scope for the improvement and electrification of the railway system, while in Germany the development of suburban train networks has become urgent.[36]

One area where public investment appears to be particularly insufficient is telecommunications. 'Every West European country will be obliged to undertake the massive initial investment to install these new networks—or risk losing its place in the ranking of the advanced industrial countries.'[37] At this stage, only France seems to have launched a long-term (twenty years) programme to install up-to-date infrastructure in telecommunications, requiring major public investments of FF 1 billion in 1983 and FF 4 billion from 1984 onwards.

Though considerable attention has been directed in some EEC countries towards the expansion of new sources of energy there is still considerable scope for improvement of energy conservation schemes by insulating buildings and better usage of heating systems. In the view of the ETUI, investment in insulation and heating controls alone could contribute to energy savings, and at the same time employ relatively unskilled workers who are most affected particularly in urban areas. Health services, schools and cultural programmes could be expanded in many countries.[38]

Trade unions of several EEC countries have developed programmes for increased public sector investments in their respective countries and have made optimistic estimates of the employment effects of such programmes.[39] Though the launching of such programmes would initially require a considerable amount of public expenditure, it is generally assumed that the employment they would create would reduce social security and unemployment compensation costs. This would result in larger tax revenues, and in increased demand in some of the slack sectors without necessarily leading to inflation. In many cases it is considered that within a few years they would become largely self-financing.[40]

The reduction of working time

Already in the mid-1970s, the ETUC began to discuss the possibility of improving the overall employment situation through the reduction of working time.[41] As the unemployment rate accelerated, trade unions increasingly leaned towards the conception that the available work should be shared—to the largest extent possible—by all workers, and that such sharing could only be accomplished by the reduction of individual working time and its redistribution among other workers. In April 1977, the ETUC Executive Committee adopted a position to this effect which was confirmed in more detail by the 1979 Congress in Munich and which called for a reduction in working time by 10 per cent without any loss of pay.[42]

Such a reduction could be brought about through several measures, either taken separately or collectively:

reduction of the work week to thirty-five hours;
extension of annual holidays to six weeks,
full pension at the age of sixty;
raising the age of leaving school to sixteen, and extending time for vocational training and further education;
introduction of a fifth shift for continuous shift work;
overtime restriction and compensation for overtime work in the form of time off.[43]

The debate about the reduction of working time has a long history. During the first decades of their existence the trade unions considered that their main preoccupation must be the reduction of working time in general and for women and children in particular. The average working time, during the first half of the nineteenth century was ten to twelve hours per day and sixty to seventy-two hours per week. By the middle of the century, this had been increased to fourteen to sixteen hours per day and to eighty to eighty-five hours per week. Trade unions are sensitive on this question and insist on pointing out that the original arguments used by employers and workers on the issue of working time have basically remained unchanged. Reduction of working time was demanded not only on humanitarian grounds, but also because the lack of free time prevented workers from engaging in political and trade-union activities. The Paris Congress of the Second Socialist International, held on 19 and 20 July 1889 declared the 1 May free of work and a day on which the workers should demonstrate for an eight-hour day. Even then attention was drawn to the fact that the reduction of working time was not only an act of social justice but also a contribution to the diminution of unemployment.[44]

Employers, on the other hand, were strictly opposed to such measures. They argued that they 'would result in the increased cost of domestic products and therefore favour foreign competition which is already difficult to face, particularly if measures will not be introduced in other countries'.[45]

It was only after the First World War that the eight-hour day was gradually introduced in European countries, and only after the Second World War that the forty-hour week became a general rule. In the German metal industry, for example, an agreement was reached only in 1958 to decrease the work week gradually from forty-five to forty hours by 1967, without a loss in wages. In fact, only 69 per cent of the metalworkers worked forty hours in 1973, whereas this percentage increased by 92.6 per cent by 1978.[46] The most important results of these developments was not so much the reduction of daily work but the introduction of work-free Saturdays practically all over Europe.

While in the past reduction of working time was considered primarily as a social measure, in the present discussion it is regarded above all as a means either to preserve employment or to create new employment.

A reduction in the work week from forty to thirty-six hours would correspond to a decrease of overall working time by 10 per cent. If such a reduction were accompanied by a decrease in production, the overall wage costs would remain the same, whereas unit production costs would increase. If, however, the firm decided to maintain its previous levels of production, it would have to take on additional manpower which would correspond to an increase in labour costs by 11 per cent.[47] According to several studies, it can be assumed that the reduction of working time would be accompanied by an increase in productivity. This increase may be brought about by several factors:

an acceleration in average work rhythm;
a reorganization of work,
a fall in absenteeism,
the exclusion of hidden pockets of unemployment,
increased motivation of the workers.[48]

Of course, an increase in productivity would not be uniform, it would vary according to different sectors, firms and other circumstances.

As shown in the following hypothetical example, if productivity increased by 50 per cent—which is what most studies assume—additional wage costs would amount to 5.5 per cent for a 10 per cent reduction in working hours. But it would also limit the positive effect on employment and open up opportunities of only 5.5 per cent additional employment.

In order to maintain previous levels of production, some additional investment might also be necessary. The ETUI estimates the additional capital cost at around 1 per cent. Excess capital and the underutilization of production capacities is already rampant in many sectors. Following the above example, this would entail an average increase of labour and capital cost of 6.5 per cent.[49] However, if the reduction of working time would be phased over a period of three years, the average annual increase of cost could be maintained at around 2.2 per cent.

On the basis of these calculations, some estimates have been made on the number of jobs created by reducing weekly working time. The German metal workers' union, for example, believes that the reduction of one working hour per week could lead to the creation of 270,000 additional jobs. The benefical

Table 5.1 Reduction of working time from 40 to 36 hours/week

Productivity increase (%)	Additional labour (%)	Additional cost (%)
0	11.1	11.1
25	8.3	8.3
50	5.5	5.5
75	2.8	2.8
100	0	0

Source: ETUI, *The Reduction of Working Hours in Western Europe*, Second Part.

effect on employment of these measures could be compounded by prolonging annual holidays from four to six weeks and by lowering the retirement age from 65 to 60. One additional condition for the effectiveness of measures to reduce working time would be to reconsider practices regarding overtime. Whenever technically possible, overtime should be eliminated. If unavoidable, it should be compensated with free time.[50]

In the view of the trade unions, the additional free time available to workers would entail a series of beneficial effects on social and economic life as a whole. It would increase the demand for cultural, educational, sporting, tourist and recreational activities. This demand would in turn, require the creation of additional jobs to provide the services and infrastructure necessary to meet this demand.[51]

The issue of the reduction of working time has given rise to considerable discussion and controversy between employers and trade unions both at the national and the European levels. In Germany, it even led to a strike which was considered by the metalworkers' union as the toughest industrial conflict in its entire history.[52]

The employers in most EEC countries firmly rejected the unions' demands in this matter. Their counterarguments centred primarily around the increased costs that such a step would incur. These would endanger the existence of small and medium-size industries that still provide about two-thirds of total employment. They rejected the idea that less work could lead to an increase in material welfare and at the same time lead to the improvement of the employment situation.[53] On the contrary, such policies, in their view, would only increase rather than decrease, employment. They would also reduce the international competitiveness of European industries already facing difficulties in maintaining their position on the world market. Moreover, increased labour costs would induce firms to accelerate the process of rationalization which, again, would lead to negative employment effects.

The trade unions countered these arguments by pointing to the evolution of modern industrial society where less work has led to more production and to higher standards of living. In most production processes, one man today can produce much more than he did some decades ago. Moreover, all union demands had invariably been considered as a danger to their competitive position by the employers. There really was no correlation between reduction of working time and rationalization. In Japan, for example, low wages and higher average working time coexist with a high degree of automization and technical progress.[54]

At the European level, the ETUC has been arguing for the coordination of policies regarding the reduction of working time and the adoption of a Community instrument to facilitate negotiations on this issue at the national, sectorial and enterprise levels.[55] The employers, on the other hand, have persistently refused to discuss the issue at the European level. In their view, reduction of working time can be considered a social measure only, aimed at ameliorating working and living conditions. But it would be unrealistic to believe that it could become an instrument for labour-market policy. Moreover, since working conditions differ from region to region and from country to country, it would be impossible to introduce uniform regulations at the national level, and even more so at the Community level. In fact, runs the argument, working time as part of general working conditions can only be discussed within the framework of collective bargaining agreements which, by their very nature, should not be influenced by government or Community measures. Finally, the argument was advanced that the European employers' committee had no mandate to negotiate about this issue at the Community level.[56]

Industrial policy

European industries are faced with a series of difficulties.

- They face a serious technological gap separating them from the United States and Japan.
- Continuously decreasing rates of capital investment have slowed down productivity rates and therefore competitiveness of European industries in the world market. This problem is only veiled by the increases in exports of some EEC countries which are due to the high United States' dollar rather than to their improved competitiveness.
- While some traditional industrial sectors in Europe—such as iron and steel, parts of car manufacturing, textiles—have been in a deep crisis situation for some time and need restructuring, there are not enough initiatives at the European level to encourage the development of industries of the future such as electronics and biotechnology.

In the ETUC's view, the establishment of a homogeneous industrial market and a Common European industrial policy are vital to avoid disruptive national competition in these areas and to succeed in achieving the establishment of high-technology industries at the European level.[57] The only experiences in industrial cooperation so far have been the joint construction of the European airbus and the development of the Ariane missile. Both have been considered by the ETUC in a positive light. The trade unions also regarded favourably the establishment of the ESPRIT programme for the development of research in the field of information technology. They insist, however, that priority should be given to the social implications of new technologies, in particular to assure that they generate employment, that they provide for education, vocational training and consultation of workers. According to a study published by the EC Commission about two million jobs could be created before 1990 if the European information technology industries manage to expand at an adequate rate. Here again, public investment should intervene to aid the development of fundamental factors in technological innovation, scientific research and development policies and employment creation.[58]

Policies towards the Third World

Frequently, the ETUC has stressed the interdependence between the European Community and the Third World. In its view, 'the social and economic development of the Third World is very much in Europe's interest, especially since about 10 per cent of our trade is with non oil-producing developing countries' which corresponds to almost twice the volume of trade with the United States.[59]

Given the close links of interest between the two groups, 'the worsening crisis in the third World is both the result of and contributes to the worsening recession in Europe . . .'[60] Thus, the growing gap between the world's rich and poor nations is in nobody's interest and has to be reduced, if not overcome, if there is to be world peace and a sustained recovery in Europe.

One of the foremost demands for development policies by the international and the European labour movements has been to push the governments to meet the United Nations' target of development aid of 0.7 per cent of GNP. The ETUC considers that foreign reserves of the non oil-producing countries have mainly been spent on imports of goods and services from industrialized countries, thereby having a positive effect on employment in those countries. The interlink model used in the aforementioned study was also applied to a multilaterally coordinated increase in development aid. The calculations showed that after two or three years nearly one million new jobs in the European export industries would be created through the increased demand of third world countries.

Labour-market policies

General economic and fiscal policies to increase employment need to be complemented by labour-market or selective employment policies. Such policies comprise a series of measures designed to facilitate adjustments of the labour market and the appropriate services for the location of employment opportunities. Generally, the policies fall into three basic categories: they can be measures for job creation through public works or investment policies in economically weak regions; they can be measures to encourage occupational and the geographical mobility of workers involving education, vocational training and retraining, including subsidies in case of geographical displacements; they can be measures affecting personnel policies of companies through employment services and subsidies for apprenticeships.[61]

In general, labour-market policies involve the planning and the forecasting of employment opportunities at the regional, industrial and company levels. In most instances, this requires the cooperation of companies. The ETUC considers that enterprises should be obliged to provide trade unions and workers with detailed information regarding their employment policies and future employment plans. This is particularly significant for the severely affected young workers for whom the ETUC 1982 Congress demanded that:

- vocational training and guidance schemes meet the particular needs of young men and women workers;
- substantial measures be taken to combat failure at school and the tendency of young people to drop out of the education system too soon; the practical

training provided by firms must also be monitored by workers' representatives;

- special attention be paid to preparing school leavers for working life and to ensuring that young men and women workers are able to acquire a high level of qualification whether at work or while unemployed;
- job creation schemes for young workers be extended and that the jobs created are of a worthwhile nature and are subject to the same pay conditions as comparable jobs in other sectors.[62]

The ETUC employment campaign

Since the 1976 London Congress, the ETUC exercised increasing pressure on the Community institutions and the national governments to adopt policies with the view to stimulating the recovery of the economy and thereby improving the employment situation. In May 1976, the Congress's position on this matter was presented to the Standing Employment Committee where it drew no response from the other Committee members. Also, it served as a basis for the ETUC's position at the June 1976 tripartite conference, which concluded with the agreement to return to full employment by 1980. While these targets were included in the Fourth Medium-Term Policy Programme of the Community, neither the Council nor the Commission were willing to commit themselves to their concrete implementation. The Standing Employment Committee and the Community Economic Policy Committee, charged with the follow-up of the conference, were also unable to develop a Community programme in this sense.[63]

In December 1976 it was already clear to the ETUC that neither governments nor the European institutions would be able to meet the tripartite objectives. The Executive Committee, therefore, asked its affiliates to press their respective governments for more recovery policies. The new Commission president, Roy Jenkins, was also approached on the matter.[64]

The Executive Committee also decided to begin to mobilize their membership at the European level by organizing a European Action Day on unemployment.[65] This initiative took the form of mass meetings, demonstrations and sometimes strikes in different parts of the Community on 5 April 1976. Although it was not very successful—it did not receive significant coverage by the press, nor did it have any sizeable impact on public opinion or government policies—it was nevertheless the first attempt by the European trade-union movement to mobilize workers for a European cause and, as such, it can be considered a further step towards a greater internal consolidation.[66]

During the course of 1978 it appeared that some positive response to ETUC positions was forthcoming. The Standing Employment Committee examined the problems of reduction of working time and employment creation in the tertiary sector; and the Economic Policy Committee discussed the question of investment and employment policies with the ETUC and the employers. In the view of the ETUC, this meeting in June 1978 was a 'constructive exchange of views' which concluded with the recognition that concerted efforts to stimulate growth were needed, that public investment should be expanded and that demand should increase with the view to stimulating private investment.[67]

The European Council, at its Bremen meeting and the world summit in Bonn in July 1978, also decided on concerted action to stimulate the European and the world economy. In this connection, the ETUC had circulated a detailed and comprehensive memorandum to all its affiliates, requesting them to bring it to their governments' attention.[68]

In spite of these encouraging results, the next meeting of the tripartite conference, also held under German leadership, proved to be highly disappointing to the ETUC. Not only were the earlier views on the recovery of the economy omitted but the ETUC positions met with negative response, from the employers' representatives and by the governments. Under these circumstances, the ETUC decided to boycott these conferences and undertook to 'make a fundamental review of the future role and nature of influencing decision-making and of promoting the interests of the working people in Europe'.[69]

As a result, the Executive Committee decided that, while continuing to exercise pressures at the national and EEC levels via the appropriate political institutions, there would be an increasing emphasis on massive campaigns and demonstrations which should mobilize the workers of Europe in support of trade-union conceptions on economic and employment policies. In this connection, a 'week of action' was organized during the last week of November 1979, during which demonstations, rallies, meetings with governments and employers' organizations, press conferences and even some work stoppages took place.[70] A number of ETUC organizations also participated in demonstrations in Venice during the meeting of the European Council in June 1980.[71] Both these demonstrations were considered a failure by the ETUC since they did not produce any positive results. The ETUC therefore decided to launch a 'Campaign for Employment and Economic Recovery'.[72]

Such a campaign was considered necessary in view of the 'increasingly ominous threat which steadily rising unemployment presents to peace in industrial relations and to the credibility of the European governments and the European institutions'.[73] On this occasion the ETUC summarized its strategy in a six-point programme:

- Higher investment must be ensured, and this presupposes active State intervention
- Measures must be taken to step up job creation and training programmes substantially
- Working time must be reduced and working conditions improved
- Aid to developing countries must be substantially increased
- Inflation must be fought with selective policies which are socially just, and not with unemployment.[74]

The campaign would be carried out through the increased mobilization of workers and through increased pressure on political groups, and should take place at national, sectorial and European levels.

At the national level, practically all ETUC organizations in EEC member states were involved, in one way or the other, in an employment campaign with the object of influencing their governments to give political priority to employment problems and to design policies according to the lines indicated by the ETUC. At the sectorial level, the ETUC began increasingly to coordinate the activities of the industry committees. At the European level, it attempted to draw the attention of political groups and parliamentary factions to its programme. In this connection, the ETUC met with leaders of the Union of Socialist Parties and of the socialist group in the European Parliament. The representatives of these parties were in full agreement with trade-union views on the unemployment situation. They favoured a 'fundamental change in present policies in order to avert economic and social disaster',[75] as well as the introduction of an economic recovery programme at the EEC level. The ETUC also had talks with the president of the European Parliament, Simone Veil, as well as with representatives of the communist faction, of the popular parties and the Christian Democrats.

The aim of the discussion with the president of the Parliament was to present ETUC positions and proposals for action and to explore the possibilities of being heard by the Parliament on problems of trade-union concern. The president confirmed that a debate on unemployment had already been scheduled at a forthcoming meeting, and that hearings by parliamentary committees were planned on different topics to which the ETUC would be invited to testify. The meetings with the party representatives also reached an understanding about the prime importance of reacting vigorously against unemployment.[76]

At the meeting of the European Council in Luxembourg on 29 June 1981 a demonstration took place which was to impress the ETUC employment strategies on the meeting and on the public. It started with a rally addressed by the ETUC president and vice-presidents, followed by a march of more than 3,000 people from all over Western Europe.[77]

The ETUC considered itself satisfied with the outcome of its demonstration in Luxembourg, not only because of the active participation of thousands of workers, but also because in its view, 'the pressure brought to bear on the Council by the workers ... has made the Council adopt a more realistic approach'.[78] This can be gauged from the fact that the Council for once granted as much priority to the unemployment problem as to inflation, and had decided to develop a social policy capable of coping with the problems at hand.[79]

Parallel with these activities, the ETUC had several times asked the Council to hold a joint meeting of Economic, Finance and Social Affairs Ministers to discuss the unemployment problem.[80] This 'jumbo-council' finally took place in June 1981. While the meeting could be considered a positive development, its results were considered insigificant by the ETUC.[81] Nevertheless, another such meeting took place in November 1982. Before it convened, a ETUC delegation led by its president, G. Debunne, met with the president of the Council to severely criticize Community policy which up to then had completely failed trade unions and their workers. Debunne complained that trade unions had been 'denied any real dialogue on an overall economic strategy in the Standing Employment Committee' and the meetings between the ETUC and the

Commission are purely a matter of form since 'they yield absolutely no positive results.'[82]

In October 1982, the ETUC decided to increase its pressure on employment policies at the national level. It was recognized that if government policies had to be influenced, this must be done primarily at the national level. Moreover, it was felt that—though most ETUC affiliates were active in pressuring their governments on employment issues—there was often a lack of mutual information and coordination among them. This was particularly regrettable since it would be more efficient for unions in several countries to be pushing the same policy measures at the same time.[83]

It was therefore decided that a ETUC delegation—composed of its president and/or secretary-general and another member of the Secretariat as well as representatives of the national confederation—would meet with each European government to discuss the unemployment problem.

These discussions should centre around four basic issues:

(1) increase in investments by 1 per cent of GNP with particular emphasis on public investments
(2) reduction of working time and the redistribution of work
(3) defense of purchasing power and social achievements and the increase of domestic demand
(4) the strengthening of international cooperation, especially in the areas of international trade, the level of interest rates, exchange rates and development policies.[84]

These meetings with national governments were to be publicized as widely as possible through press conferences and other means. The occasion should also be used to discuss national union policies related to unemployment, and to increase the flow of information about them thus opening the possibilities for better coordination among ETUC members on that matter.

During the months of January and February 1983, the ETUC president and secretary-general met with ten European governments, of which six were EEC member states (France, Belgium, Germany, Netherlands, Luxembourg, and Ireland) and three were EFTA countries (Norway, Sweden and Austria). In these meetings, all governments recognized the need for increased economic cooperation among the European countries, but among the EFTA countries exists a tendency to reserve economic cooperation to the OECD area.The trade unions, however, would prefer, at a first stage, to strenghten economic cooperation within EFTA itself and, at a second stage, develop closer economic ties between EFTA and EEC .

While the necessity to increase investments that would create employment appears to be generally recognized, some governments, in fear of inflation, continue to hesitate to launch such a programme. All of them seemed to recognize that the reduction of working time could be an instrument of employment creation, even though there are differences of view as to how efficient this measure can really be. With respect to the maintenance of purchasing power, some governments continued to defend their restrictive policies of demand management on the ground that a change in these policies would only be possible in cooperation with other governments in the area. The others, however, appeared to be impressed by the ETUC argument that to continue such policies might lead towards a downward movement ending in a situation of unacceptable poverty for many people.

While no concrete results were obtained from these meetings, the ETUC nevertheless had the impression that a fruitful dialogue had been inaugurated.[85]

The contacts between the ETUC and national governments continued and became particularly intensified before the summit meeting in Stuttgart in June 1983. By that time, all Western European governments had been visited—with the exception of the United Kingdom—by an ETUC delegation which was received at the head of government level.[86] But this did not mean that contacts at the European level had been neglected. The ETUC, in fact, tried to intensify its cooperation with the EC Commission, with the European Parliament and renewed contacts with the European employers' organization UNICE.[87]

Also, it stepped up its efforts to mobilise workers in support of its employment campaign. Under the slogan: 'Our Right: Work for All', it organized a mass demonstration of more than 80,000 workers representing all ETUC member organizations before the meeting of the European Council. In the numerous speeches made by the ETUC president and general secretary, and by the chairman of the German DGB and its regional organisation in Stuttgart, the basic ETUC demands were reiterated.

While the ETUC mass demonstration was being organized, the EC summit meeting had been postponed to a later date in June. The ETUC was deeply disappointed with the results of the June meeting since it did not make any coordinated political commitment to reduce unemployment and to promote economic growth. The ETUC considered that the European Council amply demonstrated its inability to contribute effectively towards concerted recovery, and expressed the fear that, under the circumstances, 'unemployment in Western Europe is going to increase by at least one million every six months, and there will be no economic recovery either this year or next year'. Furthermore, the ETUC considered as 'positively inconceivable' that the European Council was unable to find solutions for other problems on its agenda. For example, no clear-cut answer was found to the EC budgetary question. It pointed out that while financial problems are important, 'the real threat to the future of the Community and to its financing is the fact that the economic and social fabric of the member states is falling apart. Nothing has been done to prevent this disintegration.'

This evaluation of the economic and social situation and the inability of the Council to cope with it effectively was confirmed after the meeting of the Council in Athens which was described by the ETUC as an expression of increasing national egoism. It was considered a total failure owing to the abrogation of responsibility to resolve common problems at the Council level.[89]

In spite of all this pessimism expressed by the ETUC, some signs of positive response to its views could be discerned. In 1984 a OECD Intergovernmental Conference on Employment Growth in the Context of Structural Change took place where trade unions played an active role. The Conference came to the conclusion that OECD countries needed to abandon their defensive position on unemployment problems and, instead, take a 'forward looking stance of spurring the process of employment growth and helping the working population to prepare for, and adjust to, the new requirement of structural change'.[90]

In this connection, it is important to note that soon after taking office the new president of the Commission called for a meeting with the ETUC and the employers' organization UNICE, to demonstrate the Community's desire to work with business and labour in revitalizing the European economy.[91]

Multinational corporations

Another topic that generated considerable concern among the European trade unions was multinational corporations. The rapid expansion of American-based multinationals in Western Europe, and particularly in the Community, had become a major economic phenomenon. While United States' direct investments in Western Europe had not expanded significantly before the formation of the EEC, the stimulus generated by the Common Market contributed considerably to the establishment and the development of such enterprises.[92]

The paucity of capital in Europe, compounded with the strength of the dollar, opened the possibility of establishing new production sites; and the reduction of trade barriers between the United States and Europe after several GATT negotiations facilitated an intensified intercompany trade.[93] As a consequence, enterprises had frequently become 'Europeanized' in production, their components and sub-assemblies being produced throughout Europe.[94]

During the 1960s and early 1970s, there was a general consensus of opinion that multinational enterprises accelerated European economic integration. It was accepted that companies could strengthen the EEC directly by supporting such common industrial policies that might be in their interest, or indirectly by undermining the independence and sovereignty of the national states.[95]

A series of arguments were advanced in favour of this hypothesis.

(1) Multinational corporations (MNCs) tend to increase economic growth, productivity and mass consumption. They generate employment and general welfare thus stabilizing the framework within which the EEC could develop.[96]

(2) MNCs make optimal use of comparatively advantageous locations and mobility of the factors of production beyond national borders, thereby increasing the structural homogeneity of European integration.[97]

(3) MNCs require large markets and freedom from national restrictions regarding their production, servicing and financial activities. Since the EEC provided this framework, MNCs favour European integration.[98]

(4) MNCs transform the political awareness of economic elites. Since multinational managers think in terms of efficiency, market rationality and accelerated growth within an international framework, they are unlikely to develop strong national loyalties.[99]

(5) MNCs transnational operations create a network of complementary

interests and thus augment the level of interdependence between national economies.[100]

(6) MNCs tend to circumvent and often hinder the monetary, fiscal, credit and foreign trade policies of states.[101] It would therefore be necessary to give greater authority and competence to the European institutions to counter-vail their activities.[102]

(7) No other institution or entity has reached the same degree of inter-nationalism as MNCs. It is in no way matched by a corresponding degree of internationalization of labour.[103]

In more recent literature, however, MNCs' ability to foster the economic integration process in Europe has been contested. It has been argued that they do not have any European legal status but are established within a national framework. Their capital stock is expressed in a national currency. Their financial and investment decisions are centrally planned. Major decisions pertaining to research and development of the companies are taken by the mother firm. Yet, on the other hand, their policies are not limited to one country and its production facilities are not located in one state.[104] Neverthe-less, the conviction that American companies had favoured integration within the Community, and that the flood of direct investment into the EC had led to its 'Americanization' even before its 'Europeanization' had started had awakened the concern of some European governments.[105]

France had become concerned that its national interests would not be taken seriously into account by the American companies.[106] On several occasions, therefore, it had requested that the members of the Community should formulate a common policy towards foreign direct investment and especially towards multinational enterprises and their encroachment on domestic industrial developments. Belgium, too, had become concerned with the MNCs' impact on its economy and Germany had come out in favour of strengthening the European industries through mergers of companies within the EEC.[107] These fears were well understood by the European labour unions. In fact, they had gone even further and emphasized that the Common Market had been more beneficial to the interests of international capital than to the development of social and economic policies favourable to their members.[108]

The Commission, convinced on the one hand of the integrative impulses of transnational companies and concerned on the other by the lack of any European industrial counterpart that was able to match the American competi-tion, became an advocate of European integration policy based on an increased interdependence of its economic units.

The Treaties of Paris and Rome had already underlined the link between the growth of industrial enterprises and the development of European integration. The liberation of economic actors from national bounds was regarded as necessary if the Community were to overcome its customs union status and head towards supranational unity.

In 1970, the Commission had elaborated on this concept in a memorandum on industrial policy, defining as its object the establishment of European-structured large-scale industries which would contribute to economic growth, and which would strengthen the competitiveness of European industries on the world market. Such industrial concentration would also enable the Europeans to narrow the technological gap that existed with respect to American industries. Therefore, the industries requiring highly advanced technology should be particularly strengthened through a process of cooperation and mergers.

As a first step in that direction, the Commission considered that it was vital to adjust national company law so that a certain degree of uniformity could be introduced, permitting the establishment of European enterprises with a legal statute largely independent of national legislation.

The debate around European company law was broad in scope, involving numerous political, social and legal questions. The recurrent central theme was the problem of the decision-making structure of a company and especially, the role of the employees in relation to that structure. In this connection, the Commission made a number of proposals. In June 1970, it submitted to the Council a broad draft of a Statute for a European Company,[109] which was supplemented by a more specific proposal favouring the coordination of national laws with respect to the structure of certain types of companies;[110] and by the introduction of safeguards for employees who might be affected by mergers between companies.[111]

Parallel to these efforts, the Commission also advanced proposals with respect to MNCs with headquarters outside the EEC. In particular, a communication to the Council of Ministers entitled 'Multinational under-takings and Community regulations' was submitted in November 1973. Though recognizing that MNCs could contribute positively to the evolution of the EEC, the document highlighted extensively the negative consequences of uncontrolled power of the MNC on the integration process, thereby expressing concerns frequently articulated by the public, and in particular by the labour movement, on that matter. The Commission, furthermore, pointed out that the 'Growing hold of multinational undertakings on the economic, social and even political life of the countries in which they operate, gives rise to deep anxieties which are sufficiently widespread, especially in the areas of employment, competition, tax avoidance, disturbing capital movements and the economic independence of developing countries, as to demand the attention of the public authorities'.[112]

With the aim of creating a uniform frame of reference for MNC activities, the Commission drew up about thirty proposals concerning multinational groups of companies either directly or indirectly. It was the proposal for a Statute for a European company law that remained the focal point of lengthy deliberations between the Commission and the ETUC, as well as within the EEC's consultative bodies. The issue that continuously reappeared during these discussions centered again on the rights of workers in transnational companies and on the structure of those companies. When an amended version of the Statute was finally presented by the Commission in 1975[113] this question continued to remain largely unresolved.[114]

Before examining this issue more closely, it will be useful to analyse the evolution of the trade unions' ideas in this field. When the Commission proposals on mergers of European companies were brought forward in 1970, the European trade unions' response was mainly concerned with the social consequences of such concentrations. In their view, the formation of highly concentrated European industries should not restrict free competition, and should not jeopardise existing social achievements, including workers' participation rights.[115]

This concern regarding trade-union participation in the enterprise's decision-making process has been amply expressed by the labour movement;[116] and the development of powerful companies led it to design an international counterstrategy. From their perspective, the MNCs, by their very structure, are largely able to avoid democratic controls and social responsibility.[117] Not only can they neutralize national economic and social policy measures and thereby threaten the sovereignty of states but they can also influence national economic policies by the following practices:

- export of capital, technology, research and production facilities;
- evasion of taxes by manipulating internal prices so that profits are taxed not where they occur but in one of the 'tax havens';
- capital transfers from one part of the enterprise to another with negative effects on national balance of payments, price stability and full employment;
- abuse of investment incentives such as anti-labour legislation and low wage practices, through which some national governments try to surpass each other in order to attract MNCs' capital investment.[118]

In order to exercise some control over MNCs' business practices, the ICFTU proposed, in 1970, the convening of an international conference under the auspices of the United Nations and with the participation of trade unions to elaborate a 'code of good behaviour' for MNCs. It also submitted a wide array of proposals for dealing with such corporations, and pressed for a code of conduct within the framework of the OECD and the ILO.[119] Since the European trade unions were actively involved in the elaboration of the ICFTU proposals, in one capacity or another, they endorsed these proposals at the international level. But within the framework of the EEC they had to involve themselves in a number of specifically European issues.

In the early 1970s, trade unions generally endorsed the Commission's view that in order to lead the EEC beyond the stage of a mere customs union and in the direction of enhanced economic integration, new thinking was needed for an industrial policy.[120]

A one-sided emphasis on cooperation between and mergers of enterprises without some form of democratic control would be in contradiction of the concepts of the labour unions.[121] Economic rationalization and increased competitiveness could also lead to a concentration of economic and political power which required some form of workers' participation in order to obtain an equilibrium between the social and economic forces involved.[121] Without such an equilibrium, and without the reinforcement of the social component in general the EEC would only serve the special interests of economically powerful groups rather than those of the workers.[122]

While all this was viewed as obvious and necessary by ETUC members, its establishment was, however, problematic. To seek an increased role for labour in EEC policies, or to obtain an enlarged participation in the enterprise's decisional process, the trade unions would have to become more functional than before. They would have to carry through collective bargaining within the industrial branches at the European level; they would have to implement participation procedures within a European company; and they would need to agree to adjustments of social legislation at the European level.

But this was not easy since the labour unions were organized essentially at the national level. They had evolved and acted within their national frameworks and thus had acquired different historical traditions, formulated diverse political concepts, designed disparate means of action and had dissimilar ideas about compromise and solutions. They therefore found themselves at a disadvantageous bargaining position in respect to transnational enterprises whose locus of decision-making was often hard to identify, and whose production and future investments could be moved to plants in other states, thereby threatening employment stability.

Members of the trade unions responded to the new situation by attempting to define common policies which should enable them to confront transnational companies together at the transnational level. But numerous practical problems arose during the process of attempted consolidation at the European level. Many of them were related to the forms of workers' participation in enterprises.

The negotiation for collective bargaining agreements is the basic form of such participation and one of the fundamental activities of a labour union at the enterprise level. In the trade unions' view, the expansion of MNCs affected their bargaining position in two ways: the management representatives negotiating with the union might receive instructions from a company director located outside the country where the negotiation is taking place, as a result of which labour representatives would not be able to confront the real decision-makers directly during the negotiations; the foreign location of the decisional centre also precludes the flow of information about the company's financial structure, its investment plans and general policy intentions. This can directly or indirectly affect the workers and limit the basis of negotiation of their representatives.

In order to deal with MNCs effectively, it has often been suggested that the highly concentrated structure of international capital should be counterbalanced by an equally well-structured international labour movement.[123] This means that coordinated collective bargaining policy within industry branches and MNCs should be devised. Ideally, the objective should be to arrive at a unified collective bargaining agreement with the parent company and all the subsidiaries of an MNC regardless of the location of their production sites.

The attempts to implement this strategy, however, were stymied by a wide array of complex practical difficulties. Diverse collective bargaining practices exist at the national and at the industrial branch levels. While, in most cases, the agreements deal with questions of direct interest to employees—such as renumeration, working hours, leave and the like—in some countries, their significance and the areas they cover have been extended well beyond this framework and extend to enterprise policies as a whole. In Italy, for example, agreements concluded in the aftermath of labour conflicts in the late sixties deal increasingly with the amelioration of working conditions and frequently include provisions about workers' performance and work quality. Recently, they also contained provisions on investment policies and the maintenance of certain employment levels.[124]

This trend was also noted in Great Britain and Ireland, where management was obliged to consult with workers on all problems directly affecting them before taking any decision on such matters. In Belgium and France, agreements cover wide-ranging questions regarding guaranteed incomes, pensions, workers' education and vocational training. Furthermore, not only do contents of agreements vary considerably from one Community country to another, but they also tend to cover different economic entities. In Italy, they are generally negotiated at the plant or enterprise level, but concluded within a given industrial branch at the national level. In Germany, they are concluded industry-wide, but at a regional level. And in France, the Netherlands and Belgium, there is also a tendency to include agreements in regional industrial development plans.[125]

The time span covered by collective bargaining agreements also varies from country to country. Additionally, large differences exist in the internal structure of labour representation and the jurisdiction of their representative organs at plant, industry, regional and industrial levels. Related to this are the equally different structures of employers' representation with which the trade unions are faced. Finally, a host of discrepancies and incompatibilities exist between the national legal systems and jurisdictions dealing with labour-management relations. All these elements thus appear to constitute an important obstacle to the harmonization of collective bargaining procedures at the European level; and this is not likely to be overcome in the foreseeable future.[126]

It has been argued that under the present circumstances, the objective of concluding collective bargaining agreements at the international or at the European level is too ambitious. Although it seems to be logical to reason that the growing concentration and internationalization of capital necessitates an equally concentrated and internationalized labour movement to counteract management policies efficiently, this logic does not stand up to closer examination. The formal organization argument of countervailing the power of one by the power of the other is not sufficient since this leaves the core problem unresolved and unattended.

If anything, international agreements would weaken the historically developed thrust with which labour unions pursue their objectives at the national level without really leading to a corresponding increase in the bargaining power of the international negotiating body. This line of reasoning arrives at the conclusion that the role of the international labour movement should therefore consist esentially in giving all possible support to national collective bargaining policies.

Notwithstanding the obvious importance of functioning at the national level, some attempts have been made to coordinate trade-union action in enterprises with production sites located in different states of the Community. One of the most striking examples was the conflict with the chemical multinational AKZO, where German and Dutch trade unions were involved and achieved a sufficient level of common action to avoid the closing down of a number of plants in the Netherlands, Belgium, Germany and Switzerland.[127] Another example is the attitude of unions representing Ford workers in Britain, West Germany, Spain, Belgium and Portugal. They threatened to support industrial action 'up to and including occupation' if Ford closes a European plant.[128]

Another element which relates the grass-roots interests of workers to the issue of transnational companies in Europe is the question of the type of labour representation that should be established at the company level. This question in turn is closely linked with the structure of such a company.

In its original proposal for a Statute for a European Company, the EC Commission had introduced some regulations for the establishment of a central works' council and some rules for co-determination. But these rules did not conform to the existing concepts of the European trade unions. The draft statute stipulated a two-tier board structure largely modeled after the West German law for corporations with limited liabilities and a share capital. The direction of the company would consist of a supervisory board composed of one-third of workers' representatives and two-thirds of management representatives, plus a management board in charge of the daily business practices and controlled by the supervisory board.[129]

The ECFTU, and later the ETUC, demanded a board composed of one-third labour and one-third capital representatives with the last third selected by both these groups through a system of co-optation. The second body, the management board, in its view, should include one member in charge of social and personnel problems. Also, it requested the establishment of a central works' council elected in all the company's subsidiaries as well as in the parent company.[130]

It should be noted that the concept the ETUC and its predecesor had developed regarding company structure and workers' participation, however, did not represent a unified view of its member organizations. Firstly, it created a number of serious legal problems for those countries which did not have a tradition of a two-tier company structure. In such cases, traditional labour-management relations would have needed redefinition and readaptation, whereas they did not seem imperative to the labour unions. Secondly, a co-determination concept, acceptable to all ETUC member unions, had been debated since 1965 but it had never been solved to the satisfaction of all. Controversies on the question had arisen, particularly between the Belgian FGTB and the German DGB. The FGTB adhered to a philosophy of labour management relations which considered the capitalist system as basically incompatible with trade-union objectives of political and economic democracy.[131] It saw the realization of 'workers' control' in the form of 'permanent trade-union action', as the only effective means of representation. Workers' control was conceived as a 'strategy for broad social change and not simply another industrial reform'.[132] It is a 'transitional demand, an anticapitalist structural reform par excellence' and has to be distinguished 'from its reformist variants—co-determination and 'participation".[133]

The FGTB, therefore, strongly criticized the German concept of co-determination which was based on mixed labour-management decisions made at the plant and enterprise levels, and favoured instead the idea of a socialist and democratic society based on autogestion and geared to meeting the overall economic needs of the masses.[134] With its revolutionary outlook it could hardly accept such a prospect. The election of representatives by all workers of the enterprise, the recognition of a 'neutral' person on the supervisory board, an essential element of the German paritary co-determination system, and the inclusion of a director for social and personnel questions on the management board nominated by the trade unions was anathema to the Belgian organization. Such forms of participation in the company's decision-making process would imply a certain commitment for cooperation with the representatives of capital in an enterprise.

The DGB, on the other hand, maintained that the establishment of freedom of association, the acceptance of a collective bargaining system, and the implementation of a vast array of social policies and legislation through the years had completely changed the pattern of social conflicts, permitting thereby the efficient functioning of a co-determination system. According to its constitution, the DGB favoured a truly democratic society with all its manifestations, including the free development of the individual and the different social groups.

The differences among the European trade unions were thus indeed too great, and the harmonization of the various aspects of social and labour legislation, of the different traditions and political practices was indeed an uphill objective at this point. The ETUC role was reduced to the task of laying down general political principles acceptable to all its members. It clearly stated that 'due to the historical, economic and social differences existing between the countries of the EEC, no regulations must be imposed on workers and their trade unions which they consider to be incompatible either with circumstances in their respective countries or with their trade union convictions'.[135]

Faced with the complexity of the debate and the impasse it had generated, the Commission, in close cooperation with the ETUC, thus resorted to a different approach. Instead of proposing ambitious and across-the-board legislation, it attempted to regulate legislation on some specific issues. Closely following the Council's January 1974 resolution on social action programmes, it prepared a directive dealing with the approximation of laws of member states on collective redundancies.[136] This was followed by another directive for the approximation of legislation on safeguarding employees' rights in the event of transfer of undertakings, businesses or parts of businesses.[137]

At the same time, the Commission attempted to increase the harmonization of national laws of limited companies by issuing directives providing 'a system of publicity',[138] establishing standards for capital formation for public limited companies[139] and regulating their mergers[140] and dissolutions.[141] A codex of European accounting law was also provided through a number of directives for limited companies, including 'groups' of undertakings (parent and subsidiary companies).[142]

More recently, attempts have again been made to tackle the problem of company structure. But this has proved difficult. Such questions as employee participation, industrial relations within 'groups' of companies, liability of a parent to a subsidiary company, rights of minority shareholders, employees and credits have been intractable, still awaiting solutions.[143]

It was the issue of information rights for workers' representatives in a transnational firm that became a focal point of attention for the Commission, the trade unions and the employers alike. In the late seventies and early eighties, trade unions considered this issue vital for the pursuit of trade-union interests; and in this connection the Commission had proposed a directive of procedures for informing and consulting the employees of enterprises with a complex structure, particularly transnational firms.[144]

Faced with increasing unemployment and, at times with massive and sudden dismissals of employees, the Commission had originally aimed its proposal at MNCs to obtain some forewarning about their intended business policies which might affect employees directly and indirectly. Such advance information would have enabled workers' representatives as well as the management to introduce some planning in manpower policies. It is interesting to note that the MNCs complained of being singled out on the issue of information rights, as a result of which other enterprises called 'national companies with complex structures' in euro-terminology had also to be included.[145]

Under the Vredeling proposal, the management of a dominant, and particularly a multinational, company was required to forward information every six months to its subsidiaries in the Community, giving a clear picture of its activities and its subsidiaries. This information was expected to cover a wide array of company activities, concerning its structure and manpower policies, its economic and financial situation, the expected evolution of business, production and sales, production and investment programmes, rationalization plans, manufacturing and working methods and all planned initiatives having a substantial effect on the employees' interests.[146]

The management of each subsidiary employing at least 100 persons was required to forward this information to the workers' representatives in that firm. If it could not comply, the workers' representatives had the right to apply to the management of the dominant undertaking. The information thus received was expected to describe the activities of the parent company throughout the world and of all of its subsidiaries.[147]

Consultations with the workers' representatives were required when planned initiatives would substantially affect the interests of the workers in the dominant company or of any of its subsidiaries. In such a case, precise information would have to be forwarded to all subsidiaries within the EEC 'not later than forty days before adopting the decision'.[148] The initiative for such consultations did not have to emanate from the employers but could also be taken by the workers' representatives.[149]

Since previously established codes regarding MNCs activities—developed by such international organizations as the OECD and the ILO—were not legally binding, the proposed EEC directive was the first legally enforcible international regulation dealing with this problem. The obligations contained in the proposal were also applicable to enterprises with subsidiaries within the Common Market, even if their headquarters were located outside the region.[150]

The Commission elaborated the proposal for this directive after lengthy preparations and consultations with the social partners. It was adopted in the face of a strong opposition from the European Employers' Organization (UNICE). In a commentary presented at the request of the European Parliament's social committee UNICE, while supportive of consultation with workers' representatives regarding personnel matters voiced several reservations. Its major objection pertained to the dangers of indiscretion regarding business policies, should the companies be required to divulge information about subsidiaries situated outside the EEC. Should such directives become obligatory they would paralyse the decision-making and planning processes within the enterprises as a whole.[151] A number of American-based multinationals (IBM, ITT and General Motors) contested what they termed the 'principle of extraterritoriality' according to which the EEC jurisdiction could extend to companies based outside the EC territory.[152]

Although the Commission's October 1980 proposal fell short of the ETUC's conceptions in some points, the latter nevertheless regarded it as a political success. It considered the Commission's initiative on this question as a logical corollary to the efforts made by the Community to reach greater openness in business activities through directives on collective dismissals,[153] and on business takeovers.[154] Also, it was complementary to the proposal for a directive on associations of undertakings (ninth directive) in preparation.[155]

During the ensuing procedure, which required that the Commission proposals be submitted to the European Parliament and to the Economic and Social Committee for an opinion, the proposal provoked a serious controversy between trade unions and employers. The ETUC viewed that it was far from the original trade-union demands for workers' participation in the MNCs decisional processes and was only a modest step into the direction of informing and consulting workers since final decisions would still remain with the management. The employers, on the other hand, considered it a serious threat to the freedom of taking management decisions.

The development of a total impasse between the social partners on what was perceived to be an important issue resulted in the inauguration of an intense process of lobbying by both sides. The management lobby was particularly active. According to Commissioner Richard: 'The carpet to my door has been worn thin by the shoes of spokesmen; the multinational companies trooping in there one after another to make precisely the same points, occasionally in precisely the same language, and indeed to obtain from me precisely the same response.'[157]

Under the influence of the German trade union rapporteur, the ESC produced an opinion that was favourable to the ETUC.[158] It was not obtained without overcoming a number of hurdles. A majority of the third 'general interests' group had to be won over to the trade-union position, and this despite repeated warnings from the employers that MNCs would not be able to maintain their investments in the Community, should the proposal be passed.[159]

The situation was different in the European Parliament. Here, the proposal was submitted to the social affairs committee which debated the issue in consultation with the economic and financial affairs and the legal committees. To a large extent, the social committee's comments and proposals were close to that of the ETUC on the issue.[160] But the text was severely weakened during the debates in the plenary meetings where a conservative group held a majority since the 1979 elections.[161]

After heated debates on a series of controversial points, the Parliament introduced a number of significant amendments:

(1) while the original version stipulated the application of the directive to enterprises with at least 100 workers per subsidiary,[162] this threshhold was increased to 1,000 by the European Parliament. A considerable number of medium-sized 'complex undertakings' were, thereby, exempted.[163]

(2) Whereas the original text stipulated the convening of information sessions whenever important decisions were to be made, in the modified version the information was to be given 'at least once a year'.[164]

(3) The Parliament decided that sensitive information would be excluded from the information process. Yielding to the pressures of management regarding business secrets, it left it to the exclusive domain of company executives to determine what could be considered as confidential. This would permit management 'to omit from its coverage ... any information whose disclosure would substantially harm the company's prospects or substantially damage its interests'.

(4) The right of the workers' representatives to 'by-pass' the management of the subsidiaries and address themselves directly to the dominant company in the event of any dissatisfaction was omitted. Instead, access was restricted to the national framework which had its own legal provisions regarding information and consultation of workers and their representatives.[165]

The amendments introduced by the EP reflected to a large extent the viewpoints of the employers. In fact, the latter had obtained satisfaction on some of their most urgent concerns. To assure the implementation of its amendments, the Parliament used its new procedural powers to block the Community's proposal. Mindful of the fact that the Council could not act on any Commission proposal without having previously obtained the opinions of the ESC and the EP, the Parliament voted on its amendments, but it did not adopt its own final resolution as long as it had not obtained a sufficient commitment from the Commission that it would amend its text according to the Parliament's wishes.[166]

The Commission was not prepared to accept the Parliament's amendments unconditionally since the EP had chosen 'to amend all but two of the original eighteen articles'. In order to avoid a deadlock on procedural matters the vote on the Parliament's resolution was postponed until November 1982. During the November session, the Commission finally committed itself to modify its original proposal largely in the sense recommended by the Parliament.[167] But it did not accept all of the amendments, some of them were ignored in the new proposals.

Whereas the EP opinion had requested that information should be provided before the implementation of a management decision, the Commission proposed that it should be given to the workers before a definite decision on a certain issue had been taken. Furthermore, if measures directly affecting employees were planned, then consultations should take place which should lead to unified positions between management and labour on the matter concerned.[168]

At this stage of the procedure, the ETUC considered the proposal largely diluted and far removed from the objectives it wanted to attain. Nevertheless, the binding nature of the provisions continued to be maintained so that the unique characteristic of a legally binding 'code of behaviour' remained. As required by the procedure, the new Commission text was communicated to the EP for information, but no further consultation was required. It was now in the hands of the Council of Ministers to finalize the directives.

There appeared to be little hope that the Directive would be passed by the Council in a form desired by the ETUC. The latter, in fact, feared that intensified lobbying on behalf of the employers at the national and Council levels might well further weaken the proposal. In its view, this 'first attempt in international social history to submit multinational companies to supranational legal discipline' must therefore be considered a failure.[169]

Reform of the institutions

The EEC trade unions originally favoured the acceleration and intensification of economic and political integration. But after the establishment of the ETUC with a geographical framework that surpassed the Community, the Community idea was somewhat diluted. Its involvement with the goal of internal consolidation hardly left any time for the long-term objectives of political union.

From the short- and medium-term perspective, the trade unions had become aware of the necessity to develop common European policies, and to reinforce the powers of the European institutions as against those of the national governments. Many proposals voiced by the ETUC, therefore, referred to the 'democratization' of the European institutions, the principal objective of which was to increase the participation of the labour movement in the Community's decision-making process, and to strengthen the social component in Community policies, a factor which had indeed been neglected by the drafters of the Treaty of Rome. Besides such reforms in the eyes of the ETUC would also increase trade-union effectiveness as a pressure group within the Community.

Since many aspects of ETUC views regarding institutional aspects have already been dealt with in a previous chapter, only its salient features will be highlighted in the following pages.

On the occasion of the publication of the 'Report on European Institutions', presented by the Committee of Three to the European Council, the ETUC once again took a position on EEC institutions. It was essentially political and voluntarist. It expressed the view that a real debate on institutions as such was meaningless without the 'political will to perfect the construction of Europe';[170] and this, it felt, was lacking. If anything, the Community's socio-economic policies were actually deteriorating. Instead of improving the lives of people, they were aggravating unemployment and the inflationary situation. It was urgently necessary to manifest a real political determination to define goals and boldly design a pattern of attaining them.[171]

In this connection, it is important to note that notwithstanding its penchant for focusing on day-to-day problems the ETUC appears to have come around to the idea of a political union of Europe, since the resolution of some of the pressing socio-economic problems on the European scale seemed to be very difficult without the attainment of some of the political goals. There was, thus, a resurgence of interest in political union.

In a speech to the 1979 Congress, the ETUC general secretary, for example, reminded the audience that European integration is an all-time preoccupation having political and social peace as its major goal.[172] The Italian affiliates of the organization went even further: they insisted that the trade unions should become even more involved, and actually requested the convocation of a special meeting on the question.[173] The ETUC's new interest can also be gauged from the stand it took on the Genscher-Colombo proposal for European Union. While attacking it as a mere facade, it came out in favour of the European Parliament's more ambitious draft treaty for the establishment of a European Union. It considered it as a more valuable basis for discussion than what the German and Italian foreign ministers were proposing.[174]

Basically, the ETUC affiliates from the Common Market (with the exception of Denmark) seem to consider it fundamental that, as a first step, the Treaty provisions on European Union should be exhaustively applied, including the transfer of competence from member states to the Community in many important areas. In its view, these provisions should become a reality and cooperation among Western European countries should be increased.

The ETUC also took a clear position on the power and the working methods of the Community institutions. The trade unions were particularly concerned about the inordinate power that the European Council had acquired through the years. This was viewed as a setback to the on-going process of European integration, since it was within this institutional framework that all the narrow and conflicting national interests came into play. The preoccupation with such a development was all the more great because this had occurred outside the framework of the Rome Treaty, which did not include any stipulation to this effect.[175]

The ETUC, therefore, became a firm partisan of blocking this development by airing a series of proposals that would re-establish some degree of equilibrium among the different institutions of the Community. It demanded that the Council of Ministers should revert to a majority vote as stipulated in the Treaty, and should give more consideration than previously to the opinions expressed by the European Parliament and the Economic and Social Committee. The role of COREPER should also be limited as it had developed into an opaque bureaucratic body geared more to the objectives of representing the views of the national civil servants than that of the Community. The Commission, in turn, must regain its legally due authority of initiating and coordinating all Community policies.

The European Parliament's role should also be enhanced at all levels. In particular, it should not be limited to an advisory function, and it should be enabled to present overall political views on Community matters to the Council and the public. The authority of the Court of Justice, 'an absolutely essential institution', should be reinforced with all its decisions becoming legally binding on member states.[176]

The ETUC has thus become increasingly critical of the growing nationalism of member states and of the absence of any common policies at the EEC level. It particularly targeted its attacks on the Council for obstructing all significant progress towards European unity. The Commission too, has not been spared. It has come under severe criticism for demonstrating an inability to handle major challenges facing the Community, and this despite the obvious fact that national solutions can no longer be found for a wide array of problems, especially in the economic sector.[177] In this sector the ETUC has recommended the introduction of a wide spectrum of bold Community policies, covering such areas as investment, monetary and trade affairs, industrial and employment measures, and new infra-structural and transportation projects, etc. In this connection, it is also important to note that the Common Agricultural Policy (CAP) has been attacked for consuming an unduly large amount of the Community's limited resources. A reform of CAP has therefore become increasingly urgent at a time when the Community budget should be geared to meet the pressing needs in employment, regional and social planning.

In the trade-union view, CAP neither provides a satisfactory solution for the tax payers and consumers in general, nor does it meet the needs of most of those whose existence, employment and resources depend upon agriculture and food processing industries. While trying to bridge the wide gap between production and consumption through the purchase and storing of surpluses and finally selling them to outside markets at dumping prices, the Community was unable to assure an equitable revenue for the majority of agricultural workers.

In fact, overall real income in the agricultural sector decreased in 1981, while differences of revenues became widespread according to the productions, regions and the size of farms. In order to remedy this situation, at least 5 per cent of the agricultural budget, in the ETUC's view, should be re-allocated towards social needs. Furthermore, the Commission should develop medium- and long-term agricultural plans, including production targets for principal products with the aim of reducing the inequalities of agricultural revenues, and of improving the quality of the products as well as their marketing and distribution. It has been argued that a clear distinction should be made in such a plan between the items produced within the Community and those that are to be imported, so that the Community can cease to disturb world markets with its dumping prices.[178]

Notes

1. OECD, *Perspectives Economiques*, Paris, July 1975, p. 17; December 1975, p. 39; December 1976, p. 3; December 1979, p. 33.
2. *Eurostat*, 1984, p. 93.
3. OECD, op. cit., December 1979, p. 34.
4. OECD, *Employment Outlook*, September 1984, pp. 19, 40.
5. *Eurostat*, pp. 177, 175.
6. *30 Jours d'Europe*, Fisches documentaires pédagogiques, Supplément au Numéro, Mai 1984, p. 6.
7. OECD, *Employment Outlook*, September 1984, p. 19.
8. ETUI, *The European Economy 1980-85*, an indicative full employment plan. Brussels, 1980, p. 54.
9. *Eurostat*, p. 267.
10. ETUI, *Industrial Policy in Western Europe*, Brussels, 1981, pp. 10-15.
11. ETUI, *Negotiating Technological Change*, Brussels, 1982, pp. 3-14.
12. OECD, *Employment Outlook*, op. cit., 1984, p. 39, 40.
13. *Eurostat*, p. 97.
14. ETUI, op. cit., p. 13.
15. *Eurostat*, p. 176; comparable data for Greece are not available.
16. *30 Jours d'Europe*, op. cit., pp. 8-16.
17. ETUI, *European Trade Union Institute Background Paper*, for the ETUC Employment Conference in Strasburg, 5-6 April 1984, Brussels, 1984, p. 4. OECD, *The Challenge of Unemployment*, Paris, 1982, p. 16.
18. Ibid., pp. 6-7.
19. ETUC, *Supplement to the Report on Activities*, 1973-5, 'Secure Employment—Guarantee Income', Brussels, 1976, p. 2.; see also ETUC, 'Statement on Unemployment and Inflation', *ETUC Objectives 1976-79*, Brussels, 1976, pp. I, 1-11.
20. ETUI, *Background Paper*, op. cit., p. 3.
21. ETUC, *Secure Employment . . .*, op. cit.
22. ETUI, *Background Paper*, op. cit., p. 8.
23. ETUC, *Action Programme*, General and Specific Resolutions, 1979-82, approved by the Fourth Statutory Congress, The Hague, 19-23 April 1982, p. 9.
24. ETUC, *Report on Activities*, 1979-81, op. cit., p. 36; see also ETUC, *General Resolution and Specific Resolutions, 1982-1984*, op. cit., p. 8; ETUC, *Supplement to Report on Activities*, Fourth Statutory Congress, The Hague, 19-23 April 1982, 'ETUC Manifesto for Employment and Econmoic Recovery', pp. 31-40.
25. ETUC, *Report on Activities*, 1979-81, op. cit., p. 36.
26. ETUC, *Action Programme*, General and Specific Resolutions, 1979. 1982; Third Statutory Congress, Munich, 14-18 May, 1979.
27. OECD, *Economic Studies*, 'International Economic Linkages', Paris, November 1983. The interlink system is used to calculate the feedback effects of measures in one country upon other countries and ultimately the feedback effects upon the first country through trade.
28. ETUI, *Employment, Investment and the Public Sector*, Brussels, 1982, p. 3.
29. NFS-DGB, 'It pays to cooperate', October 1983, quoted in ETUI, *Employment . . .*, op. cit., p. 5.
30. ETUC, 'Manifesto . . .', op. cit., pp. 31-40.
31. ETUI, *Public Investment and Job Creation*, Brussels, 1984, pp. 1, 2, 7.
32. ETUC, 'Manifesto . . .', op. cit., p. 35.

33. ETUI, *Public Investment...*', op. cit., pp. 1, 15, 24.
34. Ibid., p. 65.
35. *New Scientist*, 12 May 1983, quoted in ETUI, *Public Investment...*, op. cit., p. 70.
36. Ibid., pp. 75–8.
37. *Logica*, 'Communications in Europe—The Changing Environment', 1983, quoted in the *Financial Times*, 25 August 1983.
38. ETUI, *Public Investment...*, op. cit., pp. 74, 75, 79–81.
39. For details, see: Trade Union Congress (TUC), *The Reconstruction of Britain*, London, 1981; Deutscher Gewerkschaftsbund, *Die Quelle*, Düsseldorf, June 1982; Federatie Nederlandse Vakbeweging (FNV), 'More Work', *FNV News*, Amsterdam, 1982, Walter Höhnem, 'Das DGB-Investitionsprogramm zur Sicherung der Beschäftigung durch qualitatives Wachstum: Ansätze zur Konkretisierung', *WSI–Mitteilungen*, 10/1982.
40. ETUI, *Public Investment...*, op. cit., p. 104.
41. ETUC, *Initial proposals relating to the economic situation, employment and incomes in Europe*, Brussels, 9 July 1975, p. 3. ETUC, *Executive Committee Resolution on the reduction of working hours*, Brussels, April 1977.
42. ETUC, *Third Statutory Congress*, Munich, 14–18 May, 1979, Verbatim Record, pp. 113, 125–35.
43. ETUC Action Programme, *General and Specific Resolutions 1979–82*, approved by the Third Statutory Congress, Munich, 14–18 May 1979, p. 10; see also, ETUC, *General Resolutions and Specific Resolutions, 1982–85*, Approved by the Fourth Statutory Congress, 19–23 April, 1982, p. 10.
44. Hans Mayr, '38.5 Stunden—Das Tabu ist gebrochen', *Die Mitbestimmung*, 9/84, pp. 365–7.
45. Quoted in Michael Schneider, 'Des Kampf um die Arbeitszeitverkürzung von der Industrialisierung bis zur Gegenwart', *Gewerkschaftliche Monatshefte*, 2/84, p. 79 (author's translation).
46. Ibid., p. 81. Mayr, op. cit., p. 365.
47. ETUI, *The Reduction of Working Hours in Western Europe*, Second Part: Analysis of the Social and Economic Consequences, Brussels, May 1980, p. 16.
48. Ibid., pp. 18–20. see also, Wouter Van Ginneken, 'La réduction de la semaine de travail et l'emploi: Comparison entre sept modèles macro-économoiques européens', *Revue internationale du Travail*, 123, No. 1, January–February 1984, p. 42.
49. ETUI, op. cit., p. 30.
50. IG-Metall, *Zusammenfassung der Probleme der Arbeitszeitverkürzung*, 1978, quoted in ETUI, 'The Reduction ...', op. cit., pp. 20, 30–5, 58.
51. Ibid., pp. 65, 66.
52. Mayr, op. cit., p. 365.
53. Speech of the president of the Bundesvereinigung der Deutschen Arbeitgeberverbände, Otto Esser, to the Annual Meeting, 12–13 December 1983, *Gewerkschaftliche Monatshefte* 2/84, p. 130; see also Ernst Breit, 'Arbeitszeitverkürzung—Der entscheidende Schritt voran muss gelingen', *Gewerkschaftliche Monatshefte*.
54. Breit, op. cit., pp. 79, 99.
55. ETUC Executive Committee Meeting 'Verbatim Record', 9/10 June 1983, Geneva, *ETUC Archives*.
56. CLE, *Observations du Comité de liaison d'employeurs sur le mémorandum sur la réduction et la réorganisation du temps de travail*, Brussels, 21 March 1983.
57. ETUC, *General Resolution... 1982–85*, op. cit., p. 7.
58. ETUI, *Background Paper...*, op. cit., pp. 21, 22.
59. ETUC, 'Manifesto ...', op. cit., p. 38.
60. ETUI, *Background Paper...*, op. cit., p. 23.

61. Ibid., pp. 25, 30–32.
62. ETUC, *General Resolution . . .* 1982–85, op. cit., p. 10.
63. ETUC, *Report on Activities, 1976–78*, pp. 26–7.
64. ETUC, Executive Committee meeting, 9, 10 December, 1976, 'Verbatim Record', *ETUC Archives*, see also, ETUC *Report on Activities, 1976–78*, p. 29.
65. ETUC, Executive Committee Meeting, Brussels, 13–14 April 1978, 'Verbatim Record', *ETUC Archives*.
66. ETUC, The European Action Day and the Outcome of the Action Taken, Brussels, April 1978; *Supplement to Report on Activities, 1976–78*, p. 24.
67. ETUC, *Report on Activities*, op. cit., p. 29.
68. ETUC, *Statement for preparations of Bremen European Council*, Brussels, April 1978.
69. ETUC, *Report on Activities*, p. 30.
70. ETUC Executive Committee Meeting, September 1979, 'Verbatim Record', *ETUC Archives*; see also, ETUC, *Report on Activities, 1979–81*, Brussels, 1982, pp. 36, 37.
71. ETUC, 'Concerted Action Programme for Economic Recovery' (Statement for EFTA 20th Anniversary and for the European Council, June 1980), *Supplement to Report on Activities, 1979–81*,; see also ETUC, 'Failure in Stockholm and Venice', (June 1980), *Supplement to Report on Activities 1979–81*, Fourth Statutory Congress, The Hague, 19–23 April 1982.
72. ETUC Executive Committee Meeting, Brussels, 7/8 October 1980, 'Verbatim Records', *ETUC Archives*.
73. ETUC *Information Presse*, 'ETUC Campaign: Progress Report No. 1', Brussels, 26 February 1981.
74. ETUC Executive Committee Meeting, 12–13 February, 1981, Brussels. 'ETUC Campaign Against Unemployment', Agenda, *ETUC Archives*.
75. ETUC *Information Presse*, 'ETUC and socialist leaders call for urgent action on unemployment', Brussels, 14 January 1981.
76. ETUC *Information Presse*, 'Campagne CES', Progress Report, No. 2, 12 March 1981.
77. ETUC, *Report on Activities, 1979–81*, pp. 37, 38.
78. ETUC Assesses Outcome of European Council Meeting, 29–30 June 1981, Luxembourg, *Supplement to Report on Activities 1979–81*, p. 29.
79. *Conclusions de la Présidence sur les Travaux du Conseil Européen*, tenu à Luxembourg, les 29 et 30 juin, 1981.
80. ETUC, *Information Presse*, 'Maastrich Summit; Situation continues to deteriorate', Brussels, 26 March 1981.
81. ETUC, *Information Presse*, 'Preliminary reactions to the 'Jumbo Council'', Brussels, 16 June 1981.
82. ETUC, *Information Presse*, 'ETUC meets jumbo council president', Brussels, 15 November 1982.
83. ETUC Executive Committee Meeting, 30 Sept–1 Oct., 1982, 'Verbatim Record', Brussels, 1982; *ETUC Archives*.
84. ETUC Executive Committee Meeting, 9–10 December 1982, 'Verbatim Record', Brussels, 1982, *ETUC Archives*.
85. ETUC, 'Note sur les différentes rencontres avec les gouvernements dans le cadre de la campagne CES pour l'emploi', Executive Committee Meeting, Brussels, 10 February 1983, *ETUC Archives*.
86. Interview with Mathias Hinterscheid, op. cit.
87. ETUC Executive Committee Meeting, 9–10 December, 1982, op. cit.
88. ETUC *Information Presse*, 4, 20 June 1983.
89. ETUC *Information Presse*, 4 November 1983, 25 November, 6 December 1983.
90. OECD, *Employment Outlook*, op. cit., p. 6.
91. *International Herald Tribune*, 18 January 1985.

92. Walter Hallstein, *Die Europäische Gemeinschaft*, Düsseldorf–Vienna, Econ-Verlag, 1979, p. 158.
93. Jack, N. Behrman, 'Industrial Integration and Multinational Enterprises', *The Annals of the American Academy of Political and Social Science*, September 1982, p. 50.
94. Ford Pinto, for example, has been assembled from components produced in the United States, Great Britain and Germany; see Ernst Piehl, *Multinationale Konzerne und internationale Gewerkschaftsbewegung*, Frankfurt, Europäische Verlagsanstalt (Schriftenreihe der Otto Brenner Stiftung No 2), 1974, pp. 148–50.
95. Erwin Häckel, *Multinationale Konzerne und Europäische Integration*, Forschungsinstitut der Deutschen Gesellschaft für Auswärtige Politik, (Arbeitspapiere zur Internationalen Politik, no. 5), Bonn, European Union Verlag, 1975, p. 4.
96. George Ball, 'The Promise of the MNC', *Fortune* vol. 75, No. 6, June 1967, pp. 73–81. Charles P. Kindelberger, *American Business Abroad*, New Haven and London, Yale University Press, 1969, pp. 75–7.
97. Jack Behrman, 'Industrial Integration ...', *The Annals ...*, op. cit., pp. 46–57. Lawrence Krause, 'The International Economic System', *The Annals ...*, op. cit., pp. 93–103.
98. Carl J. Friedrich, *Europa—Nation in Werden?* Bonn, Europäische Verlagsanstalt, 1972, pp. 51–78.
99. Barnard Menns and Karl P. Sauvant, 'Multinational Corporations, Managers and Development of Regional Identification in Western Europe', *The Annals ...*, op. cit., pp. 22–33.
100. Charles P. Kindelberger, 'European Integration and the International Corporation', in Courtenay Brown, ed., *World Business, Promise and Problems*, New York, Macmillan 1970, pp. 99–113; Edward L. Morse, 'Transnational Economic Processes' in Keohane and Nye (eds), op. cit., pp. 23–47.
101. Gerd Junne, 'Eurogeldmarkt, multinationale Konzerne und die verminderte Wirsamkeit von Staatsinterventionen', *Leviathan*, Jg. 2, 1974, pp. 101–32.
102. Raymond Vernon, 'Multinational Business and National Economic Goals', in Keohane and Nye, op. cit., pp. 343–55.
103. Ernst Mandel, *Europe vs. America: Contradictions of Imperialism*, New York and London, New Left Books, 1970, pp. 18–29; P. Galloway, 'Multinational Enterprise as World Wide Interest Groups', *Politics and Society*, 2, no. 1, Spring 1971, pp. 1–20.
104. Hallstein, op. cit., p. 158; Häckel, op. cit., pp. 9–10.
105. Behrman, 'Industrial Integration ...', *The Annals*, op. cit., p. 50; Häckel, op. cit., p. 11.
106. Jack N. Behrman, *National Interests and the Multinational Enterprise: Tension among the North Atlantic Countries*. Englewood Cliffs, New Jersey. Prentice Hall, Inc., 1970, pp. 32–87.
107. Behrman, 'Industrial Integration ...', op. cit., p. 50.
108. Jung, Koubek, Piehl, Scheibe-Lange, op. cit., pp. 6–8.
109. *Bulletin* of the European Communities, Supplement 8/1970, 30 June 1970.
110. 'Certain types of companies' are joint stock companies approximately equivalent to a public limited liability company in Ireland and the United Kingdom, and to a *Société anonyme* in France, Belgium and Luxembourg, to *aktieselskab* in Denmark, to *Aktiengesellschaft* in Germany, to *societa per azioni* in Italy, to *naamlose vennootschap* in Belgium and the Netherlands.
111. *Bulletin* of European Communities, 1/1973, 4 January 1973, p. 2113.
112. *Bulletin* of the European Communities, 15/1973, 8 November 1973.
113. *Bulletin* of the European Communities, Supplement 8/75.
114. ETUC, *Report on Activities 1976–78*, op. cit., pp. 69–73, 'ETUC demands for company-law regulation on multinational group of companies', March 1976, *Supplement to Report on Activities, 1973–75*.

115. ECFTU 'Industrial and Economic Concentration', The Hague Conference, April 1969; ECFTU Düsseldorf Conference 1970, *ETUC Archives*.
116. Ibid., pp. 65–68 ETUC *Objectives*, 1976–79, Brussels, April 1976, pp. II 1–5.
117. Piehl, Ernst, op. cit., pp. 249–260.
118. ICFTU, 'The Multinational Corporations', Brussels, 1971, statement by H. Maier, assistant secretary-general of the ICFTU to the hearings of the Sub-committee of Foreign Economic Policy of the US Senate, *ICFTU Economic and Social Bulletin*, no. 5, Brussels, August 1970; ICFTU, *Report 1972*, pp. 573–4.
119. ICFTU, *Trade Unions and the Transnationals*, Handbook for Negotiations, Brussels, November 1979, pp. 16–30.
120. Peter Gloystein, unter Mitarbeit von Kurt Wand, 'Europäische Industriepolitik—Die Schaffung neuer Dimensionen für Märkt und Unternehmen', in *Europäische Wirtschaftspolitik*, Programm und Realität, Bonn, Europea Union Verlag, 1973, pp. 379–80.
121. ETUC, *Action Programme*, Brussels, 1974.
122. Jung, Koubek, Schiebe-Lange, op. cit., pp. 295–6; see also, ETUC Executive Committee, 29–30 November, 1979, 'Rules for Business Takeovers', *Supplement to the Report on Activities*, 1979–81, Fourth Statutory Congress, The Hague, 19–23 April 1982, pp. 101–3.
123. ETUC, 'European Action Programme—Multinational Groups of Companies', June 1977, *Supplement to the Report on Activities*, 1976–78, Third Statutory Congress, Munich, 14–18 May 1979, p. 79; see also, Ernst Piehl, op. cit., p. 297.
124. Commission des Communautés Européennes, *Etudes*, 'Problèmes et perspectives de la négociation collective dans les pays membres de la Communauté', Série Politique Sociale no. 40, Brussels, 1979.
125. EG *Information*, Europäische Dokumentation, 'Eine grössere Rolle des europäischen Arbeitnehmens im Unternehmen', 3/1977, Brussels, 1977, pp. 6–8.
126. Karl H. Pitz, 'Internationale Tarifverhandlungen: der falsche Weg', *WSI—Mitteilungen*, 4/75, pp. 203–6.
127. P. Hoffman, A. Langwieler, *Noch sind wir da*, Hamburg, 1974. Ernst Piehl, 'Internationale Gewerkschaftssolidaritat gegen multinationale Kapitalstrategie am Beispiel des AKZO-Konzern, I und II', *Das Mitbestimmungsgespräch*, nos. 5 and 6, 7/1973, pp. 84 ff and p. 102ff. Dieter Kretschmer, 'Internationale Kampfmassnahmen gegen Multinationale Konzerne am Beispiel von AKZO', *WSI—Mitteilungen* 4/75.
128. Brian Groom, 'Multinationals turn the tables', *Financial Times*, 12 March 1985.
129. *Bulletin* of the European Communities, Supplement 8/1970.
130. ECFTU, 'Industrial and Economic Concentration', op. cit. G. Lyon-Caen, 'Beitrag zu den Möglichkeiten der Vertretung der Interessen der Arbeitnehmer in der Europäischen Aktiengesellschaft', EG Kommission no. 6, 974/XIV/69-D; *Das Mitbestimmungsgespräch*, 5–6/70.
131. Resolution, 'Refus d'intégration', 'Rapport au Congrès Extraordinaire', *Extraordinary Congress of the FGTB*, Brussels, 29–31 January 1971.
132. Frank Deppe, ed. *Arbeiterbewegung und westeuropäische Integration*, Cologne, Pahl Rugenstein Verlag 1976, p. 308; André Gorz, 'Workers' control is more than just that', in *Worker's Control*, Gerry Hunnis, G. David Carson and John Case (eds), New York, Vintage Books, 1973, p. 325.
133. Ernest Mandel, 'The Debate on Workers' Control', Ibid., pp. 344, 345.
134. FGTB, Resolution, 'Transformation de la Société', *FGTB* Congress, Brussels, 1971.
135. Updated Comments of the ETUC, 'Democratisation of the Economy and the Institutions', Committee on the '5th Directive on the structure of limited companies

and workforce representation bodies in the company law of the European Community' in *The Position of the European Trade Union Confederation (ETUC) and of the European Commission (EC) with regard to Multinational groups of companies*, Documentation, Brussels, March 1981, p. 16.

136. *Official Journal*, of the EEC, No. L48/29, 22 February 1975.
137. Ibid., No. L61/26, 5 March 1977, and No. L283/23, 20 October 1980.
138. Ibid., No. L65/815 March 1977.
139. Ibid., No. L26/1, 31 January 1977.
140. Ibid., No. L295/36, 20 October 1978.
141. Ibid., No. L378/47, 31 December 1982.
142. Ibid., No. L222/11, 14 August 1978; L193/1, 18 July 1983; L125/20, 12 May 1984.
143. Commission of the European Communities, *Company Law in the Community*, Brussels, February 1985, pp. 5, 6.
144. Commission of the European Communities, 'Proposal for a Council directive on procedures for informing and consulting employees of undertakings with complex structures, in particular transnational undertakings'. *Bulletin of the European Communities*, Supplement 3/80. A 'transnational' firm is defined as 'an undertaking whose decision-making centre is located in another member state or in a non-member country'. (Ibid., Art. 1.) An undertaking of 'complex structure' is defined as one which has 'several establishments, or one of more subsidiaries, in a single member state and where its decision-making centre is located in the same member state', (Ibid., Art. 1). This proposal is also known as the 'Vredeling initiative' or 'Vredeling Directive', named after the Dutch commissioner who launched it in 1980.
145. *Financial Times*, 17 September 1982.
146. 'Proposal . . . on procedures for informing . . .', op. cit., Art. 5, point 2.
147. Ibid., Art. 5, point 4.
148. Ibid., Art. 6, point 1.
149. Ibid., Art. 6, point 4.
150. Ibid., Art. 8. see also Ernst Piehl, 'Information und Konsultation—die 'Multi-Rightlinie' der EG', *EG Magazin*, January 1981, pp. 21–3.
151. *Neue Zürcher Zeitung*, 3 December 1981.
152. 'Proposal . . .', op. cit., Art. 8.
153. *Official Journal* of the Communities, no. L48/29, 22 February 1975.
154. Ibid., No. L61/26, 5 March 1977.
155. 'Die Positionen des EGB . . .', op. cit., pp. 19–31.
156. Communautés Européennes, Parlement Européen 1982–83. 'Procès-Verbal' de la séance du mardi, 12 octobre 1982. Intervention de Mr. H. O. Vetter.
157. European Parliament, Debates of the 1982-3 Session, Reports of Proceedings from 13–17 September 1982, no. 1–288/64.
158. Comité Economique et Social, *Avis du CES sur la 'Proposition de directive sur l'information et la consultation des travailleurs des entreprises à structure complexe, en particulier transnationale'*, Brussels, 27 January 1982.
159. ETUC Communiqué de presse, 3/82, *Directive Multi's: Les représentants du capital battus au Comité économique et social*, Brussels, March 1982.
160. Communautés Européennes, Parliament Européen, Documents de séance, 1982–83, 12 July 1982, Doc. 1–324/82/B.
161. Communautés Européennes. Parlement Européen, 1982–83, 'Procès-Verbal' de la séance du mardi 12 octobre 1982, PE 80.534.
162. Ibid., Art. 10.
163. ETUC, 'Recommendations with respect to the current deliberations of the 'Vredeling Directive' following the Opinion issued by the European Parliament', ETUC Secretariat, 1, 2 March, 1983. *ETUC Archives*.

164. Parlement Européen, 'Procès-Verbal', 12 octobre 1982, Art. 5. See also, *European Report*, 16 October 1982, no. 897.
165. Parlement Européen, op. cit., Art. 5 and Art. 15.
166. Interview with Ernst Piehl, political secretary of the ETUC.
167. Commission of the European Communities, 'Mr. Richard's Statement to the European Parliament', Employee Information and Consultation Procedures, 17 November 1982.
168. Commission of the European Communities, *Amended Proposal for a Council Directive on procedures for informing and consulting employees*, Brussels, 9 January 1984, Art. 4.
169. ETUC Executive Committee, 'Verbatim Record', 13–14 October 1983, Brussels, *ETUC Archives; ETUC Position on the EC Commission's amended proposal for a directive on 'procedures for informing and consulting employees'*, Adopted by the Executive Committee, Brussels, 14 October 1983.
170. *Report on the European Institution*, presented by the Committee of Three to the European Council, October 1979. The 'Committee of Three' or 'Committee of the Wise Men', was formed by Barend Biesheuvel, Edmund Dell and Robert Marjolin, and invited by the European Council 'to consider the adjustments to the machinery and the procedures for the Institutions which are required for the proper operation of the Communities on the basis of and in compliance with the Treaties . . .', ibid., Annex 1, p. 110.
171. ETUC, *ETUC Position on the 'Report on the European Institutions Presented by the Committee of Three to the European Council'*, Brussels, June 1980.
172. ETUC, Third Statutory Congress, *Report of Proceedings*, Munich, 14–18 May 1979, pp. 47–9.
173. ETUC Executive Committee Meeting, June 1984, in Geneva, 'Verbatim Record', Brussels, *ETUC Archives*.
174. ETUC *Statement on the European Union*, Brussels, December 1984.
175. ETUC, *Position on the Report on the European Institutions*, op. cit.; see also, ETUC *Statement on the European Union*, op. cit.
176. ETUC, *Position on the Report n the European Institutions*, op. cit.
177. ETUC, *Reform of the Community Institutions*, Brussels, 9 August 1983.
178. ETUC, Executive Committee, 2–3 April 1981, Working Document, *ETUC Archives*; see also, ETUC Resolution adopted by the Executive Committee 8–9 October 1981 on the Budget of the European Community, Brussels, October 1981, *ETUC Archives*

Chapter 6
Conclusion

The West European labour movement has come a long way in its political and ideological evolution. Since its inception in the nineteenth century until the Second World War, it had hovered between varying degrees of global internationalism and nationalism. While internationalism mirrored international solidarity, with different forms of political manifestations, including membership of ideologically-oriented labour Internationals, national concern was primarily focused on improving material standards of the working class—within the national frontiers of each state.

Since the end of the World War, however, labour's focus has shifted to regionalism. This evolution can be attributed to two major developments in Europe. First of all, there was the inauguration of a process of European integration. Though it had some historical roots that went back to the thirties and even earlier, it had acquired considerable force and urgency only at the advent of the cold war. Many West Europeans began to turn to the idea that some of the uncertainties, generated by Soviet expansionism in Eastern Europe, could be effectively contained by viable European integration.

The West European trade unions did not ignore this new and ongoing political process. Having been severely victimized by fascist regimes before the War, and having witnessed the massive destructiveness inflicted by the War itself, they strongly supported integrative movements in the hope that they would provide the appropriate guarantee for political stability and peace in the region.

The second development was economic. The increased freedom of capital movements and the internationalization of production processes had created a totally new situation, making it less and less possible to seek economic solutions within national frameworks. The phenomenon of economic interdependence, accelerated by technological progress, increased the need for an intensified economic interaction in the region. The West European trade unions could hardly turn a blind eye to such processes. In fact, they did not. Through the years, they had also become firm supporters of economic integration as the first step on the road towards political union.

The importance of this trend can be gauged from the fact that even some of the Communist-orientated trade unions, long adversaries of integration, finally came to the idea of supporting European integration and the EEC.

The West European labour movement thus had become more attentive to West European problems, and its new converging point was the European Community. The most important manifestation of this attitude was the establishment of the ETUC, the principal objective of which is to represent trade-union interests and to safeguard and ameliorate social achievements at the European level. But this projection on to the European scene necessitated the introduction of certain innovations in the organizational and functional frameworks of the new European trade-union organization.

At the organizational level, the early phase of the ETUC's existence was thus devoted to the task of accelerating the process of trade-union unification in order to overcome existing barriers between West European trade unions. The process of unification was, however, not totally completed—the French CGT and the Spanish CCOO were refused admission to the ETUC. This may be attributed to an increasing trend towards pragmatism within the European labour movement, which has generally abandoned class struggle and ideologically inspired rhetoric for reform-orientated policies.

At the functional level, the change was really important. Realizing the impossibility of extrapolating the behaviour of its national confederates at the regional level, where the circumstances were different from those prevailing within the national states, the ETUC constituted itself into a pressure group whose main activity was that of pragmatic interaction with the established Community institutions.

This was by no means an easy task, since it involved the accomplishment of some degree of cohesiveness from the existing myriad of national backgrounds and socio-political conceptions. The credibility and the effectiveness of the European labour movement as a pressure group were largely dependent on its ability to develop common policies that could be defended at the European level. The ETUC can be considered to have been successful in this task. It was able to conceive common positions on a wide array of subjects which were supported by thirty organizations from twenty countries. During the last few years it has furthermore been able to mobilize workers from Community countries for demonstrations and manifestations in support of ETUC positions.

But this type of activity is only a minor part of trade union action. In fact, it is largely superseded by a new behaviour pattern carried out by a new type of specialized personnel. The increasingly complex and technical nature of proposals in the areas of social and economic policies require a high degree of expertise, so as to be able to debate effectively with the Community and to be able to present trade union positions cogently.

As a pressure group the ETUC had established a wide network of national, European, formal and informal communication channels to influence Community policies. Most of them have been dealt with in the body of this study. Suffice it to say here that the ETUC's most regular and institutionalized interaction was with the Commission and that its most formal and superficial interaction was with the Council. This is principally due to their different functions and orientations.

Since most of the initial and basic groundwork on social issues is done by the Commission, the ETUC considered it imperative to begin the process of interaction at an early stage in order to influence the orientations of social policies from the very beginning. The Commission, in turn, was convinced of the usefulness of such a strategy, since it was naturally expedient to involve the trade-union organization for effective handling of the social issues. Besides, such interaction probably strengthened the hand of the Commission in its dealings with the Council.

How effective is the ETUC's role within the Community? Has it become an integrative force? Has it been able to influence the Community's policies? Or has its role been only marginal?

The answers to these questions can only be tentative. While ETUC's achievements are neither striking nor spectacular, it has nevertheless been able to exercise influence on many aspects of Community policies. It has successfuly pushed through a number of reforms of consultative institutions, thereby increasing its own impact on the EEC decision-making process. In many instances it has been able to incorporate its views on the Commission's proposals and has strongly influenced consultative bodies' opinions. Also, it has exercised considerable influence on social policies in the Community and has contributed substantially to the further development of such policies within the Common Market. Moreover, the ETUC's consistently held views that social problems and policies cannot be separated from the wider framework of economic and financial policies has also gained greater acceptability than before. Earlier reluctance about common consultations between economic, social and financial authorities at the EEC level has thus largely been overcome.

Notwithstanding these achievements the ETUC's impact on some of the basic issues facing the Community has not been very strong. In spite of its ability to reach cohesive policy positions on many aspects of EEC policies, it is handicapped at the Euroepan Secretariat level by too strong a dependence, both conceptionally and operationally, on its affiliated organizations. Its financial means are limited. Its capacities to increase manpower and expertise on the European forum are limited and its area of jurisdiction remains restricted. It can be wondered whether the involvement of ETUC beyond the geographical frontiers of the European Community has not diluted its capacity to play a more viable role as a pressure group within the Community. A reinforcement of its structures at the Community level might enable the ETUC to remove some of the national reins and instill a new momentum of social integration into the Community.

But even more important than all this is the fact that Europe's difficult economic situation has made a very negative impact on labour's position at the national and European levels. Due to rampant unemployment, the ETUC's dialogue with the Community's main decision-maker, the Council, as well as with its direct social partner, the employers, has become increasingly difficult, if not fruitless. On the one hand, the social and economic views and the solutions put forward by the labour movement are directly opposite to those advanced by the governments. The latter, instead of following the ETUC's prescriptions for the revival of economic activities targeted towards the removal of unemployment, have tended to pursue neo-liberal policies with a particular focus on austerity.

The employers, on the other hand, have been stressing the necessity to improve their national and international competitiveness, which they conider to have been severely hampered by high labour and social costs. Social welfare has come under serious attack, and material and human achievements obtained by the labour movement after decades of struggle are in serious jeopardy.

At both the European and national levels, labour has thus been forced into a defensive position. The continuous increase in unemployment—with the ensuing loss in membership, particularly among the traditionally unionized core workers within the 'classical' industries—has weakened the unions' position as a bargaining partner, and has led them to direct their demands more and more towards governments and European institutions. At this level, however, their voice, more often than not, remains unheard or is countered by claims for less government intervention and increased *laissez-faire*.

Whether or not the present crisis of the European labour movement, as to many before, is only a cyclical one and whether or not it will be overcome in due course, depends on many factors, including the viability of the Western European industrial and economic system. Its ability to find new conceptions and structures for industrial relations at the national and European levels will be crucial. Whatever may be the answer to this question, for the first time in history labour is endowed with a European dimension which, in spite of its shortcomings, has to be reckoned with.

Bibliography

Part I—sources

A Unpublished documents

1 ETUC—Archives

(i) ETUC—Executive Committee Minutes and Verbatim Records

1973: 4 May; 28 September
1974: 24–25 January
1975: 6 February; 1 December
1976: 9–10 December
1977: 21 January; 10–11 February; 21–22 April
1978: 13–14 April; 29 September; 29–30 November
1979: 20 September
1980: 12–13 June; 7–8 October
1981: 8–9 October; December
1982: 30 September–1 October; 9–10 December
1983: 9–10 June, 13–14 October
1984: 10 June

(ii) Memoranda and reports

ECFTU, 'Industrial and Economic Concentration', the Hague conference, April 1969.
ECFTU, Comité Exécutif du 5 juillet 1969, 'Procès-verbal', Point IV.3.
ECFTU, 'Düsseldorf conference', 1970.
CESL–OE–CMT Aide Mémoire, 'An den Ministerrat für soziale Angelegenheiten gerichtetes Aide-Mémoire des EBFG und der EO–WVA über die Errichtung eines europäischen Rates für die Beschäftigung, vom 25. und 26, Mai 1970'.
CESL–OE–CMT, 'Suggestion sur le renforcement de la collaboration entre la CESL et l'OE–CMT suite à la rencontre commune du 21 octobre 1970'. Brussels, 24 April 1971.
Sandegren, Kaare (Secretary of EFTA–TUC), 'Points on future trade union cooperation in Europe', 8 December 1971.
CESL–OE–CMT, 'Note sur la réunion des représentants CESL–OE–CMT à la Haye, le 5 février, 1972', Brussels, 8 February 1972.
CESL, Comité Exécutif du 17 février 1972, 'Procès-Verbal'.
CESL, Comité Exécutif du 30 novembre–1 décembre 1972, 'Procès-verbal'.
Coldrick, Peter, 'The Likely Development of TUC Attitudes Towards the EEC', March 1972.
'Bericht über TUC Kongress', 17 March 1972.
CESL–EFTA–TUC Working Group on Extended European Trade Union Cooperation, note, 'Summary of the discussions in the CESL–EFTA–TUC Working Group, Comments on Points of Divergence, and Proposals on a Statute for a European Trade Union Organization', Brussels, 19 April 1972.
'Report of the Working Group ECFTU–EFTA–TUC for the extension of European trade union cooperation', Brussels, 19 April 1972.

'Report of the Working Group ECFTU–EFTA–TUC for the extension of European trade union cooperation to the Meeting of Western Europe Trade Union Leaders', Geneva, 6 June 1972'.

CESL, Comité Exécutif, 'Procès-Verbal', Geneva, 6 June 1972.

'Notes of ECFTU Secretariat on Meeting of Trade Union Leaders of Western Europe', Luxembourg, 4 October 1972. *ETUC Archives*.

ECFTU–EFTA–TUC, 'Verbatim Record', Meeting of Western Europe Trade Union Leaders in Geneva, 6 June 1972.

Notes by ETUC secretary-general on Luxembourg meeting, 4 October 1972.

ECFTU, 'Notes for the Meeting of 16 European National Trade Union Confederations', 4 October 1972, Luxembourg'.

Note on telephone call by Victor Feather to the Scandinavian Confederation and the DGB on 7 November 1972.

Statement by H. O. Vetter to Luxembourg conference, 30 November 1972.

ECFTU–Secretariat, 'Notes on the Luxembourg conference, 30 November–1 December 1972'.

ECFTU–EFTA–TUC, Note, 'Problems in Connection with Future Trade-Union Cooperation in Europe', Luxembourg, 30 November–1 December, 1972, Annex I.

Note by ECFTU secretary-general on Luxembourg conference, 30 November–1 December 1972, Brussels, 8 December 1972.

ETUC, 'Comité Economique et Social: Le fonctionnement et la participation', Brussels, 27 February 1973.

ETUC Secretariat, 'Notes concernant les problèmes qui se posent dans la perspective de l'admission des Confédérations nationales, membres de l'OE–CMT et de la CES', Brussels, 3 April 1973.

ETUC Executive Committee, Rome, 18 June 1973, Item 3 on Agenda: 'Acceptance of the Industry Committees'.

ETUC Executive Committee Meeting, 28 September 1973, 'Report and Conclusions of the ETUC–EO–WCL Meeting of 12 July 1973.'

'Note sur l'entretien entre délégations de la CES et CGIL, Londres, le 20 novembre 1973', 4 December 1973.

ETUC, 'Rapport Debunne au Groupe II du Comité économique et social', 3 January 1974.

'Report on the Second Meeting between a delegation from the ETUC and the CGIL', ETUC, 3 March 1974.

OE–CMT, 'Déclaration du Comité exécutive', Brussels, 29 March 1974.

CES, Comité Exécutif, 'Rapport sur la troisième rencontre entre une délégation de la CES et une délégation de la CGIL, Bruxelles, 10 avril 1974', Brussels, 9 May 1974.

ETUC, Finance and General Purposes Committee, 30 September 1976, 'Minutes'.

ETUC, 'Memorandum on Industry Committees', Brussels, 5 November 1976.

ETUC Executive Committee, Brussels, 10–11 February 1977, Point 6 on the Agenda: 'L'emploi et la situation économique, Rapport du Comité Permanent de l'Emploi du 13 décembre 1976'.

ETUC, Executive Committee, Statement on the Elections of the European Parliament by Direct Universal Suffrage, Brussels, April 1977.

ETUC, 'Proposals on Voting Rights for Migrant Workers', Brussels, 4 April 1977.

ETUC, Executive Committee, Geneva 29–30 September 1977, 'Report on the Meeting of the Steering Group on 4 September 1977'.

ETUC, 'Projet complémentaire à la déclaration du Comité économique et social', Brussels, 9 September 1977.

ETUC, Executive Committee, 29–30 September 1977, Point 6 on the Agenda: 'Déclaration de la CES pour la relance et en meilleur fonctionnement du Comité Permanent de l'emploi', Geneva, 29–30 September 1977.

'Summary of the internal discussions held at the meeting of the trade-union press group', Luxembourg, 3–4 November 1977.

ETUC, Executive Committee, Brussels, 9–10 February 1978, 'Report on the Meeting with the Economic Policy Committee', January 1978.

ETUC, Statement of the ETUC Executive Committee, 28 September 1979, Annex: 'Working Document on Employment, Economic Development and Energy'.

ETUC, 'Memorandum on Admission Requests', Brussels, 18 February 1980.

ETUC, Position on the 'Report on the European Institutions Presented by the Committee of Three to the European Council', Brussels, June 1980.

ETUC, 'Memorandum on Frontier Workers', Brussels, 1981.

ETUC, Executive Committee Meeting, Brussels, 12–13 February 1981. Agenda: 'ETUC Campaign Against Unemployment'.

ETUC, 'Memorandum of 13 March 1981 to Finance and General Purposes Committee'.

ETUC, Executive Committee, 2–3 April 1981, 'Working Document'.

'Report by the ETUC Secretariat', Brussels, 31 August 1981.

ETUC, 'Resolution adopted by the Executive Committee, 8–9 October 1981, on the Budget of the European Community', Brussels, October 1981.

ETUC, Executive Committee, Geneva, 10 November 1982, Point 7 of the Agenda: 'ETUC position on the reform of the European Social Fund'.

ETUC, Executive Committee, 'Communication of the Secretariat', Brussels, 9–10 December 1982.

The ETUC Standing Employment Committee, 19–20 May 1983, 'Comments on the Commission's Document 'The Promotion of Employment for Young People'', Brussels, 18 May 1983.

ETUC, 'Note sur les différentes rencontres avec les gouvernements dans le cadre de la campagne CES pour l'emploi', Executive Committee Meeting, Brussels, 19 February 1983.

ETUC, 'Reform of the Community Institutions', Brussels, 9 August 1983.

ETUC, 'Position on the EC Commission's Proposal for a Directive on Procedures for informing and consulting employees', Adopted by the Executive Committee, Brussels, 14 October 1983.

ETUC, 'Statement on the European Union', Brussels, December 1984.

ETUC, 'Guidelines for the past and future cooperation amongst the ITUCs, the confederations concerned and the ETUC Executive Committee', Brussels, 15–16 December 1983.

ETUC, Executive Committee, Agenda Item 10: 'Information on the Inter-Regional Trade-Union Councils (ITUC) in the ETUC', Brussels, 15–16 December 1983.

ETUC, File on Industry Committees, January 1984.

(iii) Correspondence

Letter from the CESL, OE–CMT and UNICE to the president of the Council, Brussels, 9 May 1968.

Letter from the EO–CMT and the CESL to the president of the Council, Brussels, 18 October 1968.

Letter from T. Rasschaert, ETUC Secretary-general, to the president of the Council of Ministers, Brussels, 7 January 1971.

Letters from CGT to ETUC, 21 January 1974 and 23 August 1974.

Letter from the CISL and the UIL to the ICFTU, 29 April 1974.

Letter from H. O. Vetter, 3 July 1974, to members of the ETUC Executive Board concerning decisions of 2 July 1974 by the DGB Federation Executive Committee: that the debate about admission of the CGIL should be adjourned until the question of affiliation to the WFTU had been cleared.

Letter from G. Seguy, to H. O. Vetter, 29 August 1974.

Letters from CCOO to Victor Feather, president of the ETUC, 20 February 1973 and to H. O. Vetter, president of the ETUC, 30 May 1975.

Letter from the ETUC general secretary to the members of the ETUC Executive Committee, 18 July 1975.

Letter from H. O. Vetter to François-Xavier Ortoli, 3 March 1976, and to Gaston Thorn, 3 March 1976.

Letter from ETUC secretary general to general secretary of the CGT, 4 October 1976.

Letter to Commission vice-president Vredeling from the ETUC general-secretary, Brussels, 14 February 1978.

Letters from Marcelino Camancho, secretary-general and Serafine Aliaga, international relations secretary of CCOO to the ETUC Executive Committee, July 1978.

Letter from George Seguy to M. Hinterscheid, secretary-general of the ETUC, 28 September 1978.

Letter from M. Hinterscheid to H. O. Vetter, 11 October 1978.

Letter from A. Bergeron to all ETUC affiliates, 10 January 1979.

Letter to the president of the Commission from the ETUC general secretary, Brussels, 28 February 1979.

Letter from G. Debunne to the chairman of the ESC, Brussels, 9 November 1979.

Letter from the CGT to the ETUC, 16 January 1980.

Letter from the the the general secretary of the Council to the ETUC general secretary, Brussels, 18 February 1980, Annex I: 'Improvement of relations with the two sides of industries in the context of the Tripartite Conferences'.

Letter from Manuel Simon, UGT secretary for international relations, to Mathias Hinterscheid, ETUC general secretary, 23 May 1980.

Letter from the ETUC to the CGT, 23 June 1980.

Lettre du CCOO à toutes les centrales affiliées à la CES, Madrid, 9 September 1981, *CCOO International Informations*, Madrid, December 1981.

Letter from the UGT to all ETUC affiliates, 15 September 1981.

Letter from the UGT to the CCOO, Madrid, 10 October 1981; letter from the STV to the CCOO, Madrid, 17 November 1981.

Letter from the CCOO to the UGT and the STV, Madrid, 26 October 1981, CCOO *International Informations*, Madrid, December 1981.

Letter from the UGT to ETUC Secretariat, 5 May 1982.

2 ICFTU Archives

'Declaration—The European Recovery Programme and the Trade Unions', International Trade Union Conference, 1 March 1948; 2 July 1948.

ICFTU, 'European Regional Conference', Brussels, 1–4 November 1950.

European Regional Organization of the ICFTU, 'Report on the European Trade Union Conference for the Revival of the European Idea', Brussels, August 1955.

ICFTU–ERO, 'Observations Relative to the Draft European Market Treaty submitted to the President for the Ministerial Committee by the Free Trade Union Organization of the Community', Brussels, 30 January 1957.

IBFG, *Tätigkeitsbericht 1964–65*, 'Europäisches Aktionsprogramm', Brussels, 1966.

ICFTU Tenth World Congress, London, July 1972, 'Extraits de discours concernant l'organisation syndicale européenne'.

ICFTU, 'Extracts from Proceedings at the Sixty-first Executive Board Meeting', Brussels, 31 May 1974.

B Published documents

1 ETUC

(i) Reports and statements

Report on Activities, 1973–75;
Supplement to Report on Activities, 1973–75.
Report of Proceedings of the Second Statutory Congress held at Congress House, Great Russell Street, London on 22–24 April 1976.
ETUC *Objectives 1976–79*, approved by the Second Statutory Congress, London, 22–24 April 1976.
Report on Activities 1976–78, Third Statutory Congress, Munich, 14–18 May 1979.
Supplement to Report on Activities, 1976–78.
Third Statutory Congress, Report of Proceedings, Munich, 14–18 May 1979.
Report on Activities, 1979–81, Fourth Statutory Congress, The Hague, 19–23 April 1982.
Supplement to Report on Activities, 1979–81.
General Resolution and Specific Resolutions 1982–85, approved by the Fourth Statutory Congress, The Hague, 19–23 April 1982.
Action Programme, General Resolution and Specific Resolutions, 1979–82.
Report on Activities, 1982–84, Fifth Statutory Congress, Milan, 13–17 May 1985.
Supplement to Report on Activities, 1982–84.
CESL–EFTA–TUC, press release: 'Déclaration des représentants syndicaux européens réunis à Oslo les 5 et 6 novembre 1971'.
'Statement on Unemployment and Inflation', *ETUC Objectives, 1979–79*, Brussels, 1976.
Objective première de la CES: Le plein emploi, Brussels, 1 April 1976.
'European Action Programme—Multinational Groups of Companies' (June 1977), *Supplement to Report on Activities, 1976–78.*
'The European Action Day and the Outcome of the Action Taken', (Brussels, April 1978), *Supplement to Report on Activities, 1976–78.*
'Executive Committee Resolution on the Reduction of Working Hours', (April 1977) *Supplement to Report on Activities*, 1976–78.
ETUC, *Statement of European Trade Union Confederation to Social and Economic Conference*, Luxembourg, 24 June 1976.
Statement by the Executive Committee on the Current Economic Situation, Brussels, December 1976.
'ETUC demands for company law regulations on multinational groups of companies', March 1976. *Supplement to Report on Activities, 1973–75.*
Secure Employment—Guarantee Income; position of the European Trade Union Confederation, tripartite conference: economic and social situation in the Community and prospects, Brussels, 18 November 1975.
ETUC, *Tripartite Economic and Social Conference: A conference which must be followed up*, Brussels, 19 November 1975.
ETUC *Constitution*, Brussels, May 1974.
Coldrick, Peter, 'European Tripartite Conferences', ETUC, Brussels, 14 March 1977.
ETUC, *Initial proposals relating to the economic situation, employment and income in Europe*, Brussels, April 1977.
Tripartite Conference on 'Growth, Stability and Employment, Stock-taking and Prospects', Brussels, 21 June 1977.
Vetter, H. O., Erklärung zur dreigliedrigen Konferenz über 'Wachstum, Stabilität und

Beschäftigung: Bestandaufnahme und Aussichten', Luxembourg, 27 June 1977, mimeographed.

ETUC, *Statement for preparations of Bremen European Council*, Brussels, April, 1978.

ETUC statement to the press on *Results of 1978 ripartite Conference*, Brussels, 13 November 1978.

ETUC *Information Documents*, 'Elections of the European Parliament by direct universal suffrage', 1979.

ETUC's eight points on employment and the new microelectronic technology (ETUC statement to the Standing Committee on Employment, February 1980), *Supplement to the Report on Activities, 1979–81*.

'Concerted Action Programme for Economic Recovery (statement for EFTA twentieth anniversary and for the European Council, June 1980), *Supplement to Report on Activities, 1979–81*.

ETUC, 'Failure in Stockholm and Venice', (June 1980) *Supplement to the Report on Activities, 1979–81*.

ETUC assesses outcome of European Council meeting (Luxemboug, 29–30 June 1981) *Supplement to Report on Activities, 1979–81*.

ETUC Executive Committee, 'Rules for Business Takeovers', *Supplement to Report on Activities 1979–81*.

Piehl, Ernst, 'Information und Konsultation—die 'Multi-Richtlinie' der EG', *EG Magazin*, January 1981.

Piehl, Ernst, 'Europäische Gewerkschaften arbeiten immer mehr in Grenzregionen zusammen', Brussels, October 1982, Mimeographed.

'ETUC meets Jumbo Council President', Brussels, 15 November 1982.

Piehl, Ernst, *Die Reform des Europäischen Sozialfonds*, Brussels, 1983, Mimeographed.

(ii) ETUC Press Releases

'Erklärung zur Frage eines sozialen Aktionsprogrammes der Europäischen Gemeinschaft und damit zusammenhängende Bereiche', Brussels, 15 October 1973.

'ETUC and Socialist Leaders call for urgent action on unemployment', Brussels, 14 January 1981.

'ETUC Meeting with Thorn', Brussels, 26 January 1981.

ETUC Campaign: 'Progress Report No. 1', Brussels, 26 February 1981.

Updated comments of the ETUC, 'Democratization of the Economy and the Institutions', Committee on the '5th Directive on the structure of limited companies and workforce representation bodies in the company law of the European Community', in *The Federation of the European Trade Union Confederation (ETUC) and of the European Commission (EC) with regard to Multinational groups of Companies*, Documentation, Brussels, March 1981.

Campagne CES: 'Progress Report', No. 2, 12 March 1981.

'Maastrich Summit; Situation continues to deteriorate', Brussels, 26 March 1981.

'Preliminary Reactions to the "Jumbo Council"', Brussels, 16 June 1981.

March 1982, 'Directive Multi's: Les représentants du capital battus au Comité économique et social'.

'Stuttgart, 4 June 1983: 80,000 demonstrators for employment', Brussels, 26 May 1983.

'Address by George Debunne, ETUC president'; 'Address by Mathias Hinterscheid, ETUC general secretary'; 'Address by Ernst Breit, ETUC vice-president and DGB president'; 'Address by S. Pommerenke, president of DGB Baden-Würtenberg';–Stuttgart, 4 June 1983.

European Summit in Stuttgart, 'Irresponsible', Brussels, 20 June 1983.

'Vorbereitung des Athener Gipfels; bei den wesentlichen Problemen keine Fortschritte', Brussels, 25 November 1983.

'Zusammenkunft zwischen Papanderou und Debunne; der Rat in Athen muss erfolgreich sein', Brussels, 25 November 1983.

'Der Athener Gipfel erschüttert zutiefst das Vertrauen der Arbeitnehmer', Brussels, 6 December 1983.

2 International trade-union organizations

ICFTU, *Congress Reports*,
    1949; 1951; 1953; 1955; 1957; 1959;
    1962; 1965; 1969; 1972; 1975; 1979;

Schevenels, Walter, 'The ICFTU's European Regional Organisation', *Free Labour World*, Brussels, January 1954.

ICFTU, *Labour Management Relations in Western Europe*, Brussels, 1966.

ICFTU, 'Le mouvement syndical européen au sein de la CISL', série ' *Connaissance des faits*', CISL, Brussels, 1966, p. 140.

Cool, August, 'L'orientation des structures et de l'action du mouvement syndical dans une dimension européenne', *Rapport à la IVe Conférence Européenne des Syndicats Chrétiens*, Amsterdam, 6–8 October 1966. Brussels, OE–WCL, October 1966.

Ford, Charles, *The Rule of Trade Unions in the Economic Development of Europe*, CISL, Brussels, 1966.

EO–WCL Congress, 7–9 May 1969, *Résolution Générale*.

EO–WCL, 'Die Stellung der Arbeitnehmer in einem sich verändern den Europa', *Tätig-keitsbericht des Ersten Kongresses*, Brussels, 7–10 May 1969.

'La Confédoration Mondiale du Travail', Unité dans la Diversité, *Labor*, nos. 3–4, 1970.

ICFTU, 'Multinational Corporations', Statement by H. Maier, assistant secretary-general of the ICFTU to the Hearings of the Sub-Committee of Foreign Economic Policy of the US Senate, *ICFTU Economic and Social Bulletin*, no. 5, Brussels, August 1970.

Europäischer Bund der Freien Gewerkschaften in der Gemeinschaft, 'Der EBFG gegenüber den Umwandlungen der Gemeinschaft', Toulouse, 8–9 October 1971.

EBFG, *Der EBFG gegenüber den Umwandlunger der Gemeinschaft*, Jahresversammlung 1971, Toulouse, 8–9 October 1971.

OE–CMT, Comité Exécutif du 22 et 23 mars 1973, *communiqué de presse*.

ICFTU, *Trade Unions and the Transnationals*, handbook for negotiations, Brussels, November 1979.

3 National Trade Unions

Rosenberg, Ludwig, 'Eine Idee beschäftigt die Welt', *Gewerkschaftliche Monatshefte*, 6/1950.

'Programmation nationale et progammation Communautaire dans les pays de la CEE', texte de l'intervention prononcée par A. Novella, secrétaire-général de la CGIL à la conférence organisée par le Conseil National de l'Economie et du Travail (CNEL), 2 December 1962.

Bulletin d'information de la CGIL, 'Précisions de la CGIl sur les buts de sa politique européenne', January 1964.

'Thèmes pour le VIe Congrès de la CGIL (Italie): Politique syndicale internationale', Bologne, 31 March–4 April 1965.

Brenner, Otto, 'Die Aufgaben der Gewerkschaftsbewegung in einem integrierten Europa', in Brenner, *Gewerkschaftliche Dynamik in unsere Zeit*, Frankfurt, 1966.

Brenner, Otto, 'Für ein Grundsatzprogramm der europäischen Gewerkschaftsbewegung', *Gewerkschaftliche Monatshefte*, 8/1967.

Brenner, Otto, 'Bilanz und Perspektiven deur europäischen Integration', in Brenner, *Für eine bessere Welt*, Aufsätze zur Gewerkschaftspolitik, Frankfurt-on-Main, 1970.

Debunne, Schugens (ed.), *FGTB Congrès Contrôle Ouvrier*, Brussels, 1970.

Das Mitbestimmungsgespräch, 5–6/1970.

FGTB resolution, 'Transformation de la Société', *Extraordinary Congress of the FGTB*, 29–31 January 1971.

FGTB, 'Refus d'intégration', Rapport au Congrès Extraordinaire, *Extraordinary Congress of the FGTB*, Brussels, 29–31 January 1971.

Feather, Victor, 'Multinational Companies: The British Experience', *Free Labour World*, Brussels, May 1972.

Vetter, Heinz Oskar, 'Die Europäische Gewerkschaftsbewegung, 1972', *Die Neue Gesellschaft*, 1/72, p. 41.

Loderer, E. 'Bericht über den Londoner IBFG–Kongress', *Der Gewerkschafter*, 8/1972, July 1972.

Rosenberg, Ludwig, 'Die Verantwrotung der Gewerkschaften in einer zukunftigen Wirtschafts- und Währungsunion', (Sonderdruck), *Europa Archive*, 9/72.

Vetter, H. O., 'Zwanzig Jahre europäische Gewerkschaftspolitik', *Gewerkschaftliche Monatshefte*, 4/73.

CGT, *L'Europe des monopoles n'est pas l'Europe des travailleurs*, Paris, 21 May 1973.

'La CGT et les Firmes Multinationales', *Supplément au Journal Le Peuple*, Paris, 16/31 1973.

Lama, Servio, 'Basic Policy Statement', *VIII CGIL Congress*, Bari, July 1973.

VIII CGIL Congress, 'Political Resolution: International Relations', Bari, July 1973.

'CGIL Declaration to the Second Regional European Conference of the ILO, 19 January 1974'.

WFTU, Extraordinary meeting of the WFTU Council, Berlin, 28–29 January 1975. (German version): 'Die Verschärfung der Krise der Kapitalistischen Welt'.

'Free Labour World Interviews George Debunne', *Free Labour World*, June 1975.

CGT *39th Congress*, Le Bourget, 22–27 June 1976, 'Report by G. Seguy', Paris 1975.

DGB, 'Meinung zum Tindemans—Bericht', Düsseldorf, 2 March 1976.

'Développer notre action unitaire en Europe', report presented by Johannes Galland, *Le Peuple*, 15–30 June 1976.

DGB, Tenth Federal Congress, *Resolutions*, Düsseldorf, 1976.

Ströer Alfred, *Solidarität International*, Der ÖGB und die internationale Gewerkschaftsbewegung. Wien, Verlag des Österreichischen Gewerkschaftsbundes, 1977.

Interview with René Duhammel, CGT Secretary, in *L'Humanité*, 'La Richesse du Débat Fraternel', 28 November 1978.

IG-Metall, *Zusammenfassung der Probleme der Arbeitszeitverkürzung*, 1978.

Speech by George Seguy at the CGT meeting for the preparation of the fortieth congress in Grenoble from 26 November to 7 December 1978, in CGT *press release*, no. 30, October–November–December 1978.

CFDT-Information, *Les Syndicats dans le Monde*, Paris, Montholon-Services, 1979.

TUC, *The Reconstruction of Britain*, London, 1981.

CCOO Catalonia, *Second Regional Congress*, 'Resolution on International Affairs', Barcelona, February 1981.

CCOO Congress, 'Resolution on CCOO Affiliation to the ETUC and on the Common Market', Barcelona, 21 June 1981.

CCOO, *Informations Internationales*, Madrid, January–February 1982.

Federatie Nederlandse Vakbeweging (FNV), 'More Work', *FNV News*, Amsterdam 1982.
NFS–DGB, *It Pays to Cooperate*, October 1983.
Breit, Ernst, 'Arbeitszeitverkürzung–Der entscheidende Schritt voran muss gelingen', *Gewerkschaftliche Monatshefte*, 2/84.
Mayr, Hans, '38.5 Stunden–Das Tabu ist gebrochen', *Die Mitbestimmung*, 9/84.

4 European Communities

(i) The Commission

General Reports 1970–84
Les Problèmes de main d'oeuvre dans la Communauté en 1968, Brussels, 1968.
Lyon-Caen, G., 'Beitrag zu den Möglichkeiten der Vertretung der Interessen der Arbeit- nehmer in der Europäischen Aktiengesellschaft', EG Kommission, No. 7 974/XIV/69- D.
Memorandum der Kommission von 1970 zur Industriepolitik in der Gemeinschaft, Brussels, March 1970.
'Preliminary Guidelines for a Common Social Policy Programme', 17 March 1971, *EC Bulletin*, 1971, No. 4, Supplement 2/71.
Mitteilung der Kommission an den Rat vom 7. November 1973, 'Die Multinationalen Unternehmen und die Gemeinschaftvorschriften', 7 November 1973.
Social Action Programme, Brussels, 24 October 1973.
Tripartite Conferences, Economic and Social Stituation in the Community and Outlook, Brussels, 22 October 1975.

Trade-Union information, 1975–79.
Mitbestimmung der Arbeitnehmer und Struktur der Gesellschaften in der EG: Brüssel, 12.11.1975.
Note, 'Follow-up' der Dreierkonferenz auf Gemeinschaftsebene, Brussels, 22 June 1976.
Suites de la Conférence tripartite, Brussels, 24 November 1976.
A Community Strategy for Full Employment and Stability, Brussels, 2 April 1976.
Restoring Full Employment in the Community, Brussels, June 1976.
Annual Report on the Economic Situation in the Community, Brussels, 29 December 1976.
Le Programme de la Commission pour les Elections directes du Parlement européen, Brussels, March 1977.
Fourth Medium-term Economic Policy Programme, OJ No. L101, 25 April 1977.
Tripartite conference, 27 June 1977, 'Growth, Stability and Employment: Stock-taking and Prospects', Brussels, 23 May 1977.
Spreer, Frithjof, Vesper, Joachim, *Feasibility Studie über den Stand und die Entwicklung von vorausschauenden regionalen Arbeitsmarkt bilanzen in der Europäische Gemeinschaft*, Reihe Regionalpolitik, nr. 5, Brussels, 1979. (EG-Kommission).
Verbesserungen der Beziehungen zu den Sozialpartners im Rahmen der Dreierkonferenzen, (Mitteilung der Kommission an den Rat), Brussels, 26 April 1979.
'Problèmes et perspectives de la négociation collective dans les pays membres de la Communauté', (Série Politique Social, No. 40), Brussels, 1979.
European Economy, Special Issue, Report of the Group of Experts on Sectoral Analyses, 'Changes in industrial structure in the European economics since the oil crisis 1973– 78: Europe–its capacity to change in question!', Brussels, 1979.
Structural Change in the Community: Outlook for the 1980s, Brussels, December 1979.
Employment and New Microelectronics, Brussels, 1980.
'Proposal for a Council Directive on procedures for informing and consulting employees

of undertakings with complex structures, in particular transnational undertakings', *Bulletin of the European Communities, Supplement* 3/80.

'Directive on procedures for informing and consulting employees in undertakings with complex structures, in particular transnational undertakings', *Bulletin on the European Communities*, Supplement 3/1980.

'Le mandat du 30 mai 1980 et la relance européenne', *Le Dossier de l'Europe*, 16/81, October 1981.

'Mr. Richards' Statement to the European Parliament', Employee Information and Consultation Procedures, 17 November 1982.

Memorandum, 'Improved working methods of the Standing Committee on Employment: Problems and Prospects', Brussels, 1983.

Proposal for a Council Decision adopting the first European Strategic Programme for Research and Development in Information Technology, Brussels, 1983.

Draft Council Recommendation on the reduction of working time (submitted to the Council by the Commission), Brussels, 16 September 1983.

DG V, *Social Europe*, Supplement on Technological Change and Social Adjustment, Luxembourg, 1984.

The European Social Fund, a weapon against unemployment, Brussels, January 1984.

Amended Proposal for a Council Directive on procedures for informing and consulting employees, Brussels, 9 January 1984.

Company Law in the European Community, European File, Brussels, February 1985.

Eurostat, various issues.

(ii) The Council

Economic Programme for the 1960s, Brussels, 1968.

Communiqué à la presse, Brussels, 26 November 1970.

'*Note*: Schéma d'organisation du Comité Permanent de l'emploi des Communautés Européennes', Brussels, 3 December 1970.

Note: 'Objet: Opinions exprimées par les représentants des partenaires sociaux au sujet de l'avant projet de schéma du Comité permanent de l'emploi', Brussels, 3 December 1970.

Décision du 14 décembre 1970 portant sur la création du comité permanent de l'emploi des communautés européennes, *JO* no. L233/25.

Note 'Objet: Information du Comité permanent de l'emploi sur les décisions prises et les travaux effectués dans les domaines quo ont fait l'objet des discussions au sein du Comité', Brussels, 17 April 1972.

Memorandum by Chancellor Willi Brandt, 'Deutsche Initiative für Massnahmen zur Veröffentlichung einer europäischen Sozial und Gesellschafts politik', EC *Bulletin*, 20 October 1972.

Inventaire des Possibilités d'intervention sur le plan communautaire dans le domaine de l'emploi, 26 October 1972.

Note: 'Objet: Inventaire des possibilités d'intervention sur le plan communautaire dans le domaine de l'emploi', Brussels, 30 October 1972.

Corrigendum au doc. No. 1854/72 (CPE 40) 'Objet: Inventaire des possibilités d'intervention sur le plan communautaire dans le domaine de l'emploi', Brussels, 29 November 1972.

Note: 'Objet: Conférence réunissant les Ministres des Affaires économiques, les Ministres du Travail, la Commission et les Partenaires sociaux', Brussels, 1 October 1975.

Meeting of the Heads of State and Governments, Paris, 9–10 December 1975, *Communiqué*.

Joint Statement by the Conference on the 'Restoration of full employment and stability in the Community', press release, Luxembourg, 24 June 1976.

Note: 'Objet' Dixième session du Comité Permanent de l'emploi (13 décembre 1976), Conclusions tirées par le Président à l'issue des travaux de la session', Brussels, 28 January 1977.

Press Release, Luxembourg, 27 June 1977.

Conclusions de la Présidence sur les Travaux du Conseil Européen tenu à Luxembourg, les 29 et 30 juin 1981.

Memorandum, 'Subject: Improved Working Methods of the Standing Committee on Employment Problems and Prospects', V/766/83.

(iii) The European Parliament

Direct Elections, 1978.

Debates of the European Parliament 1978-9 Sessions, Report of Proceedings from 12 to 16 June 1978, Annex, No. 231, June 1978.

'Procès-Verbal' de la séance du mardi, 12 octobre 1982, and intervention de Vetter, PE, 80.534.

Documents de séance, 1982-3, Rapport fait au nom de la commission des affaires sociales et de l'emploi sur la proposition de la Commission des Communautés européennes au Conseil concernant une directive sur l'information et la consultation des travailleurs des entreprises a structure complexe, en particulier transnationale, 12 July 1982, Dic. 1–324/82/B.

Documents de séance, 1983-4, 'Fait au nom de la commission des affaires sociales et de l'emploi sur la proposition de la Commission des Communautés européennes au Conseil concernant une recommendation relative à la réduction et à la réorganisation du temps de travail', 16 October 1983, Doc. 1–909/83.

(iv) The Economic and Social Committee

Annual Reports, 1972-84.

Declaration by W. Hallstein to the ESC, 19 May 1958, Doc. CES/4F/58, Annex 4.

Rapport de M. Masoin, Doc. CES/17/58.

ESC president, Lappas, Alfons, 'Die Gesellschaftsgruppen brauchen Kontrollfunktionen', *Europa Union*, November 1972.

Lappas, Alfons, 'Über Höhen und Tiefen—vorwärts und rückwärts', *Die Quelle*, 9/1974.

Les Conseils consultatifs économiques et sociaux dans les Etats membres des Communautés européennes face au CES, 1977, Doc R/CES/124/77.

The Report on European Institutions, May 1980.

Amendments to the Rule of Procedure, Text adopted by the ESC at its 180th Plenary Session, Brussels, 2-3 July 1980.

Document de Travail pour la réunion extraordinaire du Groupe II, 16 December 1980, DI 131/80 (g. II).

Die Europäischen Interessenverbände und ihre Beziehungen zum Wirtschafts- und Sozialasschuss. Eine Dokumentation, NOMOS, Verlagsgesellschaft, 1980.

Le droit d'initiative du Comité économique et social des Communautés Européennes, 2e édition, Brussels, Editions Delta, 1981.

Avis du CES, sur la 'Proposition de directive sur l'information et la consultation des travailleurs des entreprises à structure complexe, en particular transnationale', Brussels, 27 January 1982.

(v) The Economic Policy Committee

Résumé de l'échange de vues, Comité de politique économique—Partenaires sociaux, Bruxelles, 11 janvier 1978, Brussels, 17 January 1978.
Conclusion from the chairman, Brussels, 2 June 1978.

5 *OECD*

OECD, *Perspectives Economiques*, various issues.
OECD, Employment Outlook, September 1983, September 1984.
OECD, 'International Economic Linkage', *Economic Studies*, Paris, November 1983.
OECD, *The Challenge of Unemployment*, Paris, 1982.

6 *Others*

UNICE (L'Union des Industries de la Communauté Européenne), *L'Industrie Européenne face à l'Intégration Economique et Sociale*, 1966.
Bulletin des Presse- und Informationsamtes, Bonn, 20 October 1972, no. 147.
UNICE, *Conférence tripartite économique et sociale*, Brussels, 22 October 1975.
UNICE, *Tripartite Economic and Social Conference*, Brussels, 21 June 1976.
Monnet, Jean, *Mémoires*, Paris, Fayard, 1976.
UNICE, *Tripartite Economic and Social Conference*, 27 June 1977, Brussels, 23 June 1977.
Report on the European Institutions, presented by the Committee of Three to the European Council, October 1979.
Institute of Mediation, Consiliation and Arbitrage (IMAC), Spain, 'Election Results', 23 January 1980.
Arbeitgeber, Jahresbericht der Bundesvereinigung der Deutschen Arbeitgeberverbände, 1980.
CLE 'Observations du Comité de liaison d'employeurs sur le mémorandum sur la réduction et la réorganisation du temps de travail', Brussels, 21 March 1983.
Speech of the president of the Bundesvereinigung der Deutschen Arbeitgeberverbände, Otto Esser to the Annual Meeting, 12–13 December 1983, quoted in *Gewerkschaftliche Monatshefte*, 2/84.

Part II—Studies and Articles

A Studies

Abendroth, Wolfgang, *Histoire du Mouvement Ouvrier en Europe*, Petite Collection, Paris, Maspero, 1967.
Albrecht-Carie, René, *One Europe: The historical background of European Unity*, Garden City, New York, Doubleday, 1965.
Auger, Jean, *Syndicalisme des autres, syndicats d'Europe, les internationales syndicales* (Collection: Comprendre pour agir), Paris, les éditions ouvrières, 1980.
Barraclough, Geoffrey, *Tendances Actuelles de l'Histoire*, Paris, Flammarion, 1980.
Beever, Colin R., *European Unity and the Trade Union Movement*, ('European Aspects', Series D: 'Social Science', No. 2), Hyden A. W. Sythoff, 1960.
Behrman, Jack, N., *National Interests and the Multinational Enterprise: Tension among the North Atlantic Countries*, Englewood Cliffs, New Jersey, Prentice Hall Inc., 1970.
Bergmann, L., *Multinational Corporations and Labour in the EEC: A Survey of Research and*

Developments. Presented at the Meeting on Multinational Corporations and Labour, The International Institute for Labour Studies, Geneva, 5–7 December 1973.

Bernard, Nadine; Laval, Claude; Nys, André, *Le Comité économique et social*, Institut d'études éuropéennes, Université libre de Bruxelles, (Thèses et Travaux politiques), Brussels, Editions de l'Université de Bruxelles, 1972.

Beykirch, Heinz; Kruppers, Heinz, *Die Autonomie der Gewerkschaften in einem integrierten Europa*, 12. Europäisches Gespräch. Recklinghausen, 19–21 Junei 1963, Cologne–Deutz, Bund 1964.

Blackmer, Donald L., *Unity in Diversity: Italian Communism and the Communist World*. Cambridge, Mass., MIT Press, 1968.

Blackmer, Donald L.; Kriegel, Annie, *The International Role of the Communist Parties of Italy and France*, Cambridge, Centre for International Studies, Harvard University Press, 1975.

Blackmer, Donald L. and Tarrow, Sydney, *Communism in Italy and France*, Princeton University Press, 1975.

Blanpain, Roger; Etty, Tom; Gladstone, Alan; Günter, Hans, *Relations between management of transnational enterprises and employee representatives in certain countries of the European Communities*, (a pilot study), Research Series No. 51, International Institute for Labour Studies, 1980.

Bouvard, Marguerite, *Labour Movements in the Common Market Countries: The Growth of a European Pressure Group* Praeger Special Studies in International Economics and Development, New York, Washington, London, Praeger, 1972.

Braukmann, Karl, (Hrst. für den DGB), *Europa 71—Der Europäische Bund Freier Gewerkschaften in der Gemeinschaft*, Europäischer Gespräch, Cologne, Bund Verlag, 1971.

Bruhat, J. et Piolet, M., *Esquisse d'une Histoire de la CGT*, Paris,CGT 1966.

Cavel, Jean-Claude; Collet, Pierre, *L'Europe au Fil des Jours: Les jeunes années de la construction européenne 1948–78*. Paris, La Documentation française 1979 (Notes et Etudes Documentaires, Nos. 4509–4510).

Collins, Doreen, *The European Communities: The Social Policy of the First Phase*, London, Martin Robertson, 1975.

Das Europäische Gespräch, June 1977, Cologne, Bund Verlag, 1979.

De Grave, Michel, *Dimension européenne du syndicalisme ouvrier*, Louvain, Université Catholique, 1968.

Della Torre, Paolo, F.; Mortimer, Edward; Story, Jonathan, *Euro-communism, Myth or Reality? Middlesex, Penguin, 1979.*

Delperee, Albert, Politique sociale et intégration européenne, Liège, G. Thone, 1956.

Deppe, Frank (ed.), *Arbeiterbewegung und Westeuropäische Integration*, Cologne, Pahl Rugenstein Verlag, 1976.

Die Europäische Sozialcharta: Weg zu einer Sozialordnung? Edition Europarat, no. 3, Baden-Baden, Nomos, 1978.

Dolleans, Edouard, *Histoire du Mouvement Ouvrier: de 1921 à nos jours*, Paris, Armand Colin, 1967.

Elsner, Wolfram, *Die EWG Herausforderung und Antwort der Gewerkschaften* Reihe: Kleine Bibliothek, Cologne, Pahl Rugenstein Verlag, 1974.

ETUI, *Employment, Investment and the Public Sector*, Brussels, 19892.

ETUI, *European Trade Union Institute Background Paper* for the ETUC Employment Conference in Strasbourg, 5–6 April 1984, Brussels, 1984.

ETUI, *Industrial Policy in Western Europe*, Brussels, 1981.

ETUI, *Public Investment and Job Creation*, Brussels, 1984.

ETUI, *The European Economy 1980–5: An Indicative Full Employment Plan*, Brussels, 1980.

ETUI, *The Reduction of Working Hours in Western Europe, Second Part: Analysis of the Social and Economic Consequences*, Brussels, May 1980.

Europa 71, *Der EBFG in der Gemeinschaft—eine neue Kraft für Europa*, Cologne-Deutz, Bund Verlag, 1971.

Feld, Werner, J., *The European Community in World Affairs: Economic Power and Political Influence*, Post Washington, Alfred Publishing Co. Inc., 1976.

Fejto, François, *The French Communist Party & the Crisis of International Communism*, Boston, MIT Press, 1967.

Fischer, Fritz, *Die institutionalisierte Vertretung der Verbände in der Europäischen Wirtschaftsgemeinschaft*, Hamburg, Hansischer Gildenverlag, 1965.

Fitzgerald, Mark J., *The Common Market's Labor Programs*, London, Notre Dame, 1966.

Fontaine, Pascal, *Le Comité d'action pour les Etats-Unis de l'Europe de Jean Monnet*, Lausanne, Centre de Recherches Européennes, 1974.

Friedrich, Carl Joachim, (ed.), *Politische Dimensione der europäischen Gemeinschaftsbildung*, Cologne, Opladen 1968.

Götz, C., *Heinz Oskar Vetter*, Cologne, Europäische Verlagsanstalt, 1977.

Häckel, Erwin, *Multinational Konzerne und Europäische Integration*, Forschungsinstitut der Deutschen Gesellschaft für Auswärtige Politik, Arbeitspapiere zur Internationalen Politik, No. 5, Bonn, Europa Union Verlag, 1975.

Hallstein, Walter, *Die Europäische Gemeinschaft*. Düsseldorf, Wien, Econ Verlag, 5, Auflage, 1979.

Haas, Ernst B., *The Unity of Europe's Political, Social and Economical Forces, 1950–7*, London, Stevens, 1958.

Heise, Bernt, *Sozialpolitik in der Europäischen Wirtschaftsgemeinschaft*, Göttingen, 1966.

Hellmann, Oesterheld, Olle (eds.), *Die Europäischen Gewerkschaften*, Berlin, Verlag Olle & Wolter, 1980.

Hürten, Heinz, *Organissierte Interessen in Europa*, Osnabrück, A. Fromm, 1966.

Ionescu, Ghita (ed.), *The New Politics of European Integration*, London and Basingstoke, Macmillan, 1972.

Jacobs, Eric, *European Trade Unionism*, London, Croom Helm, 1973.

Jensen, Firm B., and Walter, Ingo, *The Common Market*, Economic Integration in Europe, Philadelphia and New York, J.B. Lippincott, 1965.

Jungnickel, Rolf, Matthies, Claus, *Multinationale Unternehmen und Gewerkschaften*, Veröffentlichungen des HWWA-Instituts für Wirtschaftsforschung, Hamburg, Verlag Weltarchiv, GmBH, 1973.

Jung, Volker, 'Der Europäische Bund der Freien Gewerkschaften und die Wirtschafts— und Währungsunion', *Gewerkschaftliche Monatshefte*, 12/71.

Kamin, Alfred, *West European Labor and The American Corporation*, Washington, Bureau of National Affairs, 1970.

Kassalow, Everett, *In European Unionism: with some implications for American Unions* (The Frank McCallister Memorial Lecture), Chicago, Roosevelt University, December 1971.

Kendall, Walter, *The Labor Movements in Europe*, London, J. M. Dent and Sons, 1974.

Kerr, Anthony J. C., *The Common Market and How it Works*. Oxford, Pergamon Press, 1977.

Kindelberger, Charles P., *American Business Abroad*, New Haven and London, Yale University Press, 1969.

Kirchner, Emil Joseph, *An Empirical Examination of the Functionalist Concept of Spillover*, Case Western Reserve University, June 1976.

Kirchner, Emil Joseph, *Trade Unions as a Pressure Group in the European Community*, Farnborough, Hants, Saxon House, 1978.

Kittner, Michael (ed.), *Gewerkschaftsjahrbruch 1984: Daten—Fakten—Analysen*, Cologne, Bund Verlag, 1984.

Kramer, Heinz, *Ziele und Verhalten der Sozialpartner in Westeuropa als Faktoren für die Gemeinschaftsbildung*, überlegungen zu politischen Strukturfragen der Europäischen

Gemeinschaftsbildung, Ebenhausen, Stiftung Wissenschaft und Politik, Forschungs institut für Internationale Politik, 1977.

Kramer, Heinz, *Die Dreierkonferenz als 'Konzertierte Aktion' der EG*, Ebenhausen, Stiftung Wissenschaft und Politik, 1978.

Kriegel, Annie, *Un Autre Communisme?*, Paris, Hachette, 1977 (Collection 'Essais').

Kühne, Peter (ed.), *Gewerkschaftliche Betriebspolitik in Westeuropa*. (Internationale Tagung der Sozialakademie Dortmund in Verbindung mit dem Europäischen Gewerkschaftsinstitut in Brüssel), Berlin, Duncker und Humblot, 1982.

Läufer, Thomas, *Europa-Wahl '78: 22 Fragen zur Direktwahl*, (Institut für Europäische Politik, Bonn). Bonn, Europa Union Verlag, 1977.

Laviec, Jean-Pierre, *Syndicats et Sociétés Multinationales*, La Documentation Française, Paris, 1975.

Lecerf, Jean, *La Communauté en péril: Histoire de l'unité européenne*, Paris, Gallimar, 1975.

Lefranc, Georges, *Le Syndicalisme dans le monde*, (Collection 'Que sais-je?'. Le point des conaissances actuelles, No. 356), Paris, Presse Universitaire de France, 1949.

Lefranc, Georges, *Les expériences syndicales internationales des origines à nos jours*, Paris, Aubier, 1952.

Lennenberger und Gysin (eds.), *Der Historische Kompromiss: Chancen und Grenzen des Eurokommunismus*. Berlin, Colloquium Verlag, 1978.

Leohard, Wolfgang, *Europkommunismus*, Munich, Bertelsmann, 1978.

Levi, C. *Crise de l'état national, firmes multinationales et mouvement ouvrier*, Lyons, Fédérop, 1977.

Levinson, Charles, *International Trade Unionism*, London, George Allen and Unwin, 1972.

Lieber, Robert, J., *British Politics and European Unity, Parties, Elites and Pressure Groups*, Berkeley, University of California Press, 1971.

Liebhaberg, Bruno, *Relations industrielles et entreprises multinationales en Europe*, Paris, Presse Universitaire de France (CEEIM), 1980.

Lorwin, L., *The International Labour Movement: History, Politics, Outlook*, New York, Harper and Brothers, 1953.

Mandel, Ernest, *Europe vs. America: Contradictions of Imperialism*, New York and London, New Left Books, 1970.

Martinet, Gilles, *Sept Syndicalismes* (L'Histoire Immédiate), Paris, Editions du Seuil, 1979.

Marx, Eli and Kendall, Walter, *Unions in Europe*, University of Sussex, Centre for Contemporary European Studies, 1971.

Masclet, Jean-Claude, *L'Union politique de l'Europe*, Paris, Presse Universitaire Française, 1978.

Mauerhofer, Mourize, *Les syndicats italiens*, Paris, Le Monde 1974. (Notes et Etudes documentaires, No. 4068–4069, 15.3.1974.)

McInnes, Neil, *The Communist Parties of Western Europe*, London, Oxford University Press, 1975.

Meynaud, Jean; Sidjanski, Dusan, *Science Politique et Intégration Européenne*, avec le concours de Schwamm, Henri, Genève, Institut d'Etudes Européennes, 1965.

Meynaud, Jean; Sidjanski, Dusan, *Les Groupes de Pression dans la Communauté européenne*, Montreal University, 1969.

Meynaud, Jean; Sidjanski, Dusan, *L'Europe des affaires, rôle et structure des groupes*, (Bibliothèque politique et économique), Paris, Payot, 1967.

Meynaud, Jean; Sidjanski, Dusan, *Groupes de Pression et Coopération européenne, organisations professionnelles au plan régional européen*, (Série C: "Recherches", No. 14, Juin 1967), Paris, Fondation nationale des Sciences politiques, 1968.

Meynaud, Jean, *L'action syndicale et la Communauté européenne*, Lausanne, Centre de Recherches européennes, 1962.

Meynaud, Jean; Sidjanski, Dusan, *Les Groupes de Pression dans la Communauté Européenne*, Editions de l'Institut de Sociologie de l'Université de Bruxelles, 1971.

Modelski, J., *Principles of World Politics*, New York, Free Press, 1972.

Müller-Roschach, Herbert, *Die deutsche Europapolitik 1949-1977*, Bonn, Europa Union Verlag, 1980.

Nairn, Tom, *The Left Against Europe*. Middlesex, Penguin, 1973.

Neri, S.; Sperl, H., *Travaux préparatoires, déclarations interprétatives des six gouvernements, documents parlementaires*, Edité par la Cour de Justice des Communautés européennes, Luxembourg, 1962.

Nye, Joseph, and Keohane, Robert, (eds), *Transnational Relations and World Politics*, Cambridge Mass., Harvard University Press, 1971.

Olle, Werner (ed.), *Einführung in die internationale Gewerkschaftspolitik*, Berlin, Verlag Olle & Wolter 1978.

Paulus, Daniel, *La Création du Comité permanent de l'emploi*, Brussels, 1972.

Peel, Jack, *The real power game; a guide to European industrial relations*, London, McGraw Hill, 1979.

Perez-Calvo, Alberto, *L'Organisation européenne de la confédération mondiale du travail*, Essey-les-Nancy, Imprimerie Christmann, 1976.

Piehl, Ernst, 'Internationale Arbeit—Westeuropa und die Welt', in Kittner, Michael (ed.), *Gewerkschaftsjahrbuch 1984*, Daten—Fakten—Analysen, Cologne, Bund Verlag, 1984.

Piehl, Ernst, *Multinationale Konzerne und international Gewerkschaftsbewegung* (Schriftenreihe der Otto Breener Stiftung, No. 2), Frankfurt, Europäische Verlaganstalt, 1974.

Philip, Sinclair, *Les Nouvelles Perspectives du Syndicalisme International face aux Firmes Multinationales*, Thèse pour le Doctorat d'Etat en Science Politique soutenue à Grenoble, le 30 juin 1978 (miméographe).

Ribas, J. J., *La Politique Sociale des Communautés Européennes*, Paris, Dalloz, 1969.

Rittstieg, Helmut, *Wirtschaftsverbände und europäische Gemeinschaften*, eine Untersuchung zur institutionalisierten Interessenvertretung. (Schriften reihe zur europäischen integration, No. 3), Hamburg, L. Appel, 1967.

Rummel, R., *Die soziale Komponente in der Europäischen Union*, Ebenhausen, June 1974.

Rummel, Reinhardt, *Soziale Politik für Europa: ein intergrationspolitisches Konzept* (Europäische Schriften des Institutes für europäische Politik, Bonn, Band 38), Bonn, Europa Union Verlag, 1975.

Rummel, R.; und Wessel, W., (eds), *Die Europäische Politische Zusammenarbeit*, Bonn, Europa Union Verlag, 1978.

Sasse, Christophe, ed., *Decision making in the European Community*, New York, Praeger, 1977.

Schevenels, W., *Forty-five Years, 1901-1945: International Federation of Trade Unions, A Historical Precis*, ICFTU, Brussels, 1956.

Vernon, Raymond, *Sovereignty at Bay: The Multinational Spread of US Enterprises*, New York/London, Bais Books, 1971.

Von der Groeben, Hans.; Vetter, H. O.; Friedrich, O. A., *Europäische Aktiengesellschaft— Beitrag zur sozialen Integration?*, Bonn, Europa Union Verlag, 1972.

Waschke, Hildegard, *Gewerkschaften in Westeuropa*, Nationale Besonderheiten, Organisationen und Zielsetzungen in Ausland, Cologne, Deutscher Institut Verlag, GmbH, 1975.

Windmüller, John P., *Labour Internationals: A Survey of Contemporary International Trade Union Organizations*, Ithaca, New York, State School of Industrial and Labour Relations, 1969.

Zellentin, Gerda, *Formen der Willensbildung in den Europäischen Organisationen* (Kölner Schriften zur Politischen Wissenschaft), Cologne, Athenäum Verlag, 1965.

Zellentin, Gerda, *Die Kommunisten und die Einigung Europas*, Frankfurt-on-Main, Athenäum Verlag, 1964.

B Articles

Adam, Herman, 'Die Konzertierte Aktion in der Bundesrepublik', *WSI-Studien*, No. 21. Cologne, Bund Verlag, 1972.

Barry-Braunthal, Thomas, 'Will European Unions become inward-looking?', *European Community*, September 1972.

Ball, George, 'The Promise of the MNC', *Fortune*, 74, no. 6, June 1967.

Barjonet, A., 'Le Marché Commun, c'est l'Europe allemande', *Le Peuple*, no. 528, 1957.

Behrman, Jack N., 'Industrial Integration and Multinational Enterprises', *The Annals of the American Academy of Political and Social Science*, September 1982.

Beever, Colin R., 'Trade Unions and the Common Market', London, PEP, *Planning*, 1, May 1962.

Bernstein, Meyer, 'Labor and the European Communities', *Law and Contemporary Problems*, 26, no. 3, Summer 1961.

Blanpain, R., 'The Impact of Recent Developments in the EEC on National Labour Law Systems', *Relations Industrielles*, 31, no. 4, 1976.

Braun, Walter; Köpke, Günter, 'Die sozialen Auswirkungen der Wirtschaftskonzentration', *EG* 3/1971.

Braun, Walter, 'Möglichkeiten einer Politik der Europäische Gemeinschaft gegenüber den Multinationalen Konzernen', *WSI—mitteilungen*, 4/1975.

Braun, Walter, 'Für die Kontinuität verantwortlich: Die Arbeit des DGB-Sekretariats und der Ausschüsse', *Transnational 15*, Bonn, Europa Union Verlag, 1979.

Braun, Walter, 'Europäische Aktiongesellschaft und Internationale Fusion', *Gewerkschaftliche Monatshefte*, 8/71.

Bussey, Ellen M., 'Organised Labor and the EEC', *Industrial Relations*, 7, no. 2, February 1968.

Collins, Doreen, 'Towards a European Social Policy', *Journal of Common Market Studies*, 5, No. 1, September 1966.

Deheyn, Henri, 'Das Gipfeltreffen von Dublin', *Europa-Archiv*, 8/75.

'Die Kommunisten und der Gemeinsame Markt', *Europäische Schriften des Bildungswerks Europapolitik*, Band 18. Cologne, Europa Union Verlag, 1968.

Dierendonck, J. E., 'Regional Economic Integration as the Creation of an Environment Favourable for Transnational Industrial Organisations in the EEC', in Günter, Hans (ed.), *Transnational Industrial Relations—The Impact of Multinational Corporations and Economic Regionalism on Industrial Relations*. London, Macmillan, 1972.

Duma, J., 'Le PCF et l'Europe', *Cahiers de l'Institut Maurice Thorez*, 4/1974.

Engelen-Kefer, Ursula, 'Sozialpolitik in der Europäische Gemeinschaft: Eine Zwischenbilanz'. *WSI-Mitteilungen*, 12/1973.

'Europa—Wirtschaft—Der Stand der wirtschaftlichen Integration im Herbst 1971', *Gewerkschaftliche Monatshefte*, 12/71.

Feldengut, Karl, 'Die Europäische Gewerkschaftsbewegung und die Europäische Gemeinschaft', *Gewerkschaftliche Monatshefte*, 8/75.

Günter, Hans, 'Labour and Multinational Corporations in Western Europe: Some Problems and Perspectives' in Kujawa, D. (ed.), *International Labour and the Multinational Enterprise*, New York, Praeger, 1975.

Galloway, P., 'Multinational Enterprise as Worldwide Interest Groups', *Politics and Society*, 2, no. 1, 1971.

Gloystein, Peter, unter Mitarbeit von Wand, Kurt, 'Europäische Industriepolitik—Die

Schaffung neuer Dimensionen für Märkte und Unternehmen' in *Europäische Wirtschaftspolitik*, Programm und Realität. Bonn, Europa Union Verlag, 1973.

Gorz, André, 'Workers Control is more than just that', in *Workers' Control: A Reader on Labour and Social Change*, Hunnius, Gerry; Garson, David G.; Case, John (eds), New York, Vintage Books, 1973.

Groom, Brian, 'Multinationals turn the tables', *Financial Times*, 12 March 1985.

Hoffmann, P.; Langwieler, A., *Noch sind wir da*. Hamburg, 1974.

Hohnen, Walter, 'Das DGB-Investitionsprogramm zur Sicherung der Beschäftigung durch qualitatives Wachstum: Ansätze zur Konkretisierung', *WSI—Mitteilungen*, 10/1982.

Holloway, J., 'Some Issues Raised by Marxist Analyses of European Integration', *CSE Bulletin*, no. 13, 1976.

Houthuys, Joseph, 'Aspects européens et internationaux du syndicalisme', *Chronique de Politique Etrangère*, 38, July 1973.

Jung, Volker, 'Der Europäische Bund der Freien Gewerkschaften und die Wirtschafts und Währungsunion', *Gewerkschaftliche Monatshefte*, December 1971.

Jung, Volker, 'Neuer Europäischer Gewerkschaftsbund', *Gewerkschaftliche Monateshefte*, 4/73.

Jung, Volker, 'Erweiterung des Europäischen Gewerkschaftsbundes', *Die Neue Gesellschaft*, 9/1974.

Jung, Volker; Koubek, Norbert; Piehl, Ernst; Scheibelange, Ingrid, 'Aspects of union policy in Western Europe: Economic concentration and political integration as a challenge for the trade unions', Translated from *WWI-Mitteilungen*, 10/1971.

Jung, Volker; Piehl, Ernst, 'Die Entwicklung der internationalen Strukturen den Westeuropäische Gewerkschaften', WSI-Mitteilungen, 6/1972.

Junne, Gerd, 'Eurogeldmarkt, multinationale Konzerne und die verminderte Wirksamkeit von Staatsinterventionen', *Leviathan*, Jg. 2, 1974.

Kaiser, Karl, 'Transnationale Politik: Zu einer Theorie der multinationalen Politik', *Politische Vierteljahreszeitschrift*, Sonderheft, no. 1, 1969.

Kindelberger, Charles P., 'European Integration and the International Corporation' in Brown, Courteney (ed), *World Business, Promise and Problems*, New York, 1970.

Koepke, Günter, 'Aufgaben und Tätikeit des EGI', *Gewerkschaftliche Monatschefte*, May 1979.

Koepke, Günter, 'Union Responses in Continental Europe', in Flanagan and Weber (eds), *Bargaining Without Boundaries*, University of Chicago Press, 1974.

Koepke, Günter, 'Vorbereitung von gewerkschaflichen Entscheidungen: Das Europäische Gewerkschaftsinststitut (EGI)', *Transnational 15*. Bonn, Europa Union Verlag, 1979.

Kollege Nachbar, 'Die Gewerkschaftsbünde in Westeuropa', *Transnational 15*. Bonn, Europa Union Verlag, 1979.

Kramer, Heinz, 'Die Rolle der Sozialpartner im Entscheidungssystem der EG', *Aus Politik und Zeitgeschichte*, Beilage zur Wochenzeitschrift Das Parlament, B 22/77, 4 June 1977.

Krause, Lawrence, 'The International Economic System', *The Annals of the American Academy of Political and Social Science*, September 1982.

Kretschmer, Dieter, 'Internationale Kampfmassnahmen gegen Multinationale Konzerne am Beispiel von AKZO', *WSI-Mitteilungen* 4/75.

Kristoffersen, Erwin, 'Das Europa der Gewerkschaften', *Gewerkschaftliche Monatshefte*, May 1984.

Kühne, Karl, 'Eurokommunismus—Ursprünge, Wirtschaftspolitik und Rolle der Gewerkschaften', *Gewerkschaftliche Monatshefte*, 9/77.

Kuby, Heinz, 'Machtverschiebung in Europa. Rückwirkungen der Wirtschaftsunion auf die Strukturen politischer und gesellschaflicher Macht in Westeuropa', *Gewerkschaftliche Monatshefte*, 7/1971.

Lacrois, A., 'La CGT et le Plan Marshall', *Cahiers de l'Institut Maurice Thorez*, 4/1974.

Lage, Sylvain, 'La CES s'affirme', *Projet*, March 1980.

'Les premières élections européennes (juin 1979)', La campagne et les résultats, les institutions et le bilan de la CEE. *Le Monde*, Dossiers et Documents, Supplement, June 1979.

Lyon-Caen, Gérard, 'La constitution des syndicats européens est une nécessité inscrite dans les faites', *Le Monde Diplomatique*, September 1972.

Mandel, Ernest, 'The Debate on Workers' Control', in *Workers Control*, Hunnius, Gerry; Garson, David G.; Case, John (eds), New York, Vintage Books, 1973.

Mujal-Leon, Eusebio, 'Spanish Communism in the 1970s', *Problems of Communism*, March/April 1975.

Manigat, M., 'La Confédération européenne des syndicats et le syndicalisme mondiale', *Politique Etrangère*, no. 5, 1973.

Markmann, Heinz, 'Überbetriebliche Mitbestimmung in der EWG: Der Wirtschafts- und Sozialausschuss', *Gewerkschaftliche Monatshefte*, 9/71.

Menns, Bernard; Sauvant, Karl P., 'Multinational Corporations, Managers and Development of Regional Identification in Western Europe', *The Annals of the American Academy of Political and Social Science*, September 1982.

Morse, Edward L., 'Transnational Economic Processes', in Keohane and Nye (eds), *Transnational Relations and World Politics*, Cambridge, Mass., Harvard University Press, 1973.

Müller-Engstfeld, Anton, 'Ein Europa der Fünfzehn. Der Gewerkschaftliche Zusammenschluss nach der Erweiterung der Europäischen Gemeinschaft', *Europa-Archiv*, 6/73.

Niethammer, Lutz, 'Probleme der Gewerkschaften im Prozess der Integration Westeuropas', *Gewerkschaftliche Monatshefte*, 5/76.

Piehl, Ernst, 'Mitbestimmung aus der Sicht der Neuen Linken', *Das Mitbestimmungsgespräch*, 9–10/1970.

Piehl, Ernst, 'Internationale Gewerkschaftssolidaritat gegen multinationale Kapitalstrategie am Beispiel des AKZO-Konzern, I und II', *Das Mitbestimmungsgespräch*, nos. 5, 6, 7/1973.

Pitz, Karl H., 'Internationale Tarifverhandlungen: der flasche Weg', WSI-Mitteilungen, 4/75.

Pipkorn, J., 'Die Diskussion über die Wirtschaftliche Mitbestimmung der Arbeitnehmer in der EG', *Europa-Archiv*, 31. Jg. (1976) II Folge. (10.6.76).

Rhein, Eberhard, 'Europäische konzertierte Aktion', En Beitrag zur Gemeinschaftlichen Wirtschaftspolitik, *Europa-Archiv*, Folge 15/1976.

Roberts, B. C.; Liebhaberg, Bruno, 'The European Trade Union Confederation: Influence of Regionalism Detente and Multinationals', *British Journal of Industrial Relations*, **14**, no. 3., November 1976.

Roberts, Benjamin C., 'Ziele der Gewerkschaften in Westeuropa', *Europa-Archiv*, Folge 15, 1977.

Roberts, B. C., 'Industrial Relations and the EEC', *Labour Law Journal*, **24**, no. 8, August 1973.

Roberts, B. C., 'Multinational Collective Bargaining—A European Prospect?', *British Journal of Industrial Relations*, **9**, no. 1, March 1973.

Routledge, Paul, 'Les Trade-Unions voudraient que les syndicats européens descendent de la stratosphère', *Le Monde*, 6 April 1976.

Roux, R., 'The position of Labour under the Schuman Plan', *International Labour Review*, **76**, 1957.

Ruhwedel, Klaus, 'Der Europäische Gewerkschaftsbund und die Westeuropäische

Integration', in Deppe, Frank (ed.), *Arbeiterbewegung und Westeuropäische Integration*, Cologne, 1976.

Scalia, Umberto, 'Current Problems of the Trade Union Movement in the Common Market Countries', *World Marxist Review*, IV, 9 September 1963.

Schneider, Michael, 'Der Kampf um die Arbeitszeitverkürzung von der Industrialisierung bis zur Gegenwart', *Gewerkschaftliche Monatshefte*, 2/84.

Schregle, Johannes, 'Die Arbeitnehmer—Arbeitgeberbeziehungen in Westeuropa', *Gewerkschaftliche Monatshefte*, 8/74.

'Soziale Perspektiven der erweiterten Gemeinschaft', *Das Parlament*, January 1973.

'Sur la rencontre de Moscou', *Cahiers du Communisme*, XXXIX, January–February 1963.

30 Jours d'Europe, Fiches documentaires pédagogiques, Supplément au No, Mai 1984.

Vinck, F., 'Industrial Conversion in the European Coal and Steel Community', *International Labour Review*, **91**, 1965.

Wacker, Ulrich, 'Zur Europapolitik der französischen Gewerkschaft CGT', in *Arbeiterbewegung und Westeuropäische Integration*, Deppe, Frank (ed.), Cologne, Pahl-Rugenstein, 1976.

Willat, *Multinational Unions, The Financial Times*, 1974.

Weitz, Peter, 'The CGIL and the PCI' in Blackmer, Donald L., and Tarrow, Sydney, *Communism in Italy and France*, Princeton, Princeton University Press, 1975.

Windmüller, John P. (eds), 'European Labor and Politics: A Symposium (I) (II)', *Industrial and Labour Relations Review*, **28**, no. 1, October 1974.

Windmüller, John, 'European Regionalism: A New Factor in International Labor', *Industrial Relations Journal*, Summer 1976.

Van Ginneken, Wouter, 'La réduction de la semaine de travail et l'emploi. Comparison entre sept modèles macro-économiques européens', *Revue international du Travail*, **123**, no. 1, January/February 1984.

Vernon, Raymond, 'Multinational Business and National Economic Goals' in Nye, Joseph, and Keohane, Robert (eds), *Transnational Relations and World Politics*, Cambridge, Harvard University Press, 1971.

Zulee, G. Manfred, 'Die Gestalt der Europäischen Union in Tindemanns Bericht', *Europa-Archiv*, 17/76.

Index